Crane Island Journal Part Two

Vetur (Winter)

A Memoir of a Remarkable Daily Life on a Small Island in the Salish Sea

By John Ashenhurst

Walt's Second Blessing

*I have said that the soul is not more than the body,
And I have said that the body is not more than the soul,
And nothing, not God, is greater to one than one's self is,
And whoever walks a furlong without sympathy walks to his own funeral drest in his shroud,
And I or you pocketless of a dime may purchase the pick of the earth,
And to glance with an eye or show a bean in its pod confounds the learning of all times,
And there is no trade or employment but the young man following it may become a hero,
And there is no object so soft but it makes a hub for the wheel'd universe,
And I say to any man or woman, Let your soul stand cool and composed before a million universes. And I say to mankind, Be not curious about God,
For I who am curious about each am not curious about God,
(No array of terms can say how much I am at peace about God and about death.)
I hear and behold God in every object, yet understand God not in the least,
Nor do I understand who there can be more wonderful than myself.
Why should I wish to see God better than this day?
I see something of God each hour of the twenty-four, and each moment then,
In the faces of men and women I see God, and in my own face in the glass,
I find letters from God dropt in the street, and every one is sign'd by God's name,
And I leave them where they are, for I know that wheresoe'er I go,
Others will punctually come for ever and ever.*

From Song of Myself by Walt Whitman

Contents

Vetur (Winter)	1
Dedication	3
Introduction	4
Ninety-three: Shining Path	9
Ninety-four: Fly Brains and Mushroom Bodies	13
Ninety-five: Cold in the Springs	17
Ninety-six: Misplaced Pots	21
Ninety-seven: Huginn Again?	26
Ninety-eight: Press Interviews in Town	30
Ninety-nine: Speed Bump	34
One-hundred: Difficult Decisions	37
One-hundred-one: Trying to Look Ahead	41
One-hundred-two: Beauty Duty	45
One-hundred-three: Winter Dump Run	49
One-hundred-four: Dinner Party	53
One-hundred-five: Raw Recruit	56
One-hundred-six: Log Rolling	60
One-hundred-seven: We're Famous!	64
One-hundred-eight: Going for Help	68
One-hundred-nine: Sunward Bound	71
One-hundred-ten: City of Angels	75
One-hundred-eleven: Seeing Stars	79
One-hundred-twelve: The PCH	82
One-hundred-thirteen: High-speed Life	86

One-hundred-fourteen: The Bay	90
One-hundred-fifteen: Bonding	94
One-hundred-sixteen: Yvonne Cooks Up a Storm	98
One-hundred-seventeen: Enchanted	102
One-hundred-eighteen: Kayaking	104
One-hundred-nineteen: Return Flight	107
One-hundred-twenty: Return to Crane	110
One-hundred-twenty-one: Catching Up	113
One-hundred-twenty-two: Squall	117
One-hundred-twenty-three: Fifty Years?	120
One-hundred-twenty-four: Feeding Chipper	123
One-hundred-twenty-five: A Cold Swim	127
One-hundred-twenty-six: A Day on the Couch	131
One-hundred-twenty-seven: Reconciliation	134
One-hundred-twenty-eight: Boreas Blows Again	139
One-hundred-twenty-nine: First Draft	143
One-hundred-thirty: Another Volunteer	146
One-hundred-thirty-one: Books, Books	150
One-hundred-thirty-two: Multiverses	153
One-hundred-thirty-three: Oh, oh!	158
One-hundred-thirty-four: Why Do We Project Purpose?	161
One-hundred-thirty-five: More More	164
One-hundred-thirty-six: Would Wood	168
One-hundred-thirty-seven: Sad News	171
One-hundred-thirty-eight: Details, Details	175

One-hundred-thirty-nine: Eagle Walking	179
One-hundred-forty: It Works!	183
One-hundred-forty-one: What Do People Want?	186
One-hundred-forty-two: Alternate Realities	190
One-hundred-forty-three: A Roof Over Our Heads	194
One-hundred-forty-four: Waking to a Tsunami	198
One-hundred-forty-five: Thirty-one Years of Bliss	202
One-hundred-forty-six: Recovery of Lost Time	206
One-hundred-forty-seven: Survival	210
One-hundred-forty-eight: Flower Show — First Act	214
One-hundred-forty-nine: My Antonia	218
One-hundred-fifty: Specimen Day	223
One-hundred-fifty-one: Skylight Leak Detection	229
One-hundred-fifty-two: Whidbey Island	233
One-hundred-fifty-three: Forest Road	237
One-hundred-fifty-four: On Circle Road	242
One-hundred-fifty-five: Soap Opera	246
One-hundred-fifty-six: Fire Danger	250
One-hundred-fifty-seven: The Sound of Music	254
One-hundred-fifty-eight: Fire, Fire	258
One-hundred-fifty-nine: Bob Looks Good	262
One-hundred-sixty: The Five Elements	266
One-hundred-sixty-one: Green Fuse	270
One-hundred-sixty-two: Black Java	273
One-hundred-sixty-three: Soup 'n Service	276

One-hundred-sixty-four: Ties That Bind	279
One-hundred-sixty-five: Less is More	283
One-hundred-sixty-six: Timber!	287
One-hundred-sixty-seven: Burn Pile	291
One-hundred-sixty-eight: Let the Rumpus Begin	295
One-hundred-sixty-nine: Skate Park Rainout	299
One-hundred-seventy: Soup and Service	302
One-hundred-seventy-one: Victoria	306
One-hundred-seventy-two: Butchart Gardens	312
One-hundred-seventy-three: Walk Aboard	316
One-hundred-seventy-four: Talking about Walking to the North Pole	320
One-hundred-seventy-five: Roots Revealed	326
One-hundred-seventy-six: What's That?	330
One-hundred-seventy-seven: The Carrion Next Door	333
One-hundred-seventy-eight: Lonely Houses	337
One-hundred-seventy-nine: Remembering Grandma Opal	340
One-hundred-eighty: Seattle	344
One-hundred-eighty-one: Brown and White	348
One-hundred-eighty-two: Jobs I Have to Do Today	351
One-hundred-eighty-three: Morning Sun Come My Way	355
What's Next?	360

Vetur (Winter)

Vetur (Winter)

A Memoir of a Remarkable Daily Life on a Small Island in the Salish Sea

By John Ashenhurst

Crane Island Journal is a four-part memoir beginning with *Haust* and continuing with *Vetur*, *Vor*, and *Sumar* (autumn, winter, spring, and summer in Old Norse)

Publisher: Classics Unbound

V1.00 10/28/2024

Copyright © 2024 by John Ashenhurst

ISBN 978-0-9904563-3-9

All rights reserved. Created in the United States of America. No part of this book may be reproduced in any manner whatsoever without written permission except in the case of brief quotations embodied in critical articles and reviews. For information, address Classics Unbound, 5615 24th Ave NW, #43, Seattle, WA 98107

All photographs are the property of the author unless otherwise indicated.

For more information see www.craneislandjournal.com.

Dedication

Jeni, JC, Noah, Natasha, Morgan, Opal, Eric, Kristin, Jackson, Callum, James, and Keith

Introduction

Vetur (Winter) is Part Two of the *Crane Island Journal*. See Part One, *Haust (Autumn)* for the story of how we came to live on Crane Island. Part Three, *Vor (Spring)* and Part Four, *Sumar (Sumer)* follow *Vetur*.

Passing through Pole Pass in 1909

Crane Island, in the center of the San Juan Islands archipelago in northwest Washington, was settled in 1879 by Walter Caldwell who had a fruit and vegetable farm serving nearby Orcas and other islands. In 1900 a lime kiln operated on the southwestern corner of Crane and in 1906, J.C Hammond of Seattle bought the island for $5,200, eventually selling it to John Baillargeon of

Bellingham in 1936. In the 1950s, the Lundquist Brothers did selective logging, and some of the resulting huge stumps are still visible today.

Marketing Brochure Cover - 1960

In 1959, Island Properties subdivided the island into lots, created a "Club" to administer it, added a marina, airstrip, roads, and a water system - and began a marketing and sales effort.

1960 Crane Island Marketing Brochure

Here's an excerpt from their marketing brochure:

> *Have you dreamed of a beautiful, private island retreat, where you could enjoy relaxation and outdoor life—away from the cares and pressures of modern living— in a home landscaped by nature with picturesque trees and fragrant wild flowers-overlooking majestic marine and forest vistas—surrounded by famous yachting and fishing waters?*
>
> *Through the years a resourceful few have achieved their private island estates, but usually at the sacrifice of many conveniences we now consider essential. The cost of providing modern communications and utilities to most small islands has been prohibitive.*
>
> *Now at CRANE ISLAND this dream is becoming a reality for a few discriminating persons. Crane's three miles of waterfront has been endowed by nature with the most charming homesites. It has long been coveted by yachtsmen, tourists and local residents. Now*

supplied with nearly all the conveniences of suburban living, this story book island provides the practical answer for those seeking a unique private island home.

ADMINISTRATION is provided by Crane Island Club, a non-profit corporation.

One membership certificate, per lot, is issued at the time of purchase. The members elect a board of trustees to manage Crane Island.

COMMUNITY PROPERTY includes a nine-acre park tract, yacht harbor, air-strip, roads, and central water system supplying each lot.

ELECTRIC POWER is supplied by Orcas Power and Light Co., at low rates.

Lot prices in 1961

Lot	Price	Lot	Price	Lot	Price	Lot	Price	Lot	Price	Lot	Price
1	$18,000	7	$7,800	11	$9,700	16	$15,500	21	$7,500	26	$6,700
2	$27,500	7 1/2	$4,900	12	$7,200	17	$7,300	22	$9,700	27	$6,900
3	$12,500	8	$8,100	13	$9,500	18	$9,500	23	$14,800	28	$7,500
4	$8,500	9	$7,900	14	$12,800	19	$7,900	24	$7,500	29	$9,500
5	$7,800	10	$7,200	15	$5,500	20	$9,800	25	$8,800	30	$9,500
6	$24,500										

Lot	Price	Lot	Price	Lot	Price	Lot	Price
31	$9,500	39	$10,000	44	$8,500	49	$6,800
35	$8,900	40	$9,000	45	$8,900	50	$6,800
36	$7,600	41	$8,800	46	$18,800	51	$7,800
37	$6,800	42	$14,500	47	$9,500	52	$9,600
38	$7,200	43	$7,800	48	$5,700	53	$4,800

Lot prices seem modest 70 years later

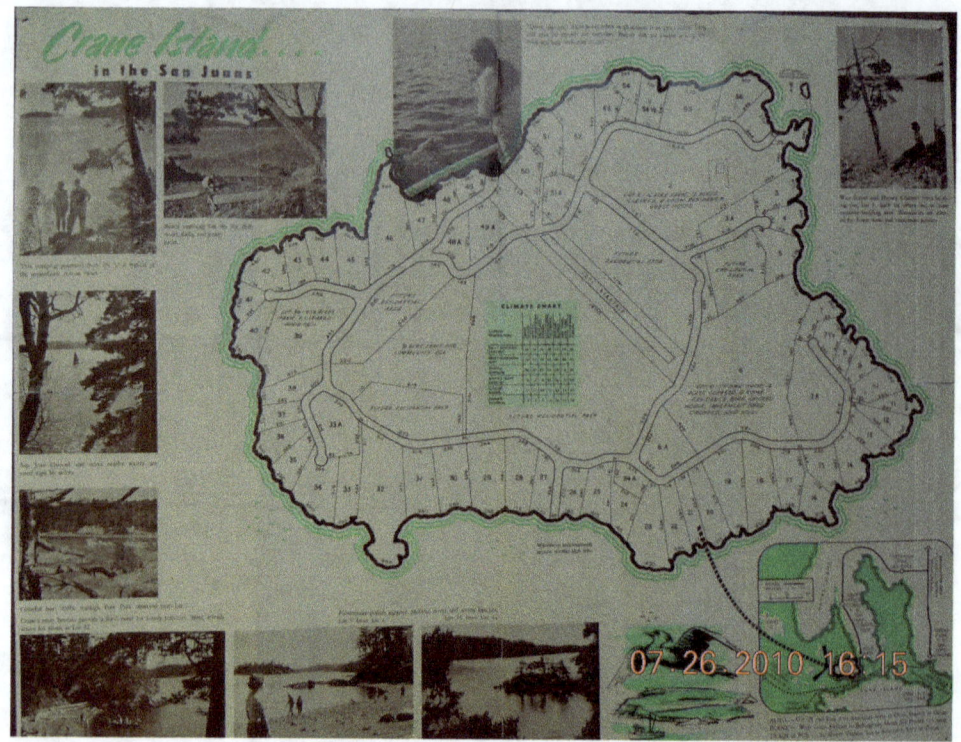

Island Map with Lot Numbers

It took years for all the lots to sell. Some owners built cabins fairly quickly; others camped on their lot for many summers before building, sometimes doing their own contracting and construction work. As the Crane Island subdivision aged, new houses tended to be larger and more comfortable. Early owners, sometimes pilots working for Boeing and living in Seattle, were later joined by owners from as far away as Alaska, California, Utah, and New Mexico.

Early owners often bought lots and built on them expecting to retire to Crane and when they did became part of the nearby Deer Harbor community on Orcas. Today most Crane houses are second homes, occupied seasonally or occasionally, and their owners often know little about life in Deer Harbor and on Orcas Island.

JCA, October 1, 2024

Ninety-three: Shining Path

"We live in succession, in division, in parts, in particles. Meantime within man is the soul of the whole; the wise silence; the universal beauty, to which every part and particle is equally related, the eternal ONE. And this deep power in which we exist and whose beatitude is all accessible to us, is not only self-sufficing and perfect in every hour, but the act of seeing and the thing seen, the seer and the spectacle, the subject and the object, are one. We see the world piece by piece, as the sun, the moon, the animal, the tree; but the whole, of which these are shining parts, is the soul." — Ralph Waldo Emerson

The evening before, Yvonne had pointed out the rising moon and its sparkling reflection on the part of the Salish Sea that makes our front yard, from Pole Pass on the west to Bell Island and Caldwell Point in the east and bounded north and south by Orcas and Shaw Islands — a half mile of salt water thousands of boats pass through, mostly in the summer, coming from Seattle and the South Sound, bound for Nanaimo, Juneau, Honolulu, or Papeete.

This morning, in the dark, the moon, now near setting, showed through the trees, enormous and still, as I turned up our driveway to climb to Eagle Lane. Then as I walked, it disappeared, lost behind the relief of the island and its thick forest. The sky was bright but didn't light my way and my LED headlamp, its batteries depleted from its use during the kitchen remodel, obscured rather than illuminated my path. As I passed the Becker farm, the eastern sky became visible and Venus was spectacularly bright but would fade as the sun rose in the next hour.

As I emerged from thick forest and the shelter of a small hill to my left and started past Rachel and Marilyn's place, or what had been their place before they moved to Orcas and had been vacant since because the buyer, who owned several properties on Crane, some with houses and some not, didn't seem to have much interest in either selling or renting his holdings, I was startled by a brighter, bigger moon, now even closer to the horizon, but obstructed by scattered trees.

093: Shining Path (2010 August)

I was certain the moon had something to say to me and I needed to put myself someplace where it could. I turned around, leaving Circle Road for Gulf Lane and the properties that had a clear view to the west. They were being developed together by three young families. I climbed onto the tent platform, now without a tent but where the carpenters who built the first house and what the families called their shared bunk house, had lived for almost a year, winter and summer, and was stunned by a glittering path of light laid down by the moon on the water below, from Sydney by the Sea on Vancouver Island, a place we'd traveled to many times by boat, past Stuart Island and Speiden and through Speiden Channel almost to my feet.

A quarter mile away, just to the right of the shining path, a white light blinked a warning about the reef it marked. At the other end of the path, perhaps 20 miles away, two radio towers near Sydney blinked back. The air was cold, but the moon, usually cold and remote, wasn't this early morning. It was warm and welcoming and spoke softly of the vast, awesome, and intimate universe that lets us see and wonder.

By the time I got to the community dock, the eastern sky showed some color, melon to rose. The frosted grass covering the path crunched as I crossed the meadow, low places flooded and wet, unfrozen. Later as I walked down the ramp and along the community dock to absent neighbor Margaret's boat to cross to Orcas for the Greybeard's, an informal retired men's group I'd been part of for many years, Wednesday morning gathering, I had to be very careful not to slip. Margaret's boat was covered in thick frost, the windshield a blank white face.

Rubbing the frost with my glove didn't make a dent and neither her boat nor ours had an ice scraper aboard. I was late, as usual. I took the red rubber bucket from the *Huginn's* cockpit, (our commuter boat) dipped it into the saltwater and poured it over the front deck of Margaret's boat to see what that would do to the frost. Melt it. I poured another bucketful on the windshield and the ice seemed to disappear — but the windshield was still translucent — until I wiped the condensed moisture off the inside of the window. I would be able to see where I was going, after all, and I pointed the boat through Pole Pass to the Crane Community dock, a quarter mile through Pole Pass on Orcas.

Later, after the Greybeard's and back on Crane, I could see that Yvonne had already left in *Huginn* for her monthly Garden Club meeting, this one featuring a presentation on landscape design by a woman from Friday Harbor who operated a nursery. I sat at my computer and worked on building a help section for the Slocum book until Gary called just after Yvonne returned to Crane in the *Huginn*.

Tom, a Crainian like me, and with whom I had a complicated relationship, was off-island, but his property caretaker, Carry, had left Gary a voice mail saying that he'd turned off the meter at the property but the meter, like a very slow odometer, was still moving and would Gary, the Water System Manager, take a look at it? Gary, on Orcas, told me about the request and asked if I could read Tom's two meters, so I printed out the last island meter readings and put a screwdriver, adjustable wrench, and a small flashlight in my pocket, clipping my camera and eyeglasses case to my belt, and retraced some of the steps I'd taken before dawn, this time turning left at Rocky Road rather than staying on Circle Road for a trip around the island, now covering about three-quarters of a mile.

When I opened the first meter box and saw it full of water, I reached for my reading glasses and found the belt box empty. My camera would have to be my magnifying glass and as it turned out it worked very well that way. Back home later, I sent Gary cropped, enlarged pictures of the meters that showed clearly their readings should any questions arise from Tom. Watching the meters, I saw no movement at all, so I took two sets of pictures at a ten-minute interval and looking carefully at the later versus earlier version, I could see no change. What had Carry seen? Was I looking at the right meters? I was certain I was but because I didn't have my glasses I couldn't read the January 1st reading spreadsheet and the photos I took of it didn't help. At home later, with my reading glasses on it was clear that I had the right meters and the readings were consistent with a half-month's use, so I sent Gary a report, with pictures attached and asked him what he'd like me to do next.

Ninety-four: Fly Brains and Mushroom Bodies

"The brain is wider than the sky." — Emily Dickinson

When Yvonne came home from Eastsound after having her hair, the wind was blowing a steady rain slantwise, not a nice day to be outdoors. She'd asked me in the past not to comment on her hair cuts so I didn't say anything but at dinner she delivered the verdict: except for the bangs — which were too short — she liked the cut. That was a relief.

I had forwarded to her an email from Suzanne, our Unitarian fellowship facilitator, that said the Orcas churches were sponsoring interdenominational soup dinners during Lent — that would include a meal and some kind of mini-service that would focus on forgiveness — and Suzanne wanted to get a sense of whether our group wanted to participate. Did Yvonne want to cook up and serve soup and help organize the meeting? She did.

I was at my desk early again, just after 4:00, eager to put the third version of the Slocum's electronically annotated *Sailing Alone Around the World* in the hands of my electronic publishing business partners, Chris and David, and get their comments so I could upload it to Amazon as (I hoped) our production version. I'd posted a second version two days before and Chris found that if an Amazon customer had already bought and downloaded an earlier version, they couldn't buy a later version but could request by email that the new version be made available for download, a process that would erase any bookmarks or notes the reader had made to the earlier version — but at least customers could get corrected versions when that was important. In this case, we weren't inconveniencing our customers by supplying defective books they'd have to explicitly request a new version of once it became available because we'd only sold three copies so far — to the three of us. Late in the day after his island electric utility, OPALCO ,Board meeting Chris suggested I simplify the Help page.

Because Chris was eager to begin annotation work on *Destroyer,* a long Slocum article, and then *Liberdade,* Slocom's first full length book, I needed to set up databases for each book that Chris could use to do eNotations — but I couldn't remember the details of how I'd done it the last time, months ago, for several classics we were considering for annotation — and my log contained only one note that looked relevant — mentioning Creator — but a search of my computer for a program of that name came up empty. I found a very early book source-to-database import but it wasn't relevant. Would I have to figure out the whole process again and write another program? Perhaps I had accidentally erased the program at some point and maybe the Mac Time Machine software that used a big external drive for automatic backups had kept a copy. I checked September, when I'd gotten the drive and turned on Time Machine and there was Creator. Whew!

Creator would read HTML files that had tags that showed where chapters began and create a database with a record for each paragraph in each chapter. Then the person doing the annotations would use the eNotator software to attach notes, eNotations, to any passages in any paragraphs. In order to import smoothly, the HTML had to be edited, mostly simplified, and poetry and other specially formatted sections like tables redone in a way consistent with the limitations of the Amazon ebook reader (Kindle) format. Some of this process could be automated but because the book source files each have their own conventions, the process would require manual intervention. I needed to write up the process so that someone else could do it.

Destroyer is short so it didn't take long to edit and then load — and I sent it off to Chris. *Liberdade* is longer, sixteen chapters, and has a table that I had to recast in a fixed-width font. Once I loaded it into a database, I could output the book through the eNotator process and compare it to the original — both viewed through a browser. After three reviews and fixes I sent the *Liberdade* database to Chris for eNotating.

And then youngest son and neuroscience grad student, James called. He was waiting for a bus on the UCLA campus to take him home and he had some time to talk. He was acting as a TA this winter and had two sections of 35 students each for an undergraduate neuroscience course that reviewed articles and heard talks on the current state of the field. He'd been taking such a course, at the graduate student level, for the last 2 1/2 years. He liked doing the class and interacting with the undergraduate students and was very impressed with perhaps 20% of his students. They did their reading, understood what they'd read, and were able to write about it clearly and even critique it. He was amused at a particularly telling example of how the students sorted themselves out.

094: At the South Side of Och's Meadow Guiding Visitors Toward the Break in the Trees and the Path to Our House (2008)

Fly brains have a structure called mushroom bodies, named that because of its shape, not because it's a fungus. And mushrooms do not have a nervous system, at least in the sense of having neurons. Only animals do. But in a multiple-choice test, some students picked the answer that suggested that fly brains have mushrooms inside. James was busier than he'd been before, finding he had to work eight to nine hours a day to keep up with his study, lab work, and teaching and both Yvonne and I said "Good" to ourselves.

After dinner we called our granddaughter, Opal Anne. It was her sixth birthday. She answered the phone and we heard about her birthday dinner — Dad (our son Noah) and Mom (Natasha), brother Morgan, cousin's Hope and Hunter, and grandma Nana (Jan) attending. She hadn't opened her presents yet, so Yvonne couldn't ask about how she liked the knit ponchos Yvonne had made for her and her doll, Crissa. It was a wild call, Opal mostly distracted by the excitement around her but trying hard to report on it. After, as is our family custom, we sang her the traditional Swedish birthday song, "Ja, må hon leva!" (Yes, Long May She Live!), we let her return to her party.

Ja, må hon leva!
Ja, må hon leva!
Ja, må hon leva uti hundrade år!
Javisst ska hon leva!
Javisst ska hon leva!
Javisst ska hon leva uti hundrade år!

Ninety-five: Cold in the Springs

"The greatest glory in living lies not in never falling, but in rising every time we fall." — Nelson Mandela

Ten years ago Karl suffered through surgery in his mouth to excise cancer there. My sister Julie's email, in my inbox this morning, reported Karl, her ex-husband, was in the hospital again, facing nine hours in the operating room and a more complicated procedure this time, since both his gum and jaw were implicated and bone would be removed from his leg to substitute for what was removed from his jaw.

Phoebe, my niece, was worried, Julie less so, and no report from Cooper, my nephew. Ted, Karl's brother, was standing by at the hospital. The surgery was serious but not, on the surface, life-threatening. The questions lay more in his recovery, recuperation, and habit revision. The first bout with cancer led Karl to quit smoking. He'd been conscientious about exercise, what he did with his body, for as long as I'd known him, at least 35 years, but he was less concerned about what he put into his body. It was his encouragement about business opportunity in Colorado that influenced me to leave Chicago in 1975 and go west to the mountains and start a business that led to several, one especially turning out well. It was very cold in the Springs and very dry but wet and dark on our island. Julie was putting out water for the birds and other thirsty wildlife since their sources were now frozen and had written and sent me a prose poem about the life of the birds in her neighborhood and what they meant to her.

On Wednesday Howard had told the assembled Greybeards that Bob would be going to the hospital in Anacortes to see about bleeding from his catheter — according to Brian not unusual. Megan, Bob's wife and older than Bob, probably in her mid-eighties, wasn't strong enough to get Bob in and out of the car. Would Howard help? Yes. So he was giving us a heads up about being ready to help. Because Bob's medical coverage was running out and their resources limited, his future nursing and rehab care and living arrangements were problematic, with Medicaid the only recourse. On Orcas primary medical care was available to all, irrespective of their ability to pay — the result of generous funding by a foundation underwritten by a few wealthy and compassionate patrons — but specialist and nursing care was a different matter.

095: Crane Community Dock (2008 December)

And Jim, who Howard paid special attention to and who suffered from MS, was running out of money for 24-hour care. What would happen to him? Would he end up in a Medicare facility and lose his connection to the Deer Harbor community, including his regular attendance — with the help of an aide of course — at monthly potlucks?

On Wednesday I had also talked to the Greybeards about Alan, his agitated depression, his death, and the note from his widow, Nora — and the way I broke off our friendship years back when I decided he had become too curmudgeonly and uncompassionate. Learning what lay behind his anger and sometime bitterness, my story, my rationalization no longer worked. I was at fault, not Alan. I had let him down, not him me. I had been self-righteous and judgmental. I thought I understood but hadn't. I had been a jerk — to Alan and Nora, who had always been friendly and generous to our family, housing our son Eric, for instance, when he started at UCSD and needed a place to stay because the dorms weren't open yet.

The group wanted to help me sustain my original story — about Alan having a choice about becoming unsympathetic to the poor and powerless — that it would have been dishonest of me and bad for Alan to in effect appease his bad behavior and values. Who knows? All I knew was that I felt guilty after finding out about his torment and that was a sign of conflict between reality and self-regard. When Yvonne and I had first talked about Nora's note and Alan's death, she suggested that I should write Nora and that I needed to acknowledge the scene in the La Jolla bakery years ago when I criticized Alan — but now looked very different — and that she would write something as well. I could now see that she was right.

With a lull in the publishing process — Chris and David were looking at the revisions of the Slocum book prior to my uploading it to Amazon — I wrote up what I thought would make sense as Crane Island Association dock policy, based on existing policies (not many and not clear), actual practice, and problems I'd observed managing the docks. In the past, for some Board members, Board policies were like laws or moral rules requiring strict observance and rigorous enforcement. My view, and the view of some others, was that reality was more complicated than the policies could treat and that since we had no real method of enforcement in almost all cases, all we could accomplish by actively getting after people was creating ill-feeling that further reduced cooperation and sense of community. It made more sense to see the policies, for the most part, as being advisory, serious suggestions for acting in a way consistent with our joint and several interests.

I'd written up suggestions for a comprehensive set of water policies and presented them at the Board meeting a week before and had included a general principle as the first policy — about conservation and protection of the quality of our limited, shared resource. I did something similar with the dock policies. Board member and water expert, Dave, would consolidate suggestions from Board members about his water policy draft and present a new draft at the next meeting, in early March, part of his chairing the long-range planning committee.

Steve, living on Orcas above the Crane Association dock there, had sent me a draft of a solicitation letter for donations to the Pole Pass No Wake Zone committee for the maintenance of existing "No wake" buoys and the installation of more, and unlike my fellow Crane Board member, Martha, who responded to Steve almost immediately, his email and attached draft had lingered in my inbox without reply. I made a few suggestions for simplifying some of his prose and sent off my reply.

I had asked Gary for Carry's phone number so I could call him about his concerns about Tom's water meter (which I'd looked into and wasn't able to find a problem) but the number Gary supplied turned out to be someone in Friday Harbor who barely knew what Crane Island was. I'd have to go to Tom for Carry's number.

I signed checks paying Association bills and Yvonne dropped them at the Post Office on her way to the Deer Harbor Community Club Friday afternoon knitting group. Besides helping one another with their knitting, this week the women decided they'd tell one another more about themselves and their lives though Bev and Yvonne and already done that to some extent because sometimes they were the only participants. They all wanted to know each other better.

Ninety-six: Misplaced Pots

"It's not what you look at that matters, it's what you see." — Henry David Thoreau

The sky was clear, but here and there over the water, especially to the east, the air was thick, misty, and the rising sun an orange disc in a white background over Shaw, though over closer Bell Island the air was crystal clear and the island seemed close enough to touch. In minutes the mist covered Bell and crossed to Crane, enveloping our house in a white gauze. Then the mist was gone, the sky blue, and the January sun warming through the dining room windows. Three seagulls took up their station on the railing outside looking for a handout but flew away when they realized nothing was coming.

Yvonne had her hair cut a few days before and I was relieved to hear that it was fine. There was no way I could tell on my own. Only she knew. Well now it wasn't OK; it was terrible, maybe the worst cut she'd ever had and she needed to get it fixed. I could only agree. Her day and some days to come were spoiled. She appealed to Jeni in Seattle and quickly got back all the details she needed to call the salon Jeni used and make an appointment. Yvonne would be going to Seattle again.

A week before, at the Deer Harbor potluck, Howard , Greybeard's host, had put the Unitarian coffee pots Sheila had been keeping into our van so that Yvonne could make coffee for this Sunday. Except that Howard had put them into the wrong van — whose? So he sent out an email plea:

> *Greetings All, At the last potluck I was supposed to hand two "Airpot" Vacuum flasks with a pumper on the top, contained in boxes and those inside an Eastsound Market bag, to Yvonne A. Instead I put them on the front seat of what I thought was her van. Big mistake, because they're still out there somewhere and I'm ketchin hell. If any of you found this bag with airpots on your front seat and*

096: Misty, Foggy, Golden Sunrise

could let me know, I might just come out of this alive! If not, Becky, could you send out an all-points. The van I put them in was parked South of the steps, near the library box. Thanks, Howard

It turned out Howard had put them in the Community Church Assistant Minister's van, a Scot, who wore his kilt and played guitar at the Robert Burns night potluck.

Yvonne began to assemble her tools and supplies for painting three kitchen walls and I brought in a 20" extension ladder I'd stored on the back deck for the occasion but when Yvonne tried to put it to work, it was too long for the 12-foot west wall. Could I get the shorter ladder? Of course. I'd left it in Margaret's house, next door, about 200 feet away, so that the window contractors could study and then estimate what it would cost to install double pane windows, something Margaret was considering but hadn't yet decided to do — from Columbus where she was teaching the spring semester.

Yvonne placed the shorter ladder and the height was right but she — and I — had a worry. The bottom of the ladder was on a rug on the kitchen floor. Would the ladder slide out from under her when she climbed it? Would the rug slide, carrying the bottom of the ladder away from the cabinets? It looked like the ladder wouldn't slide on the rug and it seemed the rug wouldn't slide — so it didn't seem necessary for me to hold the ladder and I was in the middle of a project in my office down the hall from the kitchen.

Eleven years ago when we remodeled the kitchen in our Deer Harbor house, a kitchen with a vaulted ceiling like this one but higher, I had set up a 20-foot ladder against the central roof beam so she could paint the ceiling there. A few minutes later up on the ladder she started to scream — the bottom of the ladder was sliding backwards — so the top was slipping down the face of the beam. In another second, the ladder, unsupported at the top would fall and with it Yvonne, crashing down on the kitchen floor, with dire consequences for Yvonne's health and well-being. But it didn't. I managed to grab it in time, let her climb down, shaking, and then ran blocks to the side walls so the ladder couldn't slip. Disaster invited and then prevented.

So I wasn't totally surprised when this day Yvonne screamed again. The rug had started sliding backwards — until its edge touched the kick plate on the cabinet on the east side of the kitchen. Yvonne got down, I moved the bottom of the ladder closer to the west wall, with the legs on the western most part of the rug. The rug wouldn't slide farther and the ladder wouldn't slide on the rug. But Yvonne was spooked.

Later, in order to paint at the highest point in the kitchen, Yvonne had to climb up on the top of the pantry, safe because it rested on feet on the floor and was screwed to the wall — but with her feet almost eight feet above the floor, Yvonne was nervous. Why didn't I do the ladder work? I wasn't afraid of heights and had been high on the 20-foot ladder a week before when tying a guide rope when our young Australian friend Tim (visiting with wife Kelly) and I took down three trees. I didn't even suggest to Yvonne that I take over. She didn't want me to. It was her project and she'd complete it. I knew that if she really didn't want to do this painting she'd say so.

Are you OK? Yes. I'll just stand here until I know you're OK up there on top of that pantry. OK, thanks. And then I went back to work. And now, where she wanted to change the wall color from Crunch to Mocha, it's done and it looks good. I can take the final pictures and post the kitchen project album to our family website.

Yvonne and I had agreed to get Rome to LA flight tickets for James and Keith when they return from Europe in July. I'd found a good fare with Kayak and our Chase points would just about cover them so Yvonne called James for confirmation (since it required a 14-hour layover between the two legs) while I finished up with the travel agent — who confirmed that it was the best price available around that date. Done — and it cost only $43 out of pocket — some compensation for paying all those Chase bills (well — actually Yvonne pays all the bills. She assumed that role not long after we got together, appalled at the way I did it — as she had with the laundry — never letting me touch our laundry again after I stuffed damp clothes coming out of the dryer into a basket and left them there — and maybe after I shrunk her favorite sweater). Anyway, that was done. James and Keith now had their outbound and return flights and all the Swedish relatives were already thinking about all the Lutefisk they could serve the young men.

Chris had finished the eNotations for Slocum's *The Voyage of the Destroyer* and I needed to make it into a book and upload it to Amazon for publication and hopefully sale. It was much shorter than Slocum's *Sailing Alone Around the World* and was Slocum's first publication. By late afternoon it was posted, along with what we hoped was the final improved version of *Sailing Alone,* now containing a Help file.

Yvonne's special sauce spaghetti for dinner. A new book published. The kitchen done. James and Keith with flights. A good day.

Ninety-seven: Huginn Again?

"It does not matter how slowly you go as long as you do not stop."
— *Confucius*

A solitary male bufflehead, in his elegant black tuxedo and bright white shirt, had taken a position just outside our cove, diving for breakfast, the water calm, the sun soon to rise in an almost clear sky and as I came back outside with my camera a sea gull spying my movement on the deck circled expectantly, apparently a veteran of human largess.

At the Crane community dock about 200 yards from our house, Yvonne arrived at the *Huginn* before me, got into the boat, turned on the power, put the key in the ignition, and turned it. Nothing. As I came up, she was checking the battery power switch — it was in the right position — it hadn't been left on and the batteries depleted. I turned on the cabin light and it glowed — but weakly? I retrieved the battery jump starter from the dock cart shed and connected it but that made no difference because the battery was already fully charged — as I expected because I had charged it only a few weeks before. Was the problem the throttle safety cutoff? I told Yvonne that we should just take Margaret's boat over to Orcas, that I'd look into the *Huginn* when we got back from the Unitarian service.

Phil, Library Director, and Rachel and Joan, Orcas Library Board members (Joan's tenure overlapped mine when I retired from the Board a year before) would speak on intellectual freedom, democracy, and the Orcas Island Public Library, with Suzanne moderating. I talked for a while with Megan about Bob and she explained that the doctor they had seen (not his regular urologist) had been unhelpful, even insulting, when they traveled to Anacortes this last week for help with Bob's leaking catheter. A visit to the Orcas Medical Center brought relief as Carol discovered that the tube diameter was too small causing it to become clogged so she changed it and that problem was solved — but not the issue of how Bob would be cared for because Megan simply couldn't manage it. She was hoping for a Medicaid solution and would know later in the week.

097: Ferry, Fog at Orcas Landing

Suzanne talked about what the local library had meant to her as a small child — she thought libraries and churches were the same thing — both sanctuaries, and continued to feel that way today though in a different sense. When I had been interviewed by the community at an open meeting when applying to be a Library trustee, I had pointed out that public libraries are essential to democracy in its broadest understanding, along with public schools and a free and responsible press. Unitarians are committed to the democratic process and thus to libraries. Rachel talked about Orcas Library policies that ensured open access to all and Joan about the need for libraries to be free of government control. Phil, with a stack of examples, explained how libraries contain — in their books — a wide spectrum of ideas important for fostering successful community discussion and decisions.

Now home for lunch, I put my multimeter in my backpack with our iPod as we left, returning to Orcas, again taking Margaret's boat so we wouldn't be late for the Sunday afternoon cake tasting at Don and Terri's on the hillside above the Deer Harbor tidal lagoon. Howard and Sheila had already arrived by the time we drove up and Kate was right behind us as we parked. Ken had taken the early ferry to Anacortes to pick up a 900 lb. hay bale for their horses and would appear soon. Why go all the way to Anacortes for hay? Because it cost five times as much on Orcas and with their three horses going through a bale every two weeks the accumulated differences were substantial. Don and Terri had moved into the Lahari development less than a year before after deciding they didn't want to live another winter on their sailboat in the Cayou Quay Marina, where Howard, Brian, Chris, and I (for more than ten years until last April) had moored our sailboats, cruising out to sedate and sometimes intensely exciting adventures. Brian had gone the furthest, to the South Pacific several times, bringing back stories that would have turned my hair white if it wasn't already and which may have caused him to lose most of his.

Don and Terri had had adventures as well and had lived on their boat (actually a series of them) in Mexico, Australia, Trinidad, Panama, Sausalito, and elsewhere. In Porto Vallarta they'd started what turned out to be a successful bakery, and they were now writing a book about their adventures that would include recipes and they were trying them out on willing Deer Harbor residents before committing them to print. We all agreed we enjoyed the almond cake with a slightly crunchy consistency more than the smooth one. Howard made and brought a delicious raisin cake I could only taste not eat after filling up on Don's cake. The house was small but open with a vaulted ceiling, a deck and lots of glass to the south where it looked over Cayou Valley, Pole Pass and Crane Island visible though the firs a mile and a half distant as the raven flies. Then the eight of us sat in a circle and at Howard's urging talked about adding music and dance to the Deer Harbor Community Club meetings. Yvonne favored a hootenanny, singing folk and popular songs of our youth and would look into recruiting Sharon and Michael, local gifted musicians. Howard would look into finding a contra-dance caller, and Terri would organize a percussion flash happening for the March potluck, reproducing in a small way what we'd been encouraging each other to view on YouTube.

Back on the Crane side community dock, Yvonne was already walking home on the path across Och's meadow, through the trees that screened our house, and home to make dinner. I pulled my multi-meter out of my pack and in the falling light checked the *Huginn's* two batteries and found that both were charged. The problem had to be in the throttle safety cutoff. Designed to prevent starting unless the throttle was in neutral, in the past I sometimes had problems starting even when in neutral. After a particularly harrowing experience when I was backing up to park at the Orcas dock in a strong southeast wind and the engine died and I couldn't restart it, the *Huginn* was pushed under Warren Miller's ramp to the west with both the *Huginn* and I narrowly escaping injury — while Margaret, who happened to be on the Orcas dock, watched helpless. By whacking the throttle I finally got the engine to start and then had West Sound Marina disable the cutoff. The problem was worn out contacts, they reported, so when doing their major repair in December, they installed new contacts. Now, it seemed to me, the throttle design was faulty and both Yvonne and I felt it was more dangerous not to be able to start the engine than start it in gear. I'd have to see about re-disabling it.

Ninety-eight: Press Interviews in Town

"The road to success is dotted with many tempting parking spaces."
— Will Rogers

It was raining hard and I wanted to look spiffy so I carried an umbrella to the dock rather than raise the hood of my raincoat and risk mashing my hair to my head. I was wearing fairly new Levi's (with only one food stain I could see without my glasses) and a shirt and sweater — and my three year old hiking boots — my go-to-town fancy shoes. I felt a bit uncomfortable being so fancy but if that's what it took. Recently Chris and I had used Apple's FaceTime to have face-to-face video phone calls to discuss steps in the Slocum book publication process and in doing so had to look at myself on the screen as Chris or anyone else would see me at the other end and it was a joke — unkempt white hair sticking up, a raggedy mustache and beard, glasses, a mock turtleneck with badly frayed collar under a worn out sweat shirt — dressed for dumpster diving on Crane but at the moment there weren't any.

Three years before our neighbors to the north, in the process of renovating their house, contracted to bring a dumpster to the island and invited everyone to bring their discards to it. Within minutes, it seemed, the dumpster was filled with the overflow piled next to it and the neighbors had to bring in another dumpster for their own use. Disposal is a challenge on Crane and castoffs can congregate in public places when no one is looking. A large pipe shed, built when the island water system was being laid and next to the community center and well house #1, had become a dumping ground for what no one wanted, including things like dilapidated dishwashers and batts of insulation, a messy community space that invited more of the same, so one summer day I encouraged a general cleanup and Gary and Wilma brought over their dump truck on their landing craft barge and twenty of us on the island then cleared out what didn't belong in the shed and straightened up the rest. Very satisfying.

098: Sometimes Rain Turns to Ice (2009 February)

The *Huginn* started without a hitch, no recurrence of the throttle safety interrupt problem of the day before. Yvonne, who thought she might have to go to Seattle for a repair hair cut said she would take Margaret's boat if she needed to. Our brick red Ford F-150 pickup was parked in it's usual place on Orcas in the upper Crane Island lot above Deer Harbor Road. The steps, cut into the hill side were soggy and the lot, not graveled, was flooded and muddy in spots. Unlike the other vehicles in the lot, the pickup's windows were fogged, something that had been happening for more than a year, and when I opened the driver's door I couldn't continue to ignore what I had for at least six months — a musty, wet smell, perhaps coming from whatever was growing on the vinyl as black spots and who knows where else. Some kind of mold? Maybe it would make me sick? What could I do about it that wouldn't cost anything and not be destructive or dangerous? Maybe the truck was sealed too tight and needed outside circulation, like an open window but without rain getting in.

The truck, a 1999, had only 77,000 miles on it and worked fine except that the passenger side lock would no longer work, the check engine light was always on even though I'd had it repaired, the heater temperature control required the use of a pliers, and the theft light on the dash wouldn't go out even when the ignition was off and caused the battery to become run down when I hadn't use the truck in several weeks (I needed to install a battery switch). It was very useful for taking trash and recycle to the transfer station and carry lumber and building and gardening supplies to the dock for transfer to Crane and when on Crane, as it had been in the early fall, a necessary part of picking up firewood from around the island. I'd be driving Chris to Eastsound for our two appointments and I was a bit embarrassed at the decrepitude the truck was falling into.

We'd meet first with Meredith at the *Island's Sounder* office and when I drove into the lot where it had been the last time I looked it was gone. I ducked my head into Carol's shop and she said the newspaper office had moved into the old Windemere real estate office across from the Episcopal Church. We were early so the delay didn't matter. The *Sounder*, published every Wednesday, was an Island institution, where everything of note was put into print and where the community had its sometimes passionate public conversations through letters to the editor. I had written Colleen, the editor, the week before telling her about the electronic publishing venture Chris, David, and I were embarked on, that we had published our first book and thought the project warranted coverage and she had agreed, assigning the story to Meredith. The modest offices had a newspaper look and feel, plenty of clutter and too much to do to worry about appearances. Newspapers, writing, and publishing have been in my family at least since my great-grandfather — then grandfather, grandmother, uncle, father, sister and now to me and two of my sons. One of my earliest memories is the smell of ink in a printshop that published my grandmother's community paper.

We told our story and Meredith listened, immediately grasping the concept and value of eNotating classic books. I probably talked too much. Chris was very tired from having stayed up until midnight finishing the eNotations for Slocum's *Voyage of the Liberdade*, the third in our series and the last for Slocum. Later in the day I would complete the steps needed to create an electronic book and email it to Chris for inspection. What we wanted to accomplish with Meredith and the *Sounder* was primarily a public announcement that we were actively seeking eNotators, people who had expertise, could write, had some eNotation projects in mind, had a sense of what the average reader needed or would want to know that wasn't in the primary text, and wanted to be part of the project, and secondarily we wanted the Island population to know about the Slocum books on Amazon and to buy and read them.

We moved on to Enzo's, a coffee shop and bakery in Eastsound, with lots of space and free WiFi, scheduled to meet with Margie, a published author and Alaska transplant, once editor of the *Sounder* but now publishing a competing, online, Orcas news source. Chris had an Enzo's gift certificate and being a sport, treated me to Tazo Awake tea and Margie to coffee when she came in a few minutes later, warning us that she had a cold. I told her about the origin of the idea for the business, having gotten a Kindle for my birthday and trying to read Joyce's Ulysses, using the built-in dictionary and with my Mac on my lap, looking up what I couldn't find there, a tedious and often unsuccessful effort that it seemed to me someone should have already done and built it into a version of an electronic book with the answers to my questions about the text a click or as I imagined at the time (before Apple announced the iPad) a finger tap away.

That's what we were trying to do with what we called eNotations and the Slocum books, with Chris' eNotations, were our proof of concept. Margie got it immediately and like us began to see some of the implications and possibilities. Meredith said she would put an article in the next week's *Sounder*; Margie, with her all-electronic platform, said she thought she'd publish in two days. Both Chris and I enjoyed being able to tell our story and demonstrate the concept — with *Sailing Alone* on his Kindle and iPod and my, well, Yvonne's iPad — just as I had imagined it more than a year before.

Kelly reported to Yvonne that she and Tim were bragging all over Seattle how they'd been on Crane last weekend felling trees, Natasha that Yvonne's outfit for Opal's doll Cressa had fit perfectly and Opal's birthday pool party at the Y had been a big success, and Julie that Karl's surgery had been more serious and drastic than he had let on but he had gotten through it and was communicative by note since his mouth, jaw, and face would need time to heal.

Ninety-nine: Speed Bump

"Not all those who wander are lost." — *J.R.R. Tolkien*

For forty-eight hours at least the temperature had been within a degree of 46 — at noon and at midnight — with clouds, rain, sunshine, and stars — how is this possible? Beginning my island rounds a bit before dawn, I could see that our beach ramp, displaced by high water and wind was still hanging by a thread — in this case a chain linked to a 1" diameter rope tied to a 6" diameter willow stump (I'll have to do something about it), the community water system tank was at 13 1/2 feet (as it should be), someone (Pat?) had leveled the erosion channels forming in Circle Road below the north end of the air strip, the Mallard pair were still occupying the Och's pond (and were startled into flight again as I walked nearby on the road), and the path across Och's meadow was very soggy, awash in water draining down from the higher center of the island. Heavy, moist air, at a distance everything fading into a uniform gray, unidentifiable fragrances as I left the house and when coming back over the wood chips on the north path. At noon, while I made myself a sandwich (toast, lots of butter, peanut butter, cheese, and raspberry jam) two does browsed through the yard outside the deer fence, one stopping to check Yvonne's three compost bins I'd made for her of recycled 2 x 4s, and finding nothing tempting, they continued their daily round.

Yvonne would be going to Seattle the next day for an emergency repair hair cut after the damage she suffered at the scissors of an Orcas beautician, a nice woman who wasn't paying attention, and would be visiting IKEA to pick up a few parts we needed to finally finish the kitchen project. But before she could complete her shopping list she needed to decide what under-cabinet lighting she wanted and I was drafted to help. It turned out we already had three individual lights and power source kit that would work perfectly, so she just needed to get one more kit. And rather than return a drawer she hadn't used for the pantry she found a way to rearrange what was there, added a drawer and now had more usable space in the pantry. Yvonne was intent on having a kitchen blessing/welcoming/bragging party in February.

099: Deer Outside the Deer Fence Love Yvonne's Compost

We called daughter, Jeni, on her birthday, turning 40 and maybe not so enthusiastic about it, but she didn't pick up so we deposited a "Ja, må hon leva!" into her voice mail box.

With an article about our electronic publishing effort to appear the next day, I spent the afternoon working on the website and found myself very frustrated with Apple's iWeb. It was a pleasure to use it to do WYSIWYG layout with but the resulting HTML code didn't render, properly, that is look the same in the browser as it did in iWeb. I knew I could go into the HTML code directly and fix it but that was a fix not a solution so I looked again at RapidWeaver and some other Mac packages but none were as convenient to use a iWeb — so I patched the HTML code in the offending page and posted it. The website now accomplished what we needed in the short term.

Late in the day, I got an email from Amazon, from what was now called Kindle Direct Publishing congratulating me on publishing a book. OK. But that was followed by another email that questioned our copyright to the eNotated *Voyage of the Libderdade*. How could that be? The book had first been published in 1890 so Slocum's work was clearly in the public domain. Our version, with value-added material, eNotations, written by Chris, could be copyrighted. It was original work — but not Slocum's century old original content. We had two weeks to respond — to explain our case — as to why Amazon should let us publish. It never occurred to me this might happen — but on reflection I realized that Amazon must have some kind of audit process that flags new submissions for various reasons and asks the publisher for more information than required in the standard submission process. We had been enjoying the speed at which our enterprise had been moving in the last few weeks. It was exciting, exhilarating — but Amazon, a speed bump in the road, brought us down to earth. It would continue to be a slog with thousands of steps, many forward, some sideways, and some backwards. No matter.

The tulips in the front yard were now more than an inch out of the ground and growing slowly, deliberately. How did they know when to begin? The temperature is almost constant day to day and there hasn't been much sun — yet they know spring is approaching — a beautiful time in the Northwest. The tulips are an inch-out-of-the-ground hopeful and so am I.

One-hundred: Difficult Decisions

"To be yourself in a world that is constantly trying to make you something else is the greatest accomplishment." — Ralph Waldo Emerson

Last to arrive at the "Honeymoon Cottage" up the hill from Howard's house, I took my seat on a marine-blue folding canvas chair with David to my left sitting on the sleeper couch and Howard handing me a mug of strong hot tea and taking his seat on another blue chair to my right next to the cabin door. Brian sat across from Howard and Chris from me on either side of the curtained simple bathroom. We'd been meeting nearly every Wednesday morning for six years but formerly in the less rustic more comfortable surroundings of Howard's kitchen until Sheila, retiring and home more often in the morning, realized that she'd rather be in the house and us in the cabin and told Howard to make it so. The 10 x 10 cabin was our clubhouse, I guess, where we discussed esoteric topics that women would be better off not knowing about, such as what became one of today's topics — when and how should one clean a community water tank, an important topic to four of us because we were each responsible for a water system that supplied two to forty of our neighbors.

David had been contacted by a tank cleaning service who would provide a quantify discount — or maybe more accurately not levy a surcharge — to offset their higher costs for coming to Orcas and wanting to have his tank cleaned after finding the bottom covered in silt that had settled out of the water wanted to recruit other systems for cleaning — but none of us did. Chris' homeowners association would just do it themselves from time to time, shutting down their system, emptying the tank and then entering it with buckets and shovels for the clean out — possible because their system was not yet chlorinated. The Crane tank had been cleaned more than ten years ago — also by the association members — and since the Crane system was chlorinated, the tank atmosphere was toxic and nearly overcame the members intending to clean it since they hadn't thought to wear respirators. I was in charge of the water system but didn't want to think about the silt building up in the tank. As long as it sat on the bottom it wasn't much of a problem — with the outflow pipe seven feet above. As I understood it, the silt wasn't toxic but could make valves leak if caught in them. The bottom seven feet (17,000 gallons) served as a fire reserve with the bottom valve being opened only for emergencies. I had recently let Gary, our water system manager, know that chlorine levels were low in the system and he had already adjusted them up before my email. In the end, David couldn't motivate any of us to partner in tank cleaning but Howard helpfully suggested he talk to the local representative of Evergreen Rural Water of Washington, a state association of small community systems.

Howard reminded us about the hard time Bob and Megan were having — Bob about 84 and Megan a year or two older. It was very difficult for him to get in and out of bed or a car or to walk and he'd spent quit a bit of time in the last two years in convalescent homes receiving rehabilitation care first for his partially unsuccessful knee surgery and then later for other problems, perhaps the result of being confined. He wanted to be home but practically speaking that meant Megan would be the primary caregiver and she just didn't have the strength and thought both of them would be better with Bob living where he could get 24-hour care. We wanted to help but how best to do it? If we made it easier for Bob to be home, we'd ultimately make things much more difficult for Megan — but Bob, formerly a regular member of our Wednesday morning group, hated being away from home. Howard had suggested they seek counseling to find a mutually agreeable solution but Bob wouldn't have it. We decided we'd respond to requests for help but wouldn't take the initiative to make things better. That was up to them.

100: Rain Shelter and Shops in the Snow (2008 December)

Howard asked what I had finally decided to do about Alan's death and Nora's note and my feeling that I should have been less judgmental and more gracious when I abandoned our sometime friendship because I didn't like his attitude toward those without — when he had plenty. David had missed the story the week before so I went through it briefly again saying I had written a letter of condolence and apology but hadn't mailed it because I wondered whether it was really just self-serving and a way to ease my conscience without really doing anything for Nora. David suggested I hold on to the letter for a while and then decide what to do — or write a condolence note but leave it at that until letting some time pass. Everyone had an opinion and they each were a bit different. The answer wasn't obvious to me but perhaps I was worrying about it too much — or maybe not.

Coming back from Howard's after stopping at the Post Office, I was stopped in my tracks on the Orcas dock and then the Crane dock. The water was almost still, a deep emerald green, everything on the water twice as big reflected in it. The twin floats of a crab pot that had been drifting here and there for the past year was now close to Bell Island and the nearby No Wake buoy looked big but was really too small. At the Crane marina ahead through Pole Pass, only the topmost level of breakwater rocks were visible, a narrow band with water on both sides and appearing to float on mercury. So calm, so connected, remarkable.

As we walked down to the Crane dock about 7:20 a.m., Yvonne and I observed the six mergansers close to shore on the right and the score of buffleheads to the left, in their usual place, off the end of the dock. Yvonne would catch the 8:55 ferry for Anacortes and points south, and with a 2:00 haircut appointment in Seattle in hand to repair the damage to bangs and other hirsute areas causing excruciating psychic pain inflicted on her the week before by an Orcas hairdresser. Later in the day, calling, Yvonne reported the repair was a success and that she very much enjoyed having dinner with and staying with Jeni. Yvonne told me to take an unbaked turkey pot pie out of the freezer and put it in the refrigerator. I knew the location of both major appliances but kept her on the phone until I found the pie, tomorrow's dinner, not on the middle shelf of the freezer because there was no middle shelf — there were four shelves — but on the second shelf from the top or third from the bottom depending on how you're counting.

Margie had written an article on our epublishing effort and posted it early in the day and it was deceptively pleasant to see us (David, Chris, and I) as being visionaries with a great idea and a credible start. Margie had expressed interest in eNotating her classic book favorites, having a comparative literature degree, being a published memoirist, and having done a great deal of writing and editing, so she appeared eminently qualified. But she didn't use a Mac so I'd need to create a Windows version of our software tool and test it thoroughly before she tried it. The Windows build worked almost perfectly but not quite so I'd need to spend some time analyzing and fixing. It turned out she couldn't get together until Monday — so it appeared I had time to make the fixes.

One-hundred-one: Trying to Look Ahead

"Every day, I walk out of my house / I get in my car / I drive to the gym / And sometimes I wonder where I am going." — William Stafford, *"Traveling Through the Dark"*

Having fallen asleep at 10:00 while reading David Foster Wallace's *Infinite Jest*, now well passed page 300 and beginning to enjoy and understand it, I slept straight through until 4:00 and after spending about 35 minutes doing my daily 40 slow, deep breaths, I went right into my office without laying a fire in the wood stove because I would be leaving the house soon and besides Yvonne was in Seattle at Jeni's and therefore wouldn't be disappointed on reentering the world at her usual hour of 8:30 and not finding a cozy glow coming from the corner by the living room windows facing the Salish sea.

Chris, David, and I would meet at 9:00 at David's house high on the cliffs forming the western border of Deer Harbor. At 10:30, Jens would join us, now temporarily back on Orcas with his wife Susan after driving cross country from Boston — leaving its cold and snow. Having worked hard over the last week and accomplishing a great deal, it was time to pause and take stock before beginning the next stages in the development of our electronic publishing business and an opportune time for Jens, David, and Chris to meet and get to know one another, talk about Jens inprocess*Metamorphosis* eNotations project and ideas for recruiting eNotators and marketing our books. Jens had sent me a book introduction and Kafka chronology I hadn't looked at and I wanted to add them to the *Metamorphosis* database and give it to him in case he wanted to work on it before he and Susan went to Maui for two weeks though I thought that unlikely.

Later, as I had breakfast, oatmeal cooked not in the microwave but slowly in a 1.5 qt All-Clad sauce pan without a lid over a low flame, stirred frequently but not continuously, with heavily buttered dark toast and 8 oz. of not-from-concentrate grapefruit juice, and looking at the weather report on

Weather Underground (an ironic name?), I noticed fog was reported for Deer Harbor, so I turned on the deck light, opened the dinning room door to the south deck and looked out. The report was accurate and Crane Island was socked in. No flights this morning in and out of our airstrip (that's a joke — I didn't expect any) but would it be difficult, even dangerous to make the crossing to Orcas so I could attend the meeting at David's? Certainly now in the dark it would be a problem.

101: Winter Sunrise

Two years earlier Yvonne and I had to return from Orcas in the fog and dark. 'Mantha Moo, (Samatha, our small, black, indeterminate breed pooch) was at home and would need to go out to do her business but we couldn't see more than 50 feet, lights almost useless since all they did was reflect back from the fog creating glare. The *Huginn* has GPS but not radar.

The water between the Orcas dock and the Crane dock, a bit less than a half mile, is sometimes littered with logs and even deadheads lurking just under the surface, bordered by reefs and rocks, and the currents through Pole Pass, where we would have to go, could be strong, disorienting and impossible to get through for a kayaker. That day I hadn't checked the tide tables and didn't know which direction the currents would be running tonight or how fast. The incoming tide leaves Deer Harbor going east through the pass and the outgoing tide flows west through Pole Pass, the speed of the current dependent on the difference between high and low tides (up to 13 feet) and the time between them.

After turning on the battery power, on that exciting night two years ago, I started the engine and turned on the GPS system, the navigation lights and the spotlight on the bow while Yvonne cast off the lines and came aboard, and we headed slowly into the blaze of light caused by our spotlight. Turning it off, we couldn't see anything either. But I could see our position, the direction we were heading, and where we needed to go on the glowing Furuno GPS screen mounted on the dash in the *Huginn's* cabin.

We were cruising blind, on instruments. We wouldn't see a log in our path. We couldn't see the reflective "Slow, No Wake" sign on the south side of Pole Pass, about 50 feet wide at low water with reefs on both sides, or the solar powered red flashing light on the north side on the pass, a distant descendant of the lantern our Orcas neighbor Cal McLachlan's grandfather tended there a century before. We were having an adventure. Again. Part of the Crane Island experience.

As we approached Pole Pass, according to our GPS display, Yvonne, who was outside in the cockpit for a better view thought she saw a flashing red light. I kept the *Huginn* to the middle of the channel — on the GSP screen — and slowed down to a crawl since we would be passing shallow reefs on either side.

As I looked back at the GPS, I could see that the boat was no longer headed in the right direction. The currents, opposing us, must have turned the boat. The arrow on the display shows us the direction we're traveling across the surface of the earth and it was pointing toward the rocks and then back towards where we had come from.

I turned the helm to the right to head away from the rocks and Yvonne yelled that the red flashing light was behind us, no longer on our right. Would I crash the boat on the rocks? Because she was outside I couldn't be certain but I suspected Yvonne was becoming frantic. We were going to be shipwrecked on Pole Pass. I was calm but confused. After what seemed an endless period of steering wildly back and forth, watching our position on the GPS map, and Yvonne reporting the position of the red danger light on its rock above Pole Pass, we made it through, turned left into what I hoped was the Crane marina and then could dimly see a reflector on the end of the primary dock. We would make it. We were saved.

We had been in danger, real danger. If we had ended up in the water, at 48 degrees and in the fog, we would have suffered hypothermia and been lost before we could find our way to shore, a difficult task in the night and the fog even in warm water.

As we docked, very happy to be back on our island, I realized why our passage, even with the GPS map display, had been so bizarre and disorienting. When I had slowed the boat entering the pass, its speed had dropped below the speed of the out-flowing tide and thus the *Huginn*, though pointed forward toward a safe course through the pass, was actually going backwards and the GPS system showed that. My reaction was to think I was steering us in the wrong direction. I wasn't. I just wasn't in control. The tide was. So I tried to correct what I thought was my error and that only made things worse. If I had stuck with my course and given the boat more throttle, we wouldn't have had nearly the trouble we did. Now I know. Until I forget.

Today, as the light rose and I could look at today's fog, I wasn't worried about today's crossing to Orcas. Visibility was 200 feet and it would be light when I left. Later when I crossed to Orcas, I couldn't see my destination but I could see the shore north of me and knowing it well, I followed its contours east, noting neighbor's docks and rocky points until the Crane dock came into view. Later, about 12:30, returning to Crane, the fog had risen to a position about 100 feet above the water, glowing brightly where thin and the sun almost showing through. Beautiful.

One-hundred-two: Beauty Duty

"The beauty of the world has a breath; / The shadows of the trees are not what they seem." — Wallace Stevens, "Sunday Morning"

Yvonne's trip to Seattle had been successful and her new hairdresser, Casey, had delivered beyond Yvonne's expectations; she had delighted Yvonne. The previous week her Orcas hairdresser had mangled her bangs and cut her hair so that it stuck out where it shouldn't and vice versa and for two days Yvonne was in a state. Casey fixed the bangs somehow, Yvonne wasn't quite sure how. And she turned Yvonne's cut into a bob. Jeni had stood by her mother during the crisis, pointing her to Casey and providing sympathetic listening.

I had moved one cart full of firewood to the house three days before and had burned all of it, so I loaded, moved and stacked two carts full on he front porch, out of the rain and handy for bringing in to feed the wood stove. Our electric bill had arrived, covering December 17th through January 16th, the total $250, about $100 higher than during the summer and about $150 less than our first January on the island. Our daily fire, though not our sole source of heat and maybe not even the primary source, was probably worth $100 per month in the winter, and required about 10 hours of my time (maybe more) per month for cutting, splitting, stacking, and moving so maybe my time was worth as much as $10/hour. We were down to our last stack now. I had more wood, from Tim and Kelly's visit and what I had dragged home from the beach, but those sources were green and wet and wouldn't be usable until next fall. The remaining stack was less than a cord and a cord would last about eight weeks, that is perhaps until the end of March, but the heating season wouldn't end until sometime in May. We'd be traveling for three weeks or more during that time so the wood might last until the end of April. I had my eye on a good-sized fallen tree that had been held off the ground by its branches and so probably wasn't yet rotten but I'd have to fetch it in the dock cart, a quarter mile each way and probably six loads. Next summer I'd have the pickup on the island for wood gathering and launching our day sailer. I'd have to see.

Margie, a professional writer with a comparative literature degree, was eager to begin eNotating Bronte's *Jane Eyre* and I'd meet with her Monday to sign a contract and provide the software, a database, and some training. I'd developed the software on a Mac and it needed more tweaking for Windows, so I spent several hours trying to cope with slight differences in how quitting a program and the menus work between the two operating systems. Importing the novel into a new database was still too much a manual operation, so I spent time improving the software to make it easier and perfectly accurate so we wouldn't have to spend so much time proofreading and making corrections.

Stephen, David's nephew and a college literature teacher, had heard about our project and written David to find out more. Stephen and I had agreed to talk this morning and I explained what we were doing now and what we intended over time. His school was looking into using ebooks to reduce the expenses students faced buying paper books so he'd been thinking about ebook technology and understood our idea immediately. Two possible projects made sense to him: *British Romantic Poetry* (Byron, Keats, Shelly, Wordsworth, and Coleridge, and maybe Blake — with his illustrations — and Clare) and Mary Shelly's *Frankenstein*, a popular book that many people fail to fully appreciate and for which eNotations would be very useful. I suggested he write an informal proposal to do *Frankenstein; or, The Modern Prometheus* (an 1818 novel written by English author Mary Shelley), how he wanted to approach it, and said we could get started soon.

Because Stephen would be the first non-Orcas person (he lived in Southern California) to become involved and because I hadn't met him, I felt a need to be more formal about the relationship and project, anticipating what might become our typical eNotator arrangements as we grew. Stephen and I talked about the cloud-based (Internet) teaching platform I thought we could create and its possible market.

102: Perils of Proofing

He could see the applicability to his teaching world. And we talked about the even larger picture, a linked library of classics, that for instance could serve as a base for eNotating James Joyce's *Ulysses* or Mary Shelly's *Frankenstein*. Our meeting finishing up, Chris, David, and I would turn our attention to our business plan when Yvonne and I returned from California.

Yvonne's knitting group this week numbered three: Bev, Joan, and Yvonne though Marion dropped in to pass along her current news. Yvonne told me she didn't understand how Marion knew absolutely everything about everyone. She had a long island history, felt a connection to everything, and enjoyed acquiring and spreading the news — never as gossip or in any mean way — simply because it was so interesting and important to her. Cal, a fifth generation Pole Pass resident also seemed to know everything and everyone — some of the information picked up during daily visits to the Post Office, some from monitoring the emergency radio band and VHF channel 16, the marine equivalent — and some certainly by telepathy — what else could account for it. Both Marion and her neighbor Cal could have served in the CIA, if not as operatives, as instructors.

Our days and nights continued to be very damp — even when it wasn't raining the air was saturated with moisture — discouraging evaporation outdoors — so that our wet footsteps on the deck leaving the hot tub at night were still clearly visible the next morning if there had been no rain. Nothing outside would dry — really — until June or maybe July — not a problem if you expect it but peculiar to people, like us, coming from the high desert of Colorado.

(Written in a comfortable stupor sitting next to the fire while Yvonne, on the couch, alternately napped and read Keith Richard's *Life*.)

One-hundred-three: Winter Dump Run

"The sun has to set to rise again, / The moon has to wane to wax again."
— Emily Dickinson, *"The Moon is Distant from the Sea"*

While Yvonne had her breakfast, about 8:30, I took our dock cart to the back of our lot where the *Discovery*, our 20' day sailer sits on its trailer under a copse of firs and a willow waiting for summer sun, in front of the 10' x 20' storage tent and next to the tool shed and the repurposed privy where we store trash and recycle, safe from the raccoons until we move it off the island to the transfer station on Orcas. It had been 11 weeks since the last dump run, then with Corrina, who was visiting before traveling to India (she had been back now, in Harrisburg for about a week but we hadn't yet heard from her) and was a cheerful helper when we took a good-sized load to the transfer station last fall.

There is no garbage pickup on Crane; you have to take care of it yourself and that makes one pause when buying something since the easy part is the buying — then comes carrying it to the boat, taking the boat through Pole Pass to Crane, and then carrying it to the house — and you must carry the packaging and perhaps the thing itself when it breaks back the other direction at some point.

Cooking waste, vegetable trimmings, egg shells, left-overs we didn't get around to eating and which had begun to mold, would go either to the residents of Yvonne's worm farm or onto the compost pile to be picked through by the raccoons or an occasional deer, mink, or otter. Packaging was the problem and even though most of it could go into recycle we still had to dispose of it.

The privy cum trash shed was completely full: four 55 gallon plastic trash cans — two with recycle and two with trash (some generated by the kitchen recycle and some the result of mink getting into the storage tent, breaking into a box of packing peanuts and then using them as their toilet), the broken microwave we had just replaced, a box of garbage containing clothes I had saved for working outside that were really just rags, a bag of trash, a bag of recycle, and the door to the dishwasher we had replaced in the kitchen remodel. The old dishwasher leaned against the fir that also supported cut up counter top sections. My shop shed held a huge contractors bag of recycle. Yvonne had broken up and stacked all the IKEA kitchen cartons and styrofoam in the storage tent. We wouldn't be able to take all of this in one load. Some would have to wait until the next dump run, probably until April.

As I walked back from having taken the first load to the *Huginn*, dragging our dock cart, Yvonne came looking for me wondering what she could do to help and I suggested she take the community dock cart and move cardboard from the storage tent. Neither one of us had visited it since we tried to make it mink-proof some weeks before. Had they managed to break in? Had they made a mess? As it turned out, Yvonne said they hadn't and the scent of their visit, after Yvonne's clean-up effort, was finally fading. We managed to stuff almost everything into the *Huginn*, leaving the dishwasher, microwave, and most of the kitchen construction trash for another time.

After tying up the *Huginn* at the Orcas dock, Yvonne went to fetch our pickup from the lot above Deer Harbor Road, bring it down to the lower lot, and park it near the top of the long ramp coming up from the dock while I dragged two trash cans up the ramp, left them at the top and took the Orcas-side wooden dock cart down to the boat. Much of the cardboard fit in the truck's back seat; everything else went into the bed of the truck — and it fit, though with little room to spare. As we attached the expandable web that would tie down the load, Yvonne started to give me advice; she'd mostly refrained so far and I explained that the dump process was my kitchen and she backed off asking later whether she'd been too bossy. Of course not.

There was surprisingly little activity at the transfer station, now open only three days a week and with higher fees and a charge for recycling. Our fee: $26 for the whole load — not bad — though we had to do all the work. The County Council, struggling to adjust to revenue shortfalls — primarily in sales tax I think as construction stalled and tourism dropped because of the lingering recession — appeared now to be favoring privatizing the functions of the transfer station. Only time would tell — but those of us on the outer islands would need someplace to take our trash and recycle.

103: Winter Sunrise with Blakely Island in the background, Bell Island in foreground

Though it was now rare for Yvonne or both of us to go garage saileing, there were two she wanted to stop by, given that we were on Oracs and she was on the lookout for yarn, especially. The first was on Pinneo Road off Orcas Road on the way to the ferry landing so we backtracked and drove into an area neither of us had visited before — in the 13 years we'd been on Orcas (or nearby on Crane). The host house and four outbuildings sat at the north end of a green open field, probably five acres that had been cleared of forest maybe twenty years before, a small orchard between the main house and what had probably been a garage converted into a very basic rental living unit, probably without proper county approval, like many such units on Orcas. Yvonne made her rounds and reported first that the prices were absurdly high, $2.00 for a muffin tin, and second that they had nothing she wanted. Me too.

The next stop was the American Legion hall, a half-mile east of Eastsound, where I would get gas for the truck next door at Crescent service, our source for filling propane tanks for the kitchen stove top, and occasional, minor repairs. After paying $80.00 for not much over 20 gallons — at $3.85/gallon, a bit less than $1.00 higher than what we would have to pay at Costco in Burlington on the mainland and checking the oil (down about 3/4 of a quart — I'd have to watch it), I walked into the American Legion Hall looking for Yvonne and found Jens and Susan — they were still working on fitting out their Orcas house where they'd be for the next seven months before returning to Boston. And we saw Steve and Pam and John and Caroline, Orcas neighbors to the Crane dock on Orcas who would be coming to dinner the next day. We saw them again at Island Market, where after dropping Yvonne off and going to the Library to pick up two books they'd reported had come in for her, we headed back to the Crane dock with four bags of groceries in the back seat and four empty trash cans in the bed of the truck. The rain had picked up so we left the trash cans for another time, taking only the groceries with us in the *Huginn* back to Crane.

Due for dinner with Bev and Dave at 5:45, we left Crane about 5:20, the rain light and the temperature falling, with wisps of fog here and there. I didn't expect fog for our trip home but we talked about it, Yvonne pointing out that they had a guest room with an open invitation to stay. They'd been to our house a few months before to talk about our trip to Africa in 2000 and to see the video I'd put together then on VHS tape. They'd had a wonderful time and especially enjoyed the dawn balloon ride over the Serengeti we'd recommended they do. Dave had used his photo printer to make very large prints of some of the pictures he'd taken and Bev had created a video with stills and movies and all of it brought back hundreds of memories from our trip, an extraordinary experience in the land where mankind was born. No fog on the way back home; the air clear and colder, the wind out of the north; more like winter again. Hot tub. Bed.

One-hundred-four: Dinner Party

> *"And I will show you something different from either your shadow at morning striding behind you or your shadow at evening rising to meet you." — "The Love Song of J. Alfred Prufrock," — T.S. Eliot*

Yvonne had stopped at IKEA on her way back to Crane Wednesday to pick up more 10-watt under-cabinet lighting, a cabinet end-cap, and a second valence strip. My mission for the day was to install lighting and valences before I had to pick up our dinner guests who had houses just above the Orcas dock; three pairs of lights; an end cap, and valences under three sets of cabinets so the light wiring wouldn't be be visible. Couldn't take much time....

The wall cabinets on either side of the refrigerator would each get two lights, for a total of four, all attached to the same power source. It would be plugged into a heavy-duty extension cord I ran under the floor cabinets on the left from a wall outlet behind the sink that was controlled by a wall switch that had operated the disposal — which I didn't want — and had removed when I installed the new cabinets. The wall cabinets on the north wall, next to the pantry cabinets, and over the countertop that held the phone base station and walkie-talkie charger, would also get two lights, the power cords running unobtrusively through the pantry wall at the back, then down behind the drawers and at the bottom into the base cabinet under the wall cabinets where I would install the lights, where I'd put the power source and plug it into a wireless receiver and that into the wall receptacle, putting the wireless switch on the outside of the pantry cabinet wall a bit below the wall cabinet.

And it all worked — as intended — without any real glitches — but it took all day. With our guests expecting to be picked up at the dock at 5:00 and me still working on the project at 4:00, Yvonne became a bit anxious and needed reassurance that I'd be done and the construction site cleaned up on time. She'd been cooking around me all afternoon — very patiently. When I finished we turned on all the new lights and were delighted with the effect. What had been dark, in shadow, was now bright, the glass tile Yvonne had mounted above the backsplash visible, attractive, and even glowing. I'd been careful to hide the wiring behind the valences so it wasn't visible. We were both very pleased. The kitchen was ready for public viewing — finally.

Steve and Pam had been to Crane many times and Caroline a few times but John never so we had a tour of the house, the studio we'd converted from a garage and John stayed out on the deck awhile trying to see his house on Orcas — not possible because of trees in front of his house — and appreciating how close we were to the water and that sunrises must be beautiful — as indeed they are.

Hearing that I'd decided to retire at 60 he wanted to know about my decision process and I explained that I liked to work but not go to work. He understood immediately and it turned out he had recently resigned from his management position and he and Caroline had put their house in Dana Point, Orange County up for sale. Caroline had retired from teaching two years before and spent a good deal of time on Orcas but John little since he had limited vacation time. It looked like that would change soon. Steve, a retired Boeing engineer, cited a study he'd seen that seemed to show that my retiring at 60 meant I could expect to live 10 years longer than men retiring at 65.

John wanted to know whether we had an emergency generator and I said, no we didn't need one. We had a wood stove for heat backup, a propane cooktop on the stove, and a gravity-feed community water system. He wanted to know more about the propane; how did I get refills? I explained that I had three 20-gallon bottles and kept two connected to a "Y" switch I could turn when a bottle ran out. Then I'd replace the empty bottle with one standing by and take the empty to Crescent service for refilling. One bottle would last at least three months. On cue, Yvonne called from the kitchen that the propane had just run out, so I went outside and turned the "Y" valve and she was back in business.

Caroline had brought a layered dip appetizer, Pam a salad, and Yvonne had made a spicy taco soup with a variety of fillings. Dessert — a molten chocolate mousse that we all savored to the last bowl scraping. Coming back to the Crane dock after dropping our guests at Orcas, I savored the Milky Way, blanketing the clear sky north to south, its brightness unimpeded by light or air pollution. The night would be cold, probably below freezing but Yvonne and I would soon be in the hot tub and then cozy reading in bed and then drowsiness and then….

104: Otter Slide to Our Pocket Beach (2008 December)

One-hundred-five: Raw Recruit

"And the night shall be filled with music, and the cares that infest the day shall fold their tents, like the Arabs, and as silently steal away." — "The Day Is Done," Henry Wadsworth Longfellow

The horizon was blood red to a layer of clouds not far above it, the color reflected in the two miles of calm water from the ferry landing to Crane and impressive enough to warrant the cost of digital film so I took the camera outside, zooming in on the early ferry waiting at Orcas Landing, in the dark with windows blazing, while just above it, over Blakely Island, the red sky was on fire.

The path across Och's meadow was crunchy in spots and muddy in others as we made our way to the community dock. Yvonne would attend a tool-sharpening session at the fire station and was carrying a green, long-handled clipper, a red, short-handled clipper, and a broad-bladed planting knife. In the van, the tool smelled of the earth: pungent, alive with bacteria I suppose, living their lives in the soil, sap, and whatever else clung to the blades.

Yvonne dropped me at Enzo's to meet with Margie so I could get her started with the eNotation software on Charlotte Bronte's *Jane Eyre*, while she sharpened her tools and visited with her garden club friends, about a dozen, as it turned out, who were also carrying dull-bladed tools. As we had driven along Crow Valley Road earlier on the way to town, I recalled to Yvonne my childhood memory of a man with a sharpening-stone cart, who would push it through our Chicago suburb every summer, women, at home because most didn't work outside the home, coming out to the street with their knives and scissors when they heard the tinkling bell of the cart. He must have covered at least twenty miles every day as he walked very quickly up and down every street of Chicago and its suburbs, an anachronism even then in the early 50's but a wonderful memory now.

105: Early ferry at Orcas Landing

Margie and I went over the annotation agreement, signed it, and then when I reached for my flash drive to transfer the software, Jane Eyre database and some other files to Margie's Dell notebook I realized I'd left the flash drive, disguised as a Swiss Army knife, at home. I had to borrow her flash drive, regenerate the database, and create an installation package — not having time to properly repeat what I had gotten up at 4:00 a.m. to do. What a nincompoop. Because she wouldn't be able to work in earnest on the project for two weeks, about the time we'd be returning from California, I suggested that she experiment and report any problems. When Yvonne and I returned, I'd give her a new version of the database and the software and she could officially start the process. That would give her time too to think through what it was she wanted to accomplish with *Jane Eyre*, how she would decide what text to eNotate. Chris would have the same software and database and could provide local support in my absence.

Just before noon Yvonne joined us a Enzo's and she and I drove back to the Crane lot and I took the four trash cans out of the bed of our pickup, left there two days before after returning from the transfer station in the rain, with our hands full and not willing to use the dock cart, which would add five minutes in the rain to the departure process. Wilma and her Australian cattle dog, Oscar, were leaving Crane when we arrived at the dock, Wilma having done the month-end water meter readings and reporting no meter anomalies though it was obvious to her even before entering the data into the monthly readings spreadsheet that we were pumping much more than we could account for in meter readings. Oscar, brown showing through the white, was very friendly though watching Wilma's every gesture and listening carefully to everything she said. He was on duty and was always on duty, like all well-trained shepherds, fixated on their master, waiting expectantly for a command to round something up and move it someplace.

After lunch, while I sat by the fire writing and listening to her blow-by-blow report, Yvonne struggled with the Windows notebook on the kitchen counter to create and send electronic invitations to the kitchen project open house we'd host toward the end of February. I was sympathetic but was careful not to step into the line of fire. After retyping pages of the same letter because I was literally falling asleep as I typed, I put my feet up and closed my eyes. I hadn't had enough sleep in the past week. When I opened my eyes Yvonne was ready to start the next project, Valentine's Day cards for the grandchildren, created online, printed out, and mailed, more convenient and less expensive than getting to a store from Crane Island.

Once she was set up in my office so she could use my printer, I went out for a walk around the island. The tank level was fine and it looked like Dick Clark, whose boat was at the Crane dock, had been working on some drainage project because the ditch across the road from his property had been cleaned out in two places and small ditches had been dug into the road on the other side leading off it. Here and there as I circled the island, grazing deer took off for the center of the island, trotting or bounding in their characteristic way.

As I came into the house, the phone rang and it was James waiting for a bus in Los Angeles on his way home from UCLA. With Yvonne on the phone in my office and me in the living room, we made plans about our visit the coming weekend and talked about the satisfaction he'd had teaching two beginning neuroscience sections as a TA. Yvonne finally had to get off the phone because between talking with James and trying to watch Oprah, she found herself adding Halloween jokes to the Valentine cards she was working on, her eyes straying to the contents of a paper folder where she kept copies of past cards so she wouldn't unintentionally repeat them.

Supper was some of the taco soup from the night before transformed in some mysterious way into cheese enchiladas. We called grandson Morgan after dinner — he was now ten, one of my best years I think, promise without the complexity that would soon appear and I talked with son Noah about his ski weekend with Morgan — who tried snowboarding for the first time — the snow was mostly slush at Crystal mountain —, and then about the frustrations of trying to get an agent for his second novel and that he was submitting it to Amazon for their Breakout contest. The publishing business was changing and traditional publishers and bookstores were being disintermediated by direct digital distribution — in music, books, and video, with marketing duties now falling on the creators. Big changes we were in the middle of. The hot tub took forever to warm up from its 90-degree overnight state because the temperature was now about 32. But then it did and so did we.

One-hundred-six: Log Rolling

"The logs are waiting, the forest whispering to the tools of the trade."
  — *"Logs and Forests," Theodore Roethke*

Though cold, about freezing, the day was sunny and would warm the air to 40 perhaps, the wind was calm, and the tide on the community beach though rising would be below the two logs I kept tethered to two overhanging trees, logs that had escaped a log boom a month before. I had already cut up and taken home 1 1/2 logs weeks before but a combination of bad weather and uncertainty about whether they would make good firewood had kept my enthusiasm for doing more below a threshold for action, but I had since split one of the sections (that went well) and the wood seemed more green than brine saturated so I decided that drying over the summer, preferably in a split state, would make a good addition to the next heating season's supply.

But after donning my Carhardt overalls and jacket and just leaving the house, sister Marcy returned the call I had left earlier, concerned about what sister Julie had communicated via email when telling me about Karl's surgical travails, namely that Marcy was only now recuperating from being sick for weeks and Paul had now come down with something and was suffering. Marcy explained that New Year's Day, returning from Iowa on the train with Paul, and grandchildren Aelias and Alana, she'd developed a cough that soon became almost uncontrollable and had been diagnosed with multiple, simultaneous infections, one in her ear. She was almost back to normal but not quite. Paul had had a fever, night sweats, and a bad headache for two weeks and his doctor was yet to make a diagnosis. In fact, the reason she hadn't picked up the phone when I called earlier, was that they had been to the clinic, where Paul got a chest x-ray and an MRI. Paul wanted to be healthy because after being laid off and unemployed for six months he intended to start a new job in a week that required spending a week training in Milwaukee.

Neither Marcy nor Paul got sick often, so being sick was more discouraging than expected. About 4 below zero as we spoke, the temperature was expected to drop to 20 below in Colorado Springs overnight, the coldest it had been since Christmas 1980 when Marcy had first met Paul and our Boulder family had been staying with Marcy for Christmas. From the Springs east, the weather was expected to be brutal, a terrible storm was expected for Missouri, Illinois, and points northeast, bringing a sixth major storm in as many weeks to the Northeast where snow was already piled as high as houses in spots. The moderate Crane climate seemed ideal in comparison to the extremes experienced by much of the U.S. Even the rainfall is moderate; a Board member having reported to me the night before that his weather station in Dana Point and his weather station above the Crane dock on Orcas reported exactly the same amount of rainfall year-to-date from July 1st — though by June 30th Orcas would be ahead but at 25 inches for the whole year perhaps not dramatically so.

Loading my chain saw, gas, and chain oil into our dock cart, I headed for the Crane dock beach, happy to be outside in the sunshine and delicious fresh air and eager to begin to create a firewood inventory for next winter. The daffodils were up several inches as were the tulips, and the crocuses, modest and hardy, were flowering close to the ground. Where it was shaded, the path across Och's meadow was frozen hard, so it wouldn't be damaged by the cart passing back and forth laden with log sections — but in the sun and already melted, the surface was soft, wet, in some places slippery, and becoming muddy.

Four years before we had spent a month moving items from our house on Cayou Valley Road in the Deer Harbor Hamlet to Crane, making at least 20 round trips to Orcas in the *Huginn* and about 100 dock cart round trips, with the main move January 9th and 10th, so that the path was a morass by the beginning of the year. We couldn't improve the path because it did not belong to us and though the Ochs were willing to let us use it for easy access to our house, they didn't want us to change it, so we addressed the section we owned, where it went uphill through the trees and bushes that screened our house from the Och's meadow and the community dock beyond, and laid down fir branches, plentiful on the ground after a heavy, wet Thanksgiving snow.

106: Captive Logs on the Beach Waiting for Attention

The boom-escapee logs were high on the beach to the east of the dock, just at the high water mark, where the wet sand and rocky beach turns into grass, bushes, and trees, parallel to the shore and to one another tied together at each end — in one case to an overhanging dead shore pine and in the other to an exposed root — origin unknown. In places, the logs spanned low spots in the beach and retrieving driftwood, I used it to put supports under these sections. After removing the tether ropes, I began to cut the logs into smaller sections that I could easily carry.

The process went smoothly and after making four full cart trips to the house, I took a shovel, rake, and brown paper Island Market grocery sacks to the beach to clean up the sawdust mess I'd made, bringing the sawdust/sand/gravel mix back to my splitting and wood storage area and dumping it on top of the pile from the last beach cutting next to a pile of sawdust, bark, and unusable debris left over from many cutting and splitting sessions.

Yvonne was on her way to the Food Bank Board meeting and reported later, at dinner — a new batch of enchiladas — that George had visited the plant making the new building — in two sections — and was impressed with the precision and lack of mess in the process, that the Board would officially break ground while we were in California, with occupancy expected in March, and that she had volunteered us and our pickup for moving whatever needed to be from wherever it was to the new space.

The Board Treasurer was now using QuickBooks and had been able to provide professional-style financials for the meeting and would be adding budgeting soon. Amazing developments over the last year — moving from a rat-infested storage area to the basement of the Community Church — soon to brand new space on the Church grounds.

By email, daughter-in-law Natasha had suggested spring vacation, April, as a time they could come for a visit, though surely we'd have to go see them all before that.

Earlier in the day Chris had sent an email to David and me reporting that *Liberdade* was now listed in the Amazon catalog; all three Slocum books were now available and we could each go after friends and family as a starting point, to purchase and review one or more, so I wrote Steve and Vicki, a couple that had helped with two insurance automation newsletter businesses I'd had and who were interested in our project. After saying that he didn't want to do any more eNotating, Chris asked me to prepare a *Two Years Before the Mast* database before Yvonne and I left for California and I sent it late in the afternoon, Chris having told me he preferred the edition with a preface by Dana's son, after I'd sent him two choices to look at.

I bought our *LIberdade* late in the day from Amazon and read and scanned a bit on our iPad. It looked good, reasonably professional for amateurs, and I noticed that Chris was injecting his voice, humor, and experiences into his eNotations, for instance by citing some Thomerson's sailing rules, such as "Keep the boat off the land," and "Keep the crew and passengers out of the water," exactly the kind of thing that many readers will find engaging and funny. Our project is coming along.

One-hundred-seven: We're Famous!

"In nature, nothing is perfect and everything is perfect." - Alice Walker

I peeked in the bedroom and Yvonne was awake — she too had been watching the sunrise, the eastern sky changing its palette every few seconds, beginning with dark grey with a hint of rose to its present peach and orange — and I wanted to tell her I was on my way to Howard's. Buffleheads to the left and mergansers to the right, a half dozen noisy crows overhead — up to something I couldn't imagine — and three cormorants just above the water racing through Pole Pass, long necks outstretched, elegant in their way in flight, though looking silly in the water because unlike most water birds their bodies are underwater and only their necks and heads stick out, their lack of buoyancy making it easier for them to dive in search of food but also causing their bodies to cool more rapidly than other diving birds so that they must exit the water once in a while and find someplace to stand where they can stretch out their wings and hold them there while they dry out.

To the north, the two Deer Harbor marinas, about a mile away, brooded in shadow while the top of the cliffs above the west side of the harbor were pink and the Spring Point coast running west from the harbor glowed. As I turned right to untie the *Huginn's* aft line and looking southeast over the top of Bell Island, I could see the sun, a circle of light rising out of a gap in the low hills of Shaw, the sky now ablaze in white, gold, yellow, orange, and blue. I stood paralyzed by overwhelming beauty — and then remembered I was expected at Howard's in a few minutes. As I crossed to Orcas, the rising sun twinned itself, now appearing to the left as well reflected in the windows of Steve and Pam's house above the Crane dock on Orcas. But before I reached the dock the show was over. The sky, magnificent in its glory was now only ordinary, the sun behind a gray cloud on the horizon, the radiant color gone — where?

I arrived just as Howard carried the tea tray up the garden stairs to the honeymoon cottage and he and I talked about his coming trip to France to see his daughter's family, a delight except for her husband, a math professor who could not understand why anyone would ever do what they didn't want to do but should do. Brian soon came in followed by Chris. David was — who knows where. We talked about the case of Bob and Megan, he too frail to take care of himself and wanting Megan to do it, and she too frail to care for him and not wanting to be forced into it, and without adequate resources to hire help turning to Medicaid that would mean signing over Bob's income making it impossible for her to live. A difficult situation.

107: Sun Imminent Behind Bell Island

Conversation turned to the contrast between the American and European social contracts. The American that individuals could do better for themselves than the government, the reward being modest to incredible wealth, the risk being disaster, even for the conscientious — with a social safety net that would keep people from starving but not from losing their dignity and the European, that in some areas — health care, retirement, infrastructure — the community expressed through the government could do a better job than individuals but with less opportunity for wealth and innovation but much lower risk of personal disaster. The trick was to find the right balance, we supposed, between the group and individual, a matter of experimentation and finding what works, not the result of fiat or ideology.

Back in the dock upper lot parking, I opened the F-150's hood and disconnected the positive battery cable using the tools I'd carried up from the *Huginn*, concerned that after having been gone to California almost two weeks, the battery would be dead because the theft light was always on. At the Orcas dock, Pat was loading 6 x 8 second-use beams into his Bullfrog and we talked briefly about the Circle Road repairs he'd made to erosion damage caused by hard winter rains on the grade below the North end of the airstrip. Back on Crane I made my island rounds. The water tank level was now a little higher than 13.5 feet. At 14 feet water would be lost through the overflow.

As I passed Ilze's, I could hear the carpenters at work and after hesitating, decided to say hello and see what progress they were making in the major remodel project to her cabin. Josh and his coworker seemed happy to have a little company and showed me what would be the bathroom, a new, small pie-shaped building 20 feet from the house, where the largest wall — across and top to bottom — would be all glass, with a deck outside and facing the woods and no other house. They would install a composting toilet and run only the grey water to the antiquated septic tank and tile field — as it happened — on the neighbor's property.

They had gutted the house, converting a third of it into a covered outdoor space and had raised the roof over the entryway and put in a small loft. The separate bathroom used huge, heavy beams they were placing by hand though they had a crane come out on a barge to set the steel frame that would surround the bathroom's glass wall. They had initially expected to finish the job two months before. I guessed that they'd be six months late when they finished — not unusual in big island projects where supply line delays can bring a job to a standstill. They were now using a different boat to come across from Orcas, the powered rowboat they'd used for months becoming too dangerous. With three in the boat and with supplies, there was little freeboard and they were in danger of being swamped. When a big Homeland Security / Coast Guard boat passed near Pole Pass as they approached the Crane community dock, apparently looking like suspicious characters, Josh and his companions were stopped and questioned by the crew.

Back on Circle Road, Pat came from the dock in his Gator with beams aboard and I suggested he talk to Josh about borrowing his pickup — with Pat replying that he probably wouldn't need it but that he'd like to see what they were working on. As Pat left, I saw that Tom and Liz were behind me and also headed in the direction of the community dock, so I backtracked to say hello but neither was willing to begin a conversation, Tom still fuming I guess for my telling him I no longer wanted to hear his apparently paranoid complaints about his neighbor. Oh well.

At dinner, Yvonne reported on the Deer Harbor Community Club meeting attended by a dozen women. The main topic was fundraising and the tentative decision was to hold a rummage sale at the Club in May, Yvonne volunteering to be in charge, comfortable with that role because she had managed so many in Boulder and on Orcas in the past. And she had begun to better understand the delineations of the Orcas social structure, how the very rich and those connected with them had their circle, sometimes beneficent to and sometimes volunteering for the larger community but acting more like minor, rural gentry, some even making significant efforts over the years to increase their land holdings, as Moran had done a century ago on Orcas, and more recently Kaiser and Clapp in the Deer Harbor area.

One-hundred-eight: Going for Help

"The way to get started is to quit talking and begin doing." - Walt Disney

Three couples had bought three adjacent parcels at the west end of Crane and they had begun building: one house and a shared bunkhouse were complete, built by versatile carpenters who spent a year living in a tent on the property during construction, and a second was framed with a roof on but put on hold for now. Apparently construction would start, perhaps as early as spring, on the third parcel, the owner, Larry, inquired of me, since I was the head of the Crane Island Association Water Committee, about the steps needed to have metered water available at the site. New to the job, I consulted Gary: once Larry applied for a building permit, the county would require Larry to provide a completed water availability form signed by the association. In the meantime, Gary and Larry could coordinate the installation of water for the construction period.

David had completed our eNotated Classics corporate Federal tax return and asked Chris and me to review it before he signed and mailed it. With about $4.00 of income for 2010 and more than $2000 in expenses, the business would start the year with a loss carry forward we could apply against future profits, if any. We had had a few sales of the three Slocum books in January and the first few days of February following the appearance of two articles in the Orcas press and emails to friends and relatives but we needed to do much more; we needed to have a real marketing effort for the Slocum books and then other authors and books as they were added to our eNotated Classics library. At least to start with Amazon and its Kindle catalog would be our distribution and service source but appearance in the Amazon catalog probably wouldn't sell many books on its own. Our eNotated Slocum editions were buried among many others, some free. Potential buyers would have to come to the Kindle catalog with the specific intention of buying our books, not simply because they were looking for Slocum ebooks. Our editions weren't free but they weren't as expensive as some others. If a shopper bothered to read our product description, they might understand the value we had added and pick our edition. And if we had any reviews that explained and extolled our eNotated version, that might help shoppers make up their minds in our favor. But such a passive marketing strategy wasn't likely to succeed; we needed an active and continuing marketing process.

108: Air Strip Buried in Snow (2008 December)

There were some obvious points of entry: yacht clubs (more than 1000 in the U.S.) and Slocum interest clubs, both groups with Web presences and accessible by email but neither Chris nor I could spend the time required for marketing and also eNotate another book, in his case, or further develop the software and manufacturing processes and elaborate the Web site, on mine. We needed help.

More than a year ago, I'd talked to Natasha, my daughter-in-law, a stay-at-home mom for the last 9 1/2 years - but previously a marketing manager for a company in Colorado. Would she be interested in playing a role? She was favorably disposed, but then the project stalled when the first eNotator backed out. Now we had three books to sell and more coming. Her youngest was now in kindergarten and she was spending some time taking care of her brother's two preschoolers. Knowing Natasha, her curiosity and research talents, her organizational skills, and her love of good books, I was confident she would do a great job and that we could count on her and though we had no money to pay her, we could share revenue as book sales took off due to her efforts; she didn't need a job, that is an immediate paycheck, but certainly would over time. Would she still be interested?

Yes, she would. She and Noah had been talking the evening before about how she might enter the workforce in a few years in a way that was interesting, used her talents, and was rewarding. She was considering going back to school for an MBA but that would be time-consuming, expensive, not necessarily rewarding, and probably not very interesting to her. On the other hand, she saw possibilities in eNotated Classics and thought it might be interesting to help build its sales through an organized marketing effort. Her time was limited now but she could make some time and then next fall when her niece was in kindergarten and her nephew in preschool, hopefully, she'd have more. We talked about the practicalities of finding Slocum book prospects and she'd begin doing some research. We'd talk more.

One-hundred-nine: Sunward Bound

"The gladdest moment in human life, methinks, is a departure into unknown lands." - Sir Richard Burton

Out of bed before 5:00, I began to work on my departure check list. We would be leaving Crane for Los Angles and then Los Osos, planning to be gone for almost two weeks, so the house had to be made ready. I had turned the hot tub down to 80 degrees the night before, wanting to conserve electricity but not take an excruciatingly long time to warm up we we came back. I set six of the seven thermostats to 58, omitting the master bedroom because Yvonne was sleeping and as it turned out forgot to do it. I ran the dishwasher for the half load in it and took the trash out in the pouring rain in the dark to the converted privy/trash can shed about 100 feet from the house.

After making myself an oatmeal breakfast, I went outside again in my big yellow raincoat and crawled under the south deck to turn off the propane tank, water streaming down through the interstices between deck planks above. Now I needed to tie down the hot tub lid. I'd tied a line to the southeast 4 x 4 post under the hot tub, coiled and hung on a nail. I threw the free end west over the hot tub cover but it landed in a budding red hawthorn bush. When I went to pull the line free so I could tie it across the lid to keep it from blowing off in a strong wind, the hawthorn refused again and again to give it up, curling the line around small branches so I couldn't pull it free, out of spite I suppose and wanting to keep me out in the rain so my exposed Levis would be thoroughly soaked.

Later, when Yvonne finished her shower, she told me I could turn off the water, so I put on my wet raincoat and walked the 100 yards up the driveway to our water meter and holding a small LED flashlight so I could see what I was doing, opened the meter box cover, pushed the spider webs out of the way, contorting my wrist to reach it and then turned the valve counterclockwise until it stopped. The rule on Crane was to turn your water off at the meter if you expected to be gone more than three days and too many members who had forgotten to do that found themselves facing multiple thousand-dollar water bills because they had left a hose bib on or abnormally cold temperatures had frozen and cracked a pipe that then leaked once the temperature warmed up.

109: Leo Loves Attention

We left the house at 7:30 in the pouring rain carrying our suitcases and for me a pack, went through Yvonne's bamboo gate, and then onto the path, the top part covered deep in wood chips but the bottom now muddy from water steaming down the slope to the Och's beach and then across Och's meadow, inches deep in water in spots and muddy in others. Now not fully dark, we said goodbye to the Canada geese pair paddling away from the beach after having spent the night on land and the buffleheads barely visible on the left and the mergansers on the right. Today, because we'd be gone for more than 48 hours, we moored the *Huginn* on the south side of the Crane Orcas dock with the other boats that were infrequently used and I noticed walking along the bottom of the U between the south and north fingers that four more aluminum row boats were stored on the dock, now a total of seven, upside down to keep the rain out. Why more boats? Whose were they?

We had time for something hot to drink in the Orcas Hotel coffee shop, Yvonne a Starbuck's wet latte and me Tazo Awake tea, and we each picked out a day-old pastry; a danish for Yvonne and a blueberry, almond scone for me, my second and completely unnecessary breakfast. The *Elwha* left at 8:55, on time, sparsely occupied, stopping at Shaw and then Lopez to pick up more passengers but not nearly full, arriving at Anacortes a little after 10:00. I walked into Barnes & Noble at 11:00 in Bellingham, Yvonne dropping me off while she shopped at JoAnn Fabrics not far away, finding me in the store at checkout about 11:40 buying V. S. Ramachandran's new book, *The Tell-Tale Brain*, for James, about his neuroscience research, the author's first book *Phantoms in the Brain* having influenced James to pursue neuroscience. I also picked out Bernard Haisch's *The God Theory* that I thought would provide an interesting point of view (one of a number I would present) for my upcoming UU talk on science and religion.

We stopped for lunch at Taco Time, a northwest fast food chain that offers reasonably healthy and tasty food, having a spicy pozole soup and carry-out salads to take on the plane for dinner. We left our van at the Quality Inn where we'd stay later because our return flight would arrive too late to make the last ferry at 9:05.

The van driver, taking us the two miles to the airport, was a WSU graduate in computer science trying to recover financially, I think, from an effort with two friends to start an online business that had failed. I told him about the Real Software IDE I was using to create multi-platform software and our eNotated Classics project. Two Colorado emigres we knew, but from the Western slope rather than the Front Range side, would also be on the Allegiant flight to LAX, also attracted by the convenience of being able to go south without having to deal with Seattle and SeaTac. As it turned out getting to LAX was painless.

But Friday afternoon Los Angeles traffic was terrible so it took son James forever to get to LAX from the UCLA campus and then to connect up and take off for his apartment. His partner Keith had attended an afternoon philosophy colloquium at USC and would take the bus home while the three of us stopped at Von's to pick up a pizza for James and Keith and staples for our use over the weekend. Most notable at Von's was a merchandising display James pointed out with pork rinds on the top shelf, Pringles in the middle, and 1/2 gallon plastic bottles of vodka on the bottom shelf — supplies, I suppose, for a typical Los Angles party.

One-hundred-ten: City of Angels

"To us, family means putting your arms around each other and being there." - Barbara Bush

James and Keith had done a bit more with their apartment near the intersection of Beverly Hills and Los Angeles, equidistant between UCLA and USC, and on convenient bus routes to each campus, their preferred form of transportation getting to and from school, where each was working on a PhD, James in neuroscience at UCLA with a focus on addiction and Keith at USC, specializing in philosophy of mind and of language, James in the third year of what he hoped would be a five year program, and now doing some teaching for the first time and Keith in his first year of five, teaching to begin in his second year.

We'd visited in late September and early October the previous fall, appreciating the decorating and furnishing they'd done and the meals they'd cooked us in their new apartment, after Keith came west from Atlanta, spending much of the summer with his family after graduating from Princeton, James having met him there, as a student in the class two years ahead of Keith. The big change was the brothers, Leo (as in Tolstoy) and Fyodor (as in Dostoyevsky), two four-month-old Russian Blue kittens whom they loved and who provided them continuous delight even when the kittens were sleeping. And Yvonne and I immediately loved them too — though I was a dog person, they were impossible to resist.

At 9:30, we left their apartment, going first to the UCLA building that housed James' rat lab so he could feed his charges and then to nearby Westwood Memorial Park, final resting place of many of the rich and/or famous, especially those connected with film, not two acres, I think, invisible from the street, a green oasis of trees and stone-punctuated lawn, the periphery containing the Armand Hammer family crypt and mausoleum buildings, one containing Marilyn Monroe's remains, an empty location to the left James said

Hugh Hefner owned. We lingered for almost an hour, unsuccessful in finding Frank Zappa's apparently unmarked grave. We spent the longest time at the grave of Natalie Wood Wagner, telling the boys about how we admired her in films beginning with *Splendor in the Grass*, *West Side Story*, and others.

110: Keith, James, Yvonne, Chad, Doreen at Manhattan Beach

Then to Manhattan Beach, south and a bit west, where we met nephew Chad and his girlfriend Doreen on the Manhattan Beach Pier, introduced to Doreen for the first time, a pretty and charming German emigre who worked in group travel. Chad had studied film at Loyola Marymount and then had worked in the game industry and was now, with a friend with a more technical background, building a business that provided consulting services to the transportation and game industries on the effective use of video and animation in their trade show and web marketing efforts, an area Chad said was important to companies and in which they had great interest but currently were poorly served.

Yvonne and I hadn't been to Manhattan Beach before and were struck by the long stretches of beach to the north, running all the way to Malibu, with an indentation away from the water at Marina del Rey, and then to the south to the Palos Verde peninsula, where a Crane Island couple lived when not on Crane, and above San Pedro and Long Beach, commercial areas. Oil tankers rode at anchor in the process of being loaded through pipelines that ran from refineries and tanks on the shore.

Chad and Doreen told us both grey and blue whales migrated offshore, the grey more common, on their trips down the Baja Peninsula and into the Gulf of California, but that the blues had come close to shore this season following their food source, perhaps because the water was cooler than usual. Local Homo sapiens were flocking out to mingle with the giant cetaceans, in sail and power boats and smaller craft like kayaks, something that wouldn't happen in the San Juan's or Puget sound because of protective restrictions on the distance that had to be maintained between people and whales. We told them about the orcas, killer whales, that had come through Pole Pass the previous June and how we had watched them from the Crane side of Pole Pass, the whales no more than 50 feet away, casual and unhurried in their passage, their breathing audible and visible in the plumes of condensed water vapor above them. Chad treated for lunch at a brew pub just above the pier and wouldn't let me have the check. I was impressed and pleased. James and Keith were hosting us, driving us around, and feeding us and now Chad was feeding us too.

Doreen's group travel company specialized in the geriatric set, 65 and older, my cohort, Yvonne with some years to wait, a quickly growing group being populated by aging Baby Boomers. Chad had taken up woodworking and had created Christmas presents for everyone in Colorado Springs and now gave Yvonne a serving platter, an inch-thick section of live oak. Though we had been to Los Angeles several times since James started grad school, we hadn't made an effort to visit Chad, my nephew, and I was sorry we hadn't but happy that we now had. Inextricably hearing from my sister, Marcy, that Chad was doing woodworking and had created objects for them they were impressed with had triggered something in my psyche and Chad had come into clear focus, was there, with a young woman Marcy admired, and needed visiting and paying attention to. Where had I been? Asleep?

At nearby IKEA, the boys tried for the eighth time to buy a table shown in their catalog but it seemed never to be in stock at any of the three IKEA Los Angeles stores — and it wasn't this time — and the store was packed with eager shoppers, more so than the Seattle store. Then we walked to Target where Yvonne bought them a circular, flowered tablecloth that looked good when laid on their table later. Then a stop at Trader Joe's while Yvonne and I dozed in the backseat of James' car while the boys shopped for dinner. James and Keith made a tasty macaroni casserole topped with tasty cheeses topped with sourdough crumbs and a balsamic vinegar dressing with pears and walnuts. Then off to the nearby Grove Shopping Center and nearby Farmer's Market we visited with the boys in September to see "True Grit," a film we all enjoyed considerably, James and Keith seeing it for the second time, the source of a good deal of discussion that evening and the next day.

One-hundred-eleven: Seeing Stars

"The city is not a concrete jungle, it is a human zoo." - Desmond Morris

We left the apartment about 9:30, driving first to the Melrose Trading Post, a Sunday flea market — at the Fairfax High School — where James and Keith intended to look for a cafe table they could use on their Moroccan theme deck that they also referred to as the "catio" since Leo and Fyo liked to spend time out there, generally when supervised since though the deck had a railing they had made catproof, the kittens might try to climb over it and then jump onto the roof of the deck below. The morning was lovely — cool air and warm sun — and the flea market huge with offerings from shoes (thousands of pairs) to furniture (a variety — small to large) and collectibles of many kinds. The boys found a promising chartreuse wood folding table offered for $8 they could repaint — and reviewing all the options on the grounds, bought it to take home later.

We then drove west to the UCLA campus where James would feed his rats and put them through a training regimen, one in a series in which they would learn to push a lever to receive food, moving on to test their risk-taking propensity, and then correlating that with susceptibility to addiction. He worked with two rat populations: one a standard lab rat breed and one that had been bred over three generations to be identical to the standard population except for being higher risk takers; higher risk-taking being measured with a version of the BART test, in which the subject, usually human, blows up a balloon, one step at a time and can cash out at any time. The bigger the balloon the greater the reward — except that that balloon could burst at any time, randomly, with no reward forthcoming. The rats didn't blow up balloons on computer screens; instead they would lose when the lever was withdrawn, at random. Interestingly both rats and humans, even the higher risk takers, would not take even statistically rational risks, always taking less risk than the actual situation called for.

111: Melrose Trading Post

Keith and Yvonne and I continued south and west to Santa Monica, parking at Santa Monica Place and walking the four blocks to the Pier, a site showing up in many movies, most dramatically in Spielberg's *1941*, in which the Ferris wheel at the end of the pier rolls off into the ocean. Keith pointed out Malibu, far to the north and west. Below the pier a group had set up hundreds of symbolic graves, marked by crosses, showing graphically the impact of the war in Afghanistan, with five flag-draped coffins, the most recent American soldiers fallen in that decade-old and unresolved conflict. We sat in the sunshine enjoying funnel cake — Keith hadn't had any breakfast — and then returned to Westwood to pick up James, the drive taking only 12 minutes in the light traffic of Super Bowl morning. James directed us to Pit Fire, a pizza and salad restaurant on Westwood Blvd where we'd had lunch with Laura Davis, daughter of Boulder friends, Alan and Tessa, two years before, not long after James started at UCLA, Laura having moved to Los Angeles after college looking for what turned out to be an elusive career in improvisational theatre.

In the hills north of West Hollywood, Griffith Park was a half hour away and despite being Super Sunday, parking for the Observatory and Planetarium was a challenge. As we walked uphill to the planetarium grounds we could see the Hollywood sign to the west, Santa Monica and the Pacific to the southwest, flashing in the afternoon sun, Century City, downtown LA, and the San Bernardino area to the east, the air reasonably clear with layers of clouds or smog over Palos Verdes. We bought tickets for a planetarium presentation on water in the Solar System and then walked around on the decks looking at the city below. The exhibits were especially good, I thought but the planetarium show very basic. We left the park grounds near sunset, stopping back at the apartment to recoup and make plans for dinner.

The Ethiopian restaurant James favored being closed until mid-month, James picked Awash on Pico, outside the boundaries of little Ethiopia on Fairfax. The food was wonderful. We shared three different wats — beef, chicken, and vegetable — spicy stews, on top of a sheet of injera, a large sourdough flatbread, like a crepe but spongier, and rather than using utensils, we ate by tearing off small pieces of injera — also served with the meal — and grasped the food with the bread. Back at the apartment, we played a film game, Scene It — which moved too slow and was too esoteric for me and then moved to Cranium, a more interesting game with more variety, a kind of combination of many other games, and Keith and I eked out a win against James and Yvonne, James being an unexpected warehouse of popular culture. A bit more discussion of True Grit — what was it? — and then bed — folding down a futon in the living room — the kittens behind a closed door with James and Keith so as not to disturb us. A great visit.

One-hundred-twelve: The PCH

"The greatest legacy we can leave our children is happy memories." - Og Mandino

Yvonne had reserved an Avis rental car at $150 for the next week to carry us north to Los Osos and San Luis Obispo and then back to LAX for the trip home, intentionally choosing a location on Santa Monica Blvd close to the boys apartment so it would be easy to pick up Monday morning — but in fact the rental location was IN Santa Monica not on Santa Monica — and though theoretically, James could drive us to Santa Monica he wasn't eager to since he did not want to have his car on the UCLA campus and would have to come home, park his car and then take the bus, as he always did, to the campus. Maybe we could take the bus? Of course we could.

At ten-minute intervals during rush hour, sixty-foot red articulated buses run the 720 express route from downtown LA to Santa Monica along Wilshire Blvd and back, the buses equipped with devices that adjust traffic lights along the way to make bus travel more efficient, with a bus stop across Wilshire Blvd from the Flynt Building, home of the porn king's publishing empire, only a short walk from the boys' apartment.

We crowded aboard, paying our $1.50 fare, moving farther back into the standing-room area whenever space opened up, the passengers loosely matching James' description of students and maids. The bus was a marvel compared with the electric and diesel models I'd driven two summers for the CTA in Chicago while in graduate school, powerful, comfortable, and without much of the sense of hectic anxiety palpable on the Division St. route I often drove when working the extra board in split shifts for vacationing drivers. This bus was equipped with stop request pull ropes. So that there would be no doubt, a message confirming the request was displayed on an LCD screen at the front of the bus, alternating with the date and time. James didn't mind taking the bus back and forth to campus every day and we enjoyed the 35-

minute ride to Santa Monica, exiting the bus at 14th and walking five blocks to the Avis office to pick up a Ford Focus.

112: Ventura in the Sunshine

Rather than driving the 110 to the 405 and then north to the 101, I suggested to Yvonne that we take the PCH, Pacific Coast Highway, north from Santa Monica, joining the 101 at Ventura, and that's what we did, encountering little traffic, noticing the Getty Villa and adding it to the list for our next visit, and paying attention to Malibu as we cruised along its 27-mile length, seeing signs for the state park we'd find time for in the future. In Ventura we stopped for lunch at Margarita Villa, a Mexican restaurant adjoining the marina in Ventura Harbor, sat outside in the sunshine on the upper deck, overlooking hundreds of sail and power boats wondering how often they got out and where they went — most probably not often and not far.

In Santa Barbara, we parked off State Street and Yvonne made the rounds of the stores while I sat in a Starbucks sipping tea and taking advantage of their free WiFi, catching up on email and a request from Martha to provide an up-to-date water usage report for the members, something I could do easily since Gary had sent me the meter readings a few days after the beginning of the month. After finishing and sending off a PDF version of the updated spreadsheet to Martha, I reviewed a request to the Orcas FIre Department Dan had copied me on, to move forward on a multi-year plan to bring Crane communication devices up to date to conform with Federal standards, in place after the 9/11 attack made discontinuities and inconsistencies evident in the U.S. emergency response system.

We arrived in Los Osos not long after 5:00, son Eric coming in the door a little later with Jackson and Maddie after picking them up at Bob and Diane's, Kristin's parents, who had retrieved them from school and pre-school. The kids were noticeably bigger, especially Maddie who had grown a couple of inches since we saw her in the fall, doing so without gaining weight, just stretching out. Kristin arrived as Eric was working on a fish taco dinner. As we ate, we traded news on the extended family, all the joys and concerns — as we say at our UU services — of the last month or so and the convenience of flying out of Bellingham and the great time we'd had with James and Keith and Leo and Fyo.

Here in Los Osos, we missed Katie, a crazy but loving dog, ashes now in a small box on the mantel and soon bound for delivery to the top of Peak 8 when Eric travels to Breckenridge over Presidents' weekend for his annual ski trip with his boyhood Boulder friends. Marcel, once Jeni's dog had his charms as well, I suppose, a rotund Papillon mix Eric said had lost four pounds recently but to me a hirsute insatiable appetite on four-legs.

With the kids in bed, we talked and talked about one of Eric's colleagues who was making life difficult for the Aerospace Engineering department he headed at CalPoly, continuously obscuring departmental matters in a fog of emotion, hijacking meetings and faculty energy to feed their emotional needs. I suggested that Eric keep meetings and his interaction with her and other faculty focused on the business of their department and he acknowledged that was the direction he was already beginning to take, moving from operating informally and reaching complete unanimity by making everyone happy, to operating more formally in meetings, seeking consensus, that is with everyone heard and all points of view understood but with decisions the result of a substantial majority though not unanimous vote. What a struggle — but as we liked to say in our family, a learning experience.

Bob and Diane had given up their La Jolla apartment, now living full-time in San Luis. They had passed some of their unneeded furniture on to Eric and Kristin, and among the new items were a mattress and box spring Eric had set up in their office area. It proved very comfortable as Yvonne and I turned out the light after a few pages of Keith Richard's *A Life* for her — she was enjoying reading the ghostwritten book but had decided Richards was depraved — and Bernard Haisch's *The God Theory*, a book I had picked up at Barnes and Noble in Bellingham for my upcoming UU talk on science and religion when I got Ramachandrand's *Tell Tale Brain* for James. Another big day.

One-hundred-thirteen: High-speed Life

"The universe is full of magical things patiently waiting for our wits to grow sharper." - Eden Phillpotts

Children's voices in the kitchen woke us about 7:30; the household was already moving fast, Eric managing breakfast for the kids and making their lunches while Kristin got ready and was out the door for a full day in SLO with Chamber of Commerce duties. Then Eric got ready and packed up the kids, dropping Jackson at Kindergarten and Maddie at her pre-school, one that Jackson had attended for several years before graduating — literally — to Kindergarten. Then Yvonne took the rental car and went off to San Luis Obispo, about 10 miles inland, for some quality shopping time while I caught up on my writing, email, and eNotatedClassics marketing research.

Natasha had begun thinking through elements of a marketing process and had a number of suggestions and questions: a business email address, a pitch document for the Slocum books (should she write it or Chris or?), an interview video with Chris talking about his books, what eNotation was, and why it was a valuable additional element to Slocum's century-old tellings, and a Facebook page about eNotated Classics. She wanted to identify potentially interested and influential reviewers and bloggers and supply them with review copies of one or more of the books — and I saw an easy way to do that.

I copied Chris on my reply and he quickly set up a Facebook page and expressed a willingness to do a video. Natasha had wondered whether it was possible to influence the recommendations Amazon made for additional books when you viewed a catalog entry and Chris wanted to understand how discount prices would work with Amazon. I said I'd look into those questions and then found myself looking at the variety of marketing and sales-related services Amazon offered — which I then forwarded to Chris and Natasha — and Chris began work on an Author's page for the Amazon catalog. Much to understand and choose from.

113.A: Grandpa, Maddie, and Jackson at Play

After returning from SLO and lunch, Yvonne retrieved Maddie from preschool and put her down for a nap, then going out for groceries. Before she was back, Maddie had awoken and I was feeding her cheese, crackers, and milk, the best I could think of as she cried a bit missing her mother. And later Yvonne picked up Jackson from daycare, Kristin arriving home about 5:00 and the kids stayed close to her absorbing her attention while Yvonne made a pasta, cheese, and cauliflower casserole, serving it with sautéed Brussel Sprouts, bread, and salad. Eric's CalPoly Academic Senate meeting ran late and he made it home about the time we were finishing dinner and while he ate, we each ran through our day and then brought Eric and Kristin up to date on Karl's recovery process from cancer surgery and the effect on Julie, Cooper, and others as they organized themselves to see that he was cared for — and then on to Yvonne niece, Gina and her continuing troubles and then her daughter, Cressi's request for financial help as she tried to get through high school and the hope we had for her getting to college and a better life than she had lived in her family of origin.

113B: Kristin, Maddie, and Eric

With the kids bathed and in bed, Eric set up his TV so we could view the kitchen project album I'd added to our family website and we talked through each step — the decisions we'd made, the problems we'd run into, and how we solved them. Kristin and Eric were thinking about a kitchen remodel so they were interested and may have gotten some ideas from the presentation and discussion. Before reviewing the kitchen project Kristin made some suggestions about eNotated Classics on Facebook, having taken some Facebook marketing techniques classes. We'd come back to that area another time. Though the day had been sunny, it hadn't warmed up past 65 and overnight the temperature would dip to 40. Bernard Haisch's book had become interesting as he described experiments that he and Alfonso Rueda made in which they tried to show that inertia wasn't the result of some primary constituent of the universe called mass but the zero-point field, "the background sea of quantum light filling the universe." If true, that would be a radical change from views held since Newton.

One-hundred-fourteen: The Bay

"In family life, love is the oil that eases friction, the cement that binds closer together, and the music that brings harmony." - Friedrich Nietzsche

Maddie May played hooky from pre-school and after Kristin left for SLO and then Eric left for the CalPoly campus, first dropping Jackson at kindergarten, Yvonne, and I — with Maddie in the stroller — made our way the mile to the waterfront on Morro Bay, almost entirely downhill — part of the way on a walking/bike path — to our favorite destination in Los Osos/Baywood Park, the Back Bay Cafe. The owner of the Back Bay Inn had taken over managing the coffee shop, cleaning out the clutter and installing an awning and new tables and chairs outside.

Yvonne and Maddie shared a Thomas Kemper Soda, Orange Cream, that Maddie said was sparkling and I had black tea. We sat outside in the cool air and warm sunshine of a Central Coast February Day, the shallow water of Morro Bay covering the half mile to the sand spit that protected the Bay, anchored in the south at the Montana de Oro State Park, and heading north several miles almost to Morro Rock, residue from the period 22 million years ago when nine volcanos marched from what is now the town of Morro Beach to what is now San Luis Obispo.

Flowers were everywhere, birds busy with their daily routines, with scores of seagulls near the coffee shop resting on the sand that had emerged as the tide receded out to the Pacific. On the way down to the beach, we passed several walkers in pairs coming from or going to the water, happy to be out and moving in the sun. The shop clientele were mostly older and retired — but not all. One pensioner in a billed cap, approaching a group of three at a table near us, told them he had some new gossip that they might be interested in — or not.

A flower-bordered boardwalk separates the Inn from the beach and the motley collection of canoes, kayaks, sailboats, and catamarans, some drawn up on the beach and some, with the tide out, lying in the muddy sand, waiting to be re-floated later in the day. A lush lawn edged by flowers on three sides faces a border of ten evenly spaced shore pines making its western boundary. Yvonne chased Maddie in circles for a while and then we all sat in the sunshine marveling at the spontaneous as well as deliberate beauty around us.

114A: Yvonne and Diane

It was lunchtime almost before we arrived home, Maddie eating lunch and then taking a nap. Yvonne was making cabbage and sausage for dinner and later in the day I went out for apples at Von's and mailed Valentine's Day cards to Morgan and Opal and a check to Cressie in Eastern Washington to help her with month-to-month expenses as she worked to complete high school — with good grades and the intention to go to college.

114B: Bob

Dinner was a madhouse, the kids running and screaming around the house, comfortable to act out with their parents in a way they wouldn't with us or at school. We talked more about Eric's attempt to get one of his colleagues to cooperate with the rest of the department in a change to their departmental curriculum but was again rebuffed. Kristin showed us the Chamber's three Websites and then how they used Facebook as a marketing tool, a channel to broadcast messages to groups that would be difficult to reach one by one. The Chamber director had announced that he would be retiring in July and Kristin's role would change, with more responsibility, and more people to supervise.

Then while surfing the web, Yvonne found the resume of a web developer in Long Beach who had worked on bookdoors.com, our former partner, Richard's website. I forwarded the information to Chris and David and Chris soon wrote back with links to part of the developer's website that showed what the bookdoors site looked like even though it was still behind a passworded wall. It was very attractive and impressive looking — requiring significant effort and therefore expense — and I wondered how Richard would ever recoup his investment. He'd have to sell tens of thousands of books just to break even. And how would the site be maintained and further developed? That too would be expensive. From what I understood when he withdrew from our partnership, Richard was not looking at his site as a business. It wouldn't be inaccurate to describe bookdoors.com as a form of vanity publishing, normally done with paper, here with electrons and pixels. The kids in bed and the adults worn out, we sat in front of the TV watching Modern Family, the Valentine's edition.

One-hundred-fifteen: Bonding

"There is no way to be a perfect parent, but a million ways to be a good one." — Jill Churchill

We kept Maddie May out of preschool to have more time with her and set off to SLO for some focused shopping. Dropping the two girls at Kohl's, I found the nearby Mac SuperStore and had a consultation on the fan noise coming from the left side of the keyboard when the device got warm by, for instance, sitting on a lap and being used to view video. After using compressed air to blow dust and toast crumbs out of the innards, the helpful attendant ran a diagnostic program that showed everything was hunky-dory, though he couldn't be sure about the fan because it wouldn't come on until the systems got hot and it wasn't. At my request he ran a battery test and found it basically useless, something I'd found through observation, so because he had been so helpful without even hinting that he would charge me for his efforts, I asked that he install a new battery and he did, explaining at length how I should fully discharge it once a month or so to have it last as long as possible. Then on to a nearby auto supply store for a battery disconnect device I could use on our pickup, back on Orcas, to prevent an always-on theft light from draining the battery. I met Yvonne and Maddie back at Kohl's and we walked over to Best Buy to look for a video we could watch with the kids Saturday night when Eric and Kristin had their Valentine's night away but we couldn't find "Enchanted," something we thought all four of us would enjoy. Maddie was acting a bit droopy now, not her usual smiley, talkative self.

Dropping Yvonne and Maddie at TJ Max, I bought gas at Costco and then went inside to have a nylon string glued to my right hearing-aid speaker wire to replace the one that had fallen off, an addition that made it less likely the device would fall out of my ear, as it had done more than a year earlier when we were docking the *Discovery*, our 20' Ranger day-sailer, after circumnavigating Crane with Eric and Kristin. At Home Depot I picked up a remote control wall switch I would use to replace the one I nicked from the studio loft to use in the kitchen and then next door to TJ Max where Yvonne and Maddie were shopping for Friday night's lasagna dinner. Maddie now was clearly sick, whimpering, tears in her eyes, so we headed down Los Osos Road to take her home. Within minutes Eric was calling to say that the school nurse had called and Jackson had a 101-degree fever. Could we pick him up? Of course. Soon Kristin called from Morro Bay saying she would pick up Jackson and bring him home to us. Yvonne put Maddie to bed and Jackson watched Disney short films, flushed and very quiet. The two kids had fallen ill at almost the same time, perhaps having caught something from the other kids at the Sunday Superbowl party Eric and Kristin had hosted.

At about 4:30 Eric came home and the five of us drove to Bob and Diane's, meeting Kristin there, coming from the Chamber in SLO. The kids watched TV quietly in the family room while the adults visited in the living room, a convivial session followed by a chicken enchilada dinner. We talked about the Orcas Food Bank and the generosity of some and the reluctance of others toward feeding the hungry and that led, in a roundabout way, to talking about Alan Jaffee. Though he hadn't known Alan directly, Bob reported that Alan had shut down a promising La Jolla business start-up he'd participated in just as it appeared on the verge of success, another piece of information about Alan's story in La Jolla.

At dinner, we talked about Kristin's sister, Lauren's, engagement to Dave, segueing into how Eric was introduced into Kristin's family and his dramatic, public marriage proposal to Kristin, on his knee, in a restaurant with her family and other diners fully engaged in the moment, and Noah's proposal to Natasha in the Chimayo Santuario, Diane's proposal to Bob — at his insistence — after he'd been rebuffed with his for several years, our pleasure at the relationship James and Keith were building, and wondering where things would go with Jen and JC, whom we had yet to meet.

115: Grandma and Maddie

Bob and Diane were happy enough in SLO but had found it difficult to make friends there, having left many in La Jolla and the country club not yielding prospects Bob wanted to pursue. We talked about the friendliness of Orcas and how we had met many people quickly, especially through volunteering and through the Unitarian group. About this time Eric gave me the keys to his Pilot and he and Kristin left with the kids in her VW, both tired from their work days and wanting to put the kids to bed. We continued our discussion, talking about how and why Crane felt like home — for our souls — and the conversation turned to the grandchildren and child-raising. Though Bob and Diane have a different political orientation than we do, we're in close agreement on many topics and in this case found ourselves making the same observations about how the younger generation managed their children, especially around meals and bedtime, wondering whether their unconditional love for their children, our grandchildren, and their desire to spare their children tears and frustration, sometimes resulted in situations in which parents and children ended up being more uncomfortable and frustrated than they needed to be. But then we weren't the parents and didn't see what they did — and when all was said and done they were doing a terrific job and had our complete confidence — and we would keep our lips sealed — except perhaps on those occasions when we were in charge of the grandchildren. We were bonding with Bob and Diane and we liked that a lot.

One-hundred-sixteen: Yvonne Cooks Up a Storm

"If God should hold enclosed in His right hand all truth, and in His left hand only the ever-active impulse after truth, although with the condition that I must always and forever err, I would, with humility, turn to His left hand, and say, 'Father, give me this; pure truth is for Thee alone.'" — Gotthold Ephraim Lessing

The day before, Yvonne had cooked up a big batch of marinara sauce and today she would make it into lasagna, and late the day before she had prepared no-knead bread to rise overnight and be ready to bake for the same dinner.

Jackson and Maddie woke up with smiles after falling ill the day before, not at full strength (thankfully?) but not unhappy either. But because Jackson had a fever the day before, his school asked that he stay home a day, not a bad idea because he needed to regain his strength after a bout of 24-hour flu or whatever it was. So the kids were couch potatoes for the morning and when Maddie took her nap in the afternoon, Yvonne and Jackson made cheese together from a kit Yvonne had mailed from Deer Harbor the week before. She had picked up a gallon of whole milk while shopping — with a drooping Maddie — and would use it today, her cheese kit containing rennet. A gallon of unpasteurized whole milk would make a pound or so of mozzeralla cheese after the whey was discarded. The whole process took only about 30 minutes.

Jackson was interested but his attention would wander back to the fort I had made him (at Yvonne's suggestion) in the driveway from large cartons that had been used to ship the furniture that Eric and Kristin had inherited from her parents when they decided to give up their apartment in La Jolla. Using some packing tape I was able to create an "H" shaped structure with a roof and a few cutout windows Jackson could open and close to survey his driveway domain. He put a smaller carton inside to use as a table — with packing material for a bed, making several trips to the kitchen to bring out plastic dishes to furnish his house.

At Jackson's direction, I used driveway chalk to scratch messages on the outside walls — "Private," "Friends Only," "List of Friends OK to Come In." I was a bit surprised at how much fun Jackson had with his cardboard fort and he spent a good bit of the rest of the day before dinner outside in the fresh air and sunshine except, of course, when he was actually in the fort.

116: Jackson's Driveway Fort

The cheese turned out well and Yvonne sliced up a heritage tomato she'd gotten the day before and prepared a plate of tomato and mozzarella cheese that was tasty even though the tomato wasn't particularly attractive — a dull red and green. The no-knead bread came out of the Dutch oven looking like artisan bread that might cost $6.

We had dropped the kids with Bob and Diane while we went to lunch with Eric and Kristin at Novo on San Luis Obispo Creek, in the shade with the mission on the other side. Yvonne had a Singapore chicken satay and I had a Shepard's Plate, sausage and cheese with spicy mustard — very tasty. This was the first time during our visit we'd be able to be with the young couple without the kids or others around and it was a pleasure just to be with them, adult to adult. Eric had come from a Friday afternoon departmental social time — bocci ball that they played at 11:00 Friday mornings — which had begun to draw a crowd. Yvonne and I were early and we watched Kristin schmooze someone it turned out was on their board as she came in. Eric was late. Kristin recommended Yvonne take a look at Trio, around the corner, and while she shopped, I sat on a bench below the Mission in the partial shade of a half dozen eucalyptus trees with smooth pure white bark and watched people pass through the grove on their walk above the creek. It was a Friday afternoon, a busy time in many towns and cities but not in SLO, the "happiest city in America." It was quiet, sedate, relaxed, pleasant — a very nice place to be — though it could become quite hot in the summer, unlike Los Osos, ten miles away on Morro Bay, usually ten degrees cooler.

After lunch, we went to pick up the kids, who were staying with Bob and Diane. Maddie had fallen asleep. Back in Los Osos and after some wine in the family room, we sat down to dinner, Yvonne getting compliments on her lasagna and New York Times no-knead bread James had introduced her to. The kids didn't sit still for long and were soon dressed up in their Toy Story Halloween costumes promising to dance for us — though it never came off. Dinner conversation drifted into religion, Diane asking whether we believed in God, something foundational for her and we replied in the negative. I talked briefly about panentheism, God not separate from the creation but the world in God. I had just begun reading *The Belief Instinct* and wanted to talk about how the human capacity for postulating theory of mind in other people, that is being able to see them from the inside, was a highly successful evolutionary adaptation but was mistakenly, perhaps inevitably, applied to the universe — it must have a purpose, be the handiwork of a mind, and so on — but I thought the audience wouldn't be a bit interested so I let it drop.

Kristin went to bed early and Yvonne, Eric, and I, tired from the day's activities held down the couch while we watched *Lonesome Jim*, a movie Yvonne and I had seen before and enjoyed.

One-hundred-seventeen: Enchanted

"Belief is a beautiful armor, but makes for the heaviest sword." — John Mayer

Yvonne and I had seen *Enchanted* several times, including with Morgan and Opal, and liked the film a great deal, thinking it would be appropriate for the kids while we babysat them when Eric took Kristin went out for the night to a place on the ocean close to the Hearst Castle, north of Los Osos. As it turned out we liked *Enchanted* more than the kids did but they were quiet and patient, happily eating the kettle corn we picked up at the Morro Bay Saturday afternoon Farmers' Market.

Earlier at 5:00 we were at the Morrow Bay waterfront park adjacent to the public dock with the marina a little farther south. A group of eight young people, mostly boys, had a paddle board, and two at a time would go out among the sailboats attached to mooring buoys, standing on the board, their feet wet since the board was nearly submerged. A 14-year-old girl, wearing shorts and a brown and white checked jacket, took her turn, a black terrier behind her on the board. Protected from the Pacific by the sand bar, Morro Bay is generally smooth and shallow, especially at low tide.

As the setting sun neared the crest of the dunes across the estuary, the sky turned a hazy orange, the sound of the surf on the ocean side drifting the quarter mile to the park. Here Jackson spent his time going from hiding place to hiding place, though it wasn't clear who he was hiding from since he was clearly visible to Yvonne and me and to Maddie.

During the movie, a knock on the front door turned out to be a neighbor driving by, seeing the table and other goods Kristin had left at the curb with assigned prices. The kids went to bed without any objections, Yvonne reading to Maddie and me to Jackson, in his case a Disney version of *A Christmas Carol*. Kristin had expected to make a little money on her sale but the neighbor wouldn't offer any so we sent him on his way and I moved the sale items into the garage where they would be safe from the dew or being carried off in the darkness.

117: Walking Across the Morro Spit to the Pacific

Stephen Lehigh was making progress on a proposal to eNotate *Frankenstein* and we exchanged emails as he explained what he had in mind and I explained more about what we were looking for.

I began to make progress reading Jesse Bering's *Belief Instinct* which looked interesting at the beginning but became less so as I got farther into the book. His claim that humans can't help believing in God because their minds automatically project a perception of other minds not just on people, where it makes sense, but also on random events and the universe as a whole wasn't convincing.

One-hundred-eighteen: Kayaking

"The clearest way into the Universe is through a forest wilderness."
— John Muir

The kids woke up about 7:00, not worried that Eric and Kristin weren't home. They watched television for a while and then their parents returned from their overnight at 10:00. It took a while to get ready but soon we were all out the door headed for the Morro Bay Kayak Shack to rent a canoe for Eric, Kristin, and the kids and a double kayak for Yvonne and me. We intended to head across the bay to the sand spit and the attendant cautioned us to go north first and then turn west since the tide was on its way out and if we headed directly across we might end up stuck in the mud.

The sand spit was a quarter mile away as the seagull flies but our course with its meanderings north, then west, then back south might have been closer to a half mile, the wind blowing from the south and pushing us north away from where we wanted to go. A group of five kayaks were ahead of us though they didn't seem certain of their course or destination. I'd wondered about the depth of the bay and now I knew — at least for a major part of it. The high tide, at about 5 a.m. was a little over five feet. The low tide, after 1:00 would be -0.10. As we paddled across at 11:30 or so we had inches to perhaps two feet of water under the kayak — and that was in the deeper channel. The shallower locations would dry (well, at least to mud) at low tide, so much or most of Morrow Bay was less than five feet deep at high tide.

The bay is protected from the Pacific by the seven-mile-long sand spit and the bay is mostly an estuary fed by a creek from Los Osos valley, bordered by volcano remnants, as Eric explained, plugs not the volcanoes themselves. As we paddled we saw familiar feathered fauna: seagulls, of course, but also buffleheads and turkey vultures and species we didn't have in the San Juans: pelicans, plovers, swans (we did have but rarely). And basking in the shallow water just off the sand spit beach, a sea otter stared at us unafraid and not very interested.

118: Picnic on Morro Bay Spit

Finding a place to beach the canoe and kayak took some searching since we didn't want to have to wade through the mud. Eventually, we found a steep stretch of beach that was mostly sand at low tide and that's where we pulled out. Crossing the dunes to the Pacific, the kids dawdled, playing in the sand, and probably not enthusiastic about the difficult walking in the loose sand. Looking back across the dunes and Morro Bay, the town stretched from the bay uphill a quarter mile or so, a colorful hillside. Morro Rock now stood out more definitively from the land, a breakwater created by quarrying the rock, a kind of apron around its base. Behind the town were the volcano plugs, about 1500 feet high, and now, in the rainy season quite green.

We spent a little time on the beach, long enough to encounter some skeletal remnants — one from a seal and another probably from a gull. We could not figure out how the bones, still connected by ligaments here and there, were originally arranged. It was puzzling to be so puzzled but we were. We couldn't imagine the bones into a shape that, once dressed in skin, would look like something we knew. Retreating from the windy beach, we found a quieter location and Eric spread the colorful Mexican blanket he had been carrying — as well as sandwiches — and we sat in the sun enjoying our time on the dunes. As we walked back towards the landward side of the spit, we passed a midden of oyster shells. Though it didn't make much sense, I wondered aloud whether the shells had been left years ago by camping Native Americans. Eric thought not; more likely birds that had nested in the area — long ago but not now when even infrequent human visitors to the area would make it unacceptable to nesting birds.

On our way back, the tide was nearly at its lowest point and the difference between the channel and shallows was clearly visible and easier to navigate. We had talked about doing this little trip for at least four years and now we had.

Home again in Los Osos, with Jackson at Donovan's house for a play date and Maddie down for her nap, Yvonne soon succumbed and I followed suit. So much sun and fresh air had made us drowsy.

Yvonne heated up the last of the lasagna for dinner and once the kids were in bed, Kristin suggested we watch an episode of Mad Men, as it turned out the last one of the first year — and that turned into the first of the second year. Yvonne and I had enjoyed the shows but I couldn't get very interested this evening. Kristin went off to bed and then Yvonne and I talked with Eric for a while, especially about the reading I was doing for a UU talk on science and religion — the latest view — and he found connections to what he was working on with his teaching and as department chair. Yvonne who now was definitely coming down with something but listened to what was a typical conversation in our family — ideas, humor, imagination, experience. We gave Eric a hug. We'd be leaving in the morning right after Eric, Kristin, and family drove off to begin their busy Monday and busy week.

One-hundred-nineteen: Return Flight

"The more I read, the more I acquire, the more certain I am that I know nothing." — *Voltaire*

Removing the schmaltzy Valentine's Day Card and Reese's Bits bag from my suitcase while Yvonne took a shower in preparation for leaving Los Osos for LAX, I signed my card to her, "Motorman," a name I'd used sometimes for affectionate purposes. Ten years ago when James was a student at Middlesex School in Concord, Massachusetts, the three of us had taken the train into Boston. I was mansplaining something about motormen and subways — which they inexplicably found very funny — and the name stuck.

I laid the card and candy on the iPad on the kitchen table for her to find. Yvonne had already placed cards for Jackson and Maddie on the kitchen counter where they would find them later in the afternoon when arriving home from Bob and Diane's where they were staying because the school had an in-service day.

Since our February 2011 trip to Ireland, I'd tried to be conscientious about my Valentine's Day ritual since at that time Yvonne had somehow gotten and then given me a Valentine and embarrassed, all I could think to do was cross my name off the envelope and add hers, then cross her signature off the card and add mine, returning it to her. She had laughed, sort of. Now she wasn't concerned about a card to me; only about the grandchildren. I didn't spend any time thinking about the change.

Overnight the clouds had moved in, the rain starting just as we loaded the rental car for our return to LAX. We'd been fortunate to have such good weather in LA and Los Osos during the California rainy season. Determined to avoid the 405 as we had done on the way north, we turned off the 101 south of Ventura and followed the Pacific Coast Highway to Malibu, where we stopped for lunch at the Beachcomber straddling the Malibu pier at its entrance. By now the sun had returned and even though the air was chilly, sitting behind the glass panel walls on the deck we could feel the warmth of the southern California February sun. At the table behind Yvonne, two tanned seventy-something men who had seen better days were engaged in a conversation about car collecting between intermittent cell phone calls each was having to discuss business deals. I imagined they were former producers. Who knows.

119: Malibu Lunch

Our destination now LAX, we stayed on the PCH through Santa Monica, stopping for 30 minutes at a park where Yvonne, now suffering the full brunt of her grandkid-induced cold took a nap and I continued through *The Belief Instinct*, now on the last chapter. We found the Avis return facility without much trouble, taking their bus to the United terminal where Allegiant had a gate. Half a dozen young men, each carrying three plastic cartons of six deluxe muffins joked with each other as they waited in the security check line, acting out what looked like a reality show. Yvonne didn't like them or the pall of grunge that spread over the scene. They were on their way back to Texas and we had no idea what they did to earn a living; they weren't businessmen or tradesmen. Maybe they were musicians. Ten young women, in their late teens or early twenties, were traveling together, all with long dark hair and eyes and mostly flawless skin. They spoke English as a first language but weren't American. Yvonne later discovered they we Pakistani, returning home to the Vancouver, BC area on our Allegiant flight to Bellingham, just a few miles south of the border, enjoying a lower fare from LAX than they would have to pay flying directly to Canada.

Lew and Katie were on their way back too having enjoyed their visit with a son in LA and because they had checked in after we had passed on the information that the flight would be late. It had left Bellingham for LAX on time but had to turn back because of a mechanical problem. We now had time for some dinner since we would be at least two hours late and relaxed in a nearly empty sports bar in the terminal sipping taco soup, acceptable and desirable to me since our lunch had left me queasy. Finishing "The Belief Instinct" on my Kindle, I started Brian Greene's "The Hidden Reality," a layman's account of the latest in cosmological thinking, especially on the multi-verse, something I'd heard and read about and that "The God Theory" considered an important element of an argument for an intelligence that created our universe. Green's prose was crystal clear and I came to have a grasp (or thought I did) of many of the concepts of contemporary cosmology referenced in popular science articles. My UU talk on science and religion was beginning to take shape.

Our flight left almost three hours late and it was after 1:00 a.m. before we climbed into bed at the Quality Inn in Bellingham. Their shuttle wasn't running at that hour but they arranged and paid for a cab ride. Earlier as our flight approached Bellingham, we passed over Anacortes, its peninsular form outlined by the lights that stopped at the water line. In the distance, we saw the lights of Victoria and Sydney to the west and closer the lights of what must have been Friday Harbor — almost everything else to the west was black. No sign of Eastsound, hiding behind Mt Constitution. It was very evident that the San Juans, Orcas, and especially Crane were rural area, sparsely inhabited in comparison with where we had been staying in the last twelve days — and that's just what we like. We were eager to return to our small island home.

One-hundred-twenty: Return to Crane

"The ache for home lives in all of us, the safe place where we can go as we are and not be questioned." — Maya Angelou

A Belgian waffle with strawberries and a hardboiled egg seemed like a good idea so I helped myself at the Bellingham Quality Inn breakfast bar but because her cold had worsened and her appetite gone Yvonne settled for a piece of raisin bread toast and tea and then we were off to Trader Joe's to pick up wine for the Saturday kitchen project brunch — tentative and dependent on how Yvonne felt Friday. In light traffic, under gray skies, and with intermittent rain we drove the 20 miles south to Costco in Burlington. From there it would be another 20 miles to the Anacortes landing where the ferry we intended to catch would depart for Shaw and Orcas at 11:20 — the 3:05 alternative would delay us getting home until after 5:00 — not what we wanted.

Gas prices at Costco had risen but were about $.25 lower than SLO and close to $.75 per gallon lower than on Orcas, where gasoline tanker trucks had to come by barge since they were not, understandably, allowed on the ferries. I filled the tank but since the store wouldn't open for another 25 minutes I picked up my Kindle to continue my Brian Greene book while Yvonne resumed the nap she had started when leaving Bellingham and then had interrupted as we exited I-5 for Costco. Many though not all of the cars in the parking lot contained white-haired seniors, always early for meals, shopping, and bed. We were approaching that demographic, at least I was.

Our goal was to be back in the van by 10:30 and since the store would open at 10:00, we'd have 30 minutes for our shopping and no time for wandering around. Yvonne instructed me to stay close so she could send me on short missions, to find Guerre cheese for instance, and not to get distracted by books or tools or technology.

While retrieving a jar of mixed nuts, my favorite snack, I spotted Pierette, like me a retired Orcas Library Board member, now president of the Friends of the Library, a fundraising group that provided a significant revenue stream to the Library, earned primarily through their February and August book fairs, stocked with tens of thousands of volumes donated by island residents, avid readers who checked out books at twice the Washington State average and from the looks of the book fair tables must buy at a much higher rate as well. Could I help with the upcoming fair? Yes. Someone would call me — and did in the evening after we arrived home on Crane.

At the drive-through ticket kiosk at the landing, we bought a five-ride car and driver Wave2Go ticket and a single senior passenger ticket, $125.85 and good for five months for the former and $5.75 for the latter — both covering the round trip since the return to Anacortes whenever we did that was free. Yvonne had missed the last Wednesday's *Islands' Sounder* because we were gone and wanted to read the current *Seattle Times* so after depositing some trash I bought the two papers from vending machines ($.75 and $1.00) and returned to the van for a Trader Joe's turkey and cheese sandwich while we waited for the *Sealth* to dock and unload. Yvonne stayed in the van on the car deck and napped while I walked upstairs so I could write during the trip, several booths with tables equipped with wall sockets, a convenience for passengers who needed 120-volt power during the voyage. Though I didn't count the vehicles boarding the *Sealth*, it wasn't many on this February late morning, 30 at the most.

Driving off at Orcas landing I could see that a strong southeast wind was blowing and at the Crane dock on Orcas Yvonne and I had a hard time holding the *Huginn* close to the dock once we'd loaded one cart-full, leaving the balance for the next day. Walking along the bottom of the dock "U" I was almost blown off my feet twice and the water outside the breakwater was choppy but not really a problem. At the Crane community dock, Yvonne walked home on the path across Och's meadow, wetter now than when we left, and I followed with the dock cart, making ruts in the path in places, and creating more mud. Something would have to be done for Saturday's brunch — perhaps planks over the wettest and muddiest areas.

120: The Yakima Approaches Orcas Ferry Landing

The house was cold so after releasing the 58-degree hold on the thermostats, turning on the propane and replacing the empty 20-gallon bottle on the Y-switch with a third, full bottle, turning on the water at the road, removing the tie-down rope on the hot tub lid, adding chlorine and shock to the hot tub, and unlocking the remaining doors, I laid a fire in the wood stove and began working on a Web photo album of the trip. Yvonne had bought a roast chicken at Costco and made mash potatoes and peas for dinner, comfort food she said. After dinner I caught up with Noah and then Natasha, hearing about their swim fun in Hoquiam and problems with school server technology. Later the hot tub felt very good, something we missed during our trip, and soon we were happy to be sleeping in our own bed.

One-hundred-twenty-one: Catching Up

"Time flies over us but leaves its shadow behind." — Nathaniel Hawthorne

Not realizing that it was actually raining outdoors but knowing that it was cold, about 40, I hadn't dressed accordingly but continued to the community dock anyway; I needed to be at the Deer Harbor Community Club to leave a sack to be picked up by one of Yvonne's colleagues on her way to Eastsound, first for a yoga class and then the Garden Club meeting where Yvonne was in charge of greeting but would miss the meeting because of her bad cold. Because it was raining I waited in the van for the sack pickup rather than risk the contents getting wet.

I couldn't show up a Howard's until 8:00 for Greybeards, so once I handed over the sack I backtracked to the Post Office to drop off Crane Association mail and then turned around and drove down Channel Road and across the bridge passing Howard's and stopping in the parking lot at the Cayou Quay Marina where I moored one or another of our boats over a ten year period. The marina had unrestricted WiFi available — and Ron, Yvonne's brother, had used the service when he lived on our Nauticat pilothouse sailboat studying for his Oriental Medicine certification exams the previous winter — and since I had my MacBook Pro with me I could get on the Internet and do some emailing while waiting for 8:00 a.m. to roll around.

Howard would leave for England and France in a few days to visit family so we'd suspend our meetings until mid-March but today only Chris, who continued to be sick, failed to show up at the honeymoon cottage on the hillside next to the fenced vegetable garden and above the house and shop. Howard reported he'd done his first spring planting, potatoes, showing us the patch of cultivated soil near the steps up into the garden. The day's topics revolved around the irrationality or immorality of elements of our economy and government, with especially negative reactions to our society's self-destructive urge to defund education and other critical public services that all benefit from directly or indirectly.

121: Deer Harbor Fog (2010 December)

On the way back to the Crane dock on Orcas I stopped at the marina to pick up the *Seattle Times* and *Islands' Sounder*, Yvonne's regular Wednesday treat. She'd spend most of the day on the living room couch reading and napping — for about two hours — after which she said she was beginning to feel better. I wasn't feeling very good myself and had taken some vitamin C hoping to avoid a full-fledged cold. After lunch, I crossed to Orcas to mail Crane checks to Jason for a second signature and to pick up the sack coming back from the Garden Club meeting but it was nowhere to be seen around the Deer

Harbor Community Club. At the Crane parking lot two OPALCO employees, a man and a woman were wandering around the lot carrying technology of some kind that they explained, when I asked, they were using to find the electrical supply cable for Bell Island, about a quarter mile south of the Crane dock on Orcas. OPALCO wanted to be fully prepared to deal quickly with any underwater cable failures and so was undertaking a complete inventory of their system. Crane Island, they said, was supplied from Shaw, the only outer island with two cables, making it more resilient than the other islands.

Returning, I took my first walk around the island since leaving for California, noticing a new, promising deadfall near Circle Road and Eagle Lane, less than a quarter mile from the house and thus a candidate to be cut up and carried home in our dock cart and then split for firewood. The community water tank was just shy of 13 feet, a bit lower than when we left but in the right range and a small dead fir had fallen across Circle Road next to the Becker farm so I moved it to the side. Six deer browsed on the airstrip and I remembered that the *Sounder* had recently reported that deer populations in the San Juans, the Gulf Islands, and Vancouver Island, were changing the plant population by the way they grazed, with the result, for instance, that bird populations were falling by 50%. Too many deer and no predators.

I'd written Chad to thank him and Doreen for their hospitality copying in Eric and James' contact information to encourage them to get together and Chad wrote back from 30,000 feet over Illinois that his new business was considering Seattle for a home base, so I replied describing where Jeni, Noah and family, and we lived inviting him and Doreen to visit anytime. Doreen wrote Yvonne about how much she had enjoyed our visit and conversation.

Sisters Marcy and Julie had both written to remind me that today would have been the hundredth birthday of our father, James Harold Ashenhurst; I had to say something about it to our family, so I wrote:

> *To all Borg units,*
>
> *Marcy and Julie reminded me that our father, Jim, would have been 100 years old today.*
>
> *Jim would have marveled at today's world, especially technology like the iPad, smartphones, instant information access, digital cameras, and the connectivity of Facebook. He used to say that when*

your phone bill was high that was a good thing because it meant you were talking to friends and family.

Jim would have acknowledged all the problems in the world — climate change, endless wars, bizarre priorities, the resurgence of ultra-conservative religion and politics but would have remained optimistic nonetheless. He would have been enormously proud of all of you — engaged, directed, loving, giving, earnest — evidence that his optimism was well founded.

He was my teacher and I continue to learn from him — from time to time finally understanding something he said forty years ago. And once in a while I visit him in a dream — and we talk — it's wonderful — no sadness, just love.

Love,
John/Dad

One-hundred-twenty-two: Squall

"Every landscape is a state of mind." — Peter Doig

The days had been longer in California during our visit, about an hour this time of year, but that would change after the spring equinox, when Crane days would be longer and the nights stronger than moonshine. Since the annual amount of daylight is the same all over the planet, always twelve hours at the equator and varying from zero to 24 hours per day at the poles, it has seemed to me, once I began living in the Pacific Northwest, that there were real advantages in having very long days in the summer when you're likely to be outdoors and short days in winter when you're not.

In California, I had been trying to pay attention to what the landscape felt like compared with Crane, the San Juans, and the Pacific Northwest generally and had come to a conclusion. For me, the California landscape though beautiful is profoundly lonely. It's not just because it's a desert; so is Colorado but it doesn't evoke the same feeling. The California landscape is empty because something is hinted at but missing, that the process of creation east to west, north to south had run out of inventory by the time it got to central and southern California. The Pacific, in most places unrelieved by islands, contributes to the sense of emptiness as well. And there is something about the horizon in California and Colorado in places that is troubling and ominous.

As Yvonne and I drove south from Bellingham two days earlier through the range of hills, mountains really, that separates the enormous Fraser River delta from the smaller Skagit River delta, I was aware of a kind of fullness in the landscape, a peacefulness and richness, an abundance that spills out everywhere in excess. Lots of living and dying; nature doesn't hold back here, scattering trees here and there and then packing them so close together that the sun doesn't reach the ground in places. Some would say the crowding of the trees, the difficulty of seeing through them is suffocating but I don't feel that; I feel protected from the horizon, the place of nothingness.

122: Snow on Chinook at Becker's Farm (2008 December)

Crane has forest but also wide open expanses of water, from our house all the way to Blakely Island, perhaps ten miles away — but the water is contained within the land or appears to be, protecting us from the empty horizon. Forests are dark; water is bright. We have both and they complement each other satisfying together in ways they can't be separately. The ocean is a kind of desert, after all, with its life underground and a perfect disguise above.

Back at my customary place in a wicker chair next to a glowing wood stove, talking to me in its way, as logs crackled and expanding iron pinged and dinged, with my MacBook Pro on my lap also providing some welcome heat as the house warmed up from its overnight sleep, the sun a few degrees over Shaw Island to east, I noticed that the water and air had a steely look, remote, cold, unfriendly — what winter can look like in many parts of the U.S. I couldn't figure it out. Where was the benign mildness, the comforting light and feel of the San Juans? The juice was gone. We could be anywhere. I was alarmed.

In a few minutes, drinking her coffee at the kitchen counter, Yvonne interrupted my meditation on the loss I'd just felt by directing my attention outside. A snow squall had kicked up and globs of big wet flakes on the verge of being sleet were falling and immediately melting as they hit the deck, the ground or our big skylight at the peak of the living room ceiling. Ah — so that was it. The coldness, the steel gray, the separation I'd seen a few minutes before was real — it was snow headed west. But it was gone in a few minutes and the friendliness of our island landscape returned, the air glowing in it's way, stroking our souls with its message of peace, love, life, abundance.

After dinner, Alan and Tessa called as we started a second Netflix movie (after giving up on a French film that made no sense) to tell us they were leaving for six weeks in New Zealand in the morning, by way of their daughter, her partner, and their baby son in Mountain View. Alan explained that he'd survey a project a colleague had started but died without completing and his widow had asked for help. We'll see them in Colorado and New Mexico for our annual Chimayo pilgrimage. It was wonderful to talk to our dear Boulder friends we so missed. They'd be our way in the summer too — along with Ann and Dave and Barb and Dean. Yvonne and I glowed.

One-hundred-twenty-three: Fifty Years?

"Success is where preparation and opportunity meet." — Bobby Unser

A fast walk around the island showed the tank at about 13 feet and scared up a few deer but mostly I was thinking about the upcoming meeting with Chris and David and left the house, late, after making sure I had the shopping list Yvonne had prepared for me. Some sun, partly cloudy and a southeast wind.

I walked into David's house eight minutes after 9:00, not as bad as I feared, Chris was at the dining room table and David was working on coffee. The day before I had talked with Natasha for quite a while about how we might go about marketing the eNotated sailing books Chris had created and then produced an outline of what I thought we had agreed on: roles for Natasha (a structured communication process with sail bloggers, yacht clubs, Slocum interest groups — what I called pitching) and Chris (an Amazon author's page, an author Facebook page, and a blog — what I called catching). At some point, Chris might cross-connect with bloggers. And I would expand the eNotated classics Web page to allow people to sign up to do reviews, get newsletters, suggest a book for eNotation, or volunteer to eNotate (more catching functionality).

I had prepared an agenda and the first item was whether we should become more structured and regular about our meetings, to have them monthly with a regular agenda. We would have other, special purpose meetings but we needed to begin to become more organized. Chris and David agreed. David volunteered to handle bookkeeping and reporting for a while and would need access to the Amazon publishing account, as would Chris and Natasha to retrieve sales figures. I had some thoughts about eNotator contracts, suggesting we include a reference to exactly which text file we would use and a project plan the eNotator would produce. While David excused himself for a conference call, Chris and I talked about the eNotator software and decided it would make sense to reduce the functionality so that all eNotators would do with it would be to do eNotations. Everything else, the more complicated steps, would be done by eNotated Classics. I liked the idea because it would simplify support and creating and maintaining commercial software. We wouldn't try to provide software that provided for lots of choices — since we didn't even know beforehand what that would be. If variety and exceptions were handled in-house rather than expecting the eNotators to do it, our part might be more labor intensive in some ways — that is having to do special-purpose scripting or even manual intervention — but we would save time by not having to provide the software to the eNotators and train them on it. We then talked through what we would begin doing with marketing and Natasha's "pitching" role and Chris' and my "catching" role. We finished up by talking about our personal and business goals — growing the company to a point where we could sell it for enough to make it worthwhile.

Then off to town and Island Market. With the help of a young woman in the produce department, I picked out the vegetables Yvonne wanted and a few other grocery items and back to Deer Harbor to pick up the mail. It was now after 1:00. Following an egg salad sandwich, I wrote up and distributed meeting minutes. After operating in an ad hoc manner, it felt good to begin to structure ourselves like a real, ongoing organization.

One more business item: Chris had shown himself to be fully committed to the project and had worked hard to annotate three, almost four books. I wanted to give him an opportunity to buy more stock, to bring himself up to David's level. I called David and he said he'd been thinking about that as well and was in favor. When I called Chris he was pleased at the acknowledgment of his effort. He would double his holdings by investing another $50.

Yvonne was feeling much better and wanted to go ahead with the brunch scheduled for Sunday so we began a round of calling people to check whether they intended to attend and then assigned them specific times to show up at the Crane dock on Orcas for a ride over to Crane.

123: Living Room Deck Facing the Water

And then I listened to a voicemail Yvonne told me about Tuesday but which I had so far ignored. It was Gene Hallongren, a Willowbrook High School classmate I didn't much know (we had a graduating class of about 400) telling me about plans for a 50th reunion — 1961 to 2011. So soon? He answered on the first ring and said Larry Rockwood had told him I was living in Washington and he'd found me through White Pages listings. He hadn't been able to find about 140 of us (16 he counted as dead) and would send me the list to see if I could help. The reunion would be held together with York High School where we spent our first two years before a new school was built for us anticipating the baby boomers who were bulging the lower grades across the country. The reunion would conflict with the Crane Annual meeting — at which I was to provide a Treasurer and Water report. I told Yvonne I wanted to go to the reunion. We'd be going to Chicago in August.

One-hundred-twenty-four: Feeding Chipper

"Pleasure in the job puts perfection in the work." — Aristotle

Sunday would be the big day, our Kitchen Project Grand Opening Brunch. We would have twenty-two guests and most would need ferrying from Orcas to Crane. Don and Terri would use their own boat, cruising from Cayou Quay Marina and bring Sheila and Kate along. Howard was gone to France to visit his daughter and family. Ken would be coming from Eastsound where he would attend an Orcas Seedbank meeting. Tom and Liz were coming from Crane — by foot or boat. Ken and I would take the rest, in two waves, using the *Huginn* and Margaret's boat. We'd had other, larger gatherings, for instance of the Unitarians when we brought about forty across from Cayou Quay Marina with our Nauticat and Roger and Joan's Alexander. Nancy and Steve had come by kayak.

Besides getting everyone (nearly) back and forth from Orcas, we needed to get them back and forth from the Crane Community dock. Normally that wouldn't be a problem since it was only a 200-yard walk. But Brian had difficulty walking and usually carried a camp stool so he could rest every 100 feet or so. And because the weather had been so wet the path was muddy or wet or both — at the north end where the path starts at the community parking lot, coming through the Och's split rail fence and at the south end where it cuts through 30 feet of trees and bushes that screens our house from view. I decided that it would be reasonable to use the Crane Fire and Rescue vehicle parked near the dock to bring Brian to the house, going west on Dock Road, then south on Circle Road, east on Eagle Lane, and then north on our driveway, a half-mile trip to accomplish 200 yards. But the path was another matter.

At our end, as it rose toward the house, we had first used fir boughs when we were moving in, and then later, when we bought a chipper with Margaret and Mike, two adjacent property owners, and we'd chipped branches littering the property that had fallen in a bad storm — before we bought the house — and spread the chips on our part of the path. The Ochs didn't want us to improve their part of the path so I laid down planks over sections of the north part of the path and then removed them once the path dried out. We'd need to do the same thing for the Kitchen Brunch. I still had the planks, left by Dean, the previous owner and builder, though by this time, having lain on the ground between my shop and the 10 x 20 storage tent, they were on their way to returning to the soil. The more difficult problem was how to make new chips for the path; we had few branches we'd collected so they wouldn't make many chips. But we did have bark I'd saved.

124: Preparations for the Kitchen Completion Party

Two years before when I'd brought a big fir in sections to Crane that Chris had felled and wanted to get rid of, and in the process that put my back out of commission for a week, splitting these big sections, some over two feet in diameter, had yielded a pile of bark, some in neat split-cylinder form, and I'd stacked the bark thinking that I might be able to chip it. In another pile I'd thrown other bark sections that had separated from the wood during splitting sessions last autumn. The chipper was a low-end orange DR commercial chipper powered by a 10 hp gas engine with a 30 lb flywheel and had a 3 1/2" wood diameter capacity. I hadn't used it much in the last year but had taken care of it, changing the oil and installing a new blade after the original dulled after a great deal of chipping by Margaret, Mike, and us. It worked great with tree limbs and small trunks but how would it do with bark?

The chipper had an axel and two wheels and though heavy and clumsy, I could generally move it where I needed it. We had stored it wrapped in a tarp under the rain shelter next to Yvonne's shop so the other two owners would have easy access to it. The gas tank was full and the oil still clean so after starting it, just to check, I moved it from the south to the north end of our property positioning it next to the debris pile that contained some bark sections and then put the 7 cu ft agri-fab yard cart (that makes a wonderful dock cart) under the chip output chute and began to chip bark. The chipper input chute is made of heavy gauge steel so I used that edge to break the bark into narrower sections, two or three inches, and then would feed those 3-inch by 16-inch strips into the chipper — and out came 1/2" chips sprayed into the yard cart. Whenever the cart started to fill up, I'd take it to the path nearby, dump the chips and then rake then to cover the right parts of the path to the right depth. It worked like a charm. Once I exhausted the bark supply in the debris pile I moved the chipper and cart close to the bark pile and began to chip from there. In some cases, the bark was so thick and strong that I couldn't break it across the mouth of the feed funnel. Some day I'll pick up where I left off and use an axe to split difficult bark sections but once I'd done four cart loads, total, I'd managed to cover the parts of the north end of the path that needed it. What fun!

My next task was to wash the outside of windows — master bedroom, living room, dining room, and kitchen — that were covered with salt spray. At its closest point the house was less than 20 feet from the water on rock 15 feet above high tide but since it faced east-south-east, where the prevailing and often the strongest winds came from, the sides of the house and east and south windows became salt covered, though sometimes washed by the right combination of wind and rain. Yvonne said she wanted the windows washed for the brunch — and wanted me to do it by spraying the windows, squeegeeing them, and then wiping them with a rag. I wanted to use Boat Zoap, a liquid soap for boat washing that I'd found does well with salty windows but my instructions were not to get so fancy, so I did as I was told — except that I found wiping with a rag left smear marks — so I omitted that step from the procedure. But it did work pretty well, though in the 40 degree air my hands got numb — but the sunshine felt great.

Yvonne spent the entire day cooking, cleaning, and coordinating with guests. She felt mostly recovered from her cold caught in California but by the end of the day was very tired and both of us took naps midday and recovered enough to go on to the next chore.

One-hundred-twenty-five: A Cold Swim

"The best time to plant a tree was 20 years ago. The second best time is now." — Chinese Proverb

The community water system tank level seemed to be falling, now about 13 feet — down half a foot and perhaps 1500 gallons from a few days earlier. Something to keep an eye on. With air temperatures overnight below freezing the path across Och's meadow was frozen in places, where it hadn't yet dried from the recent sunny weather. As it thaws it would turn to mud — so with guests coming who would walk across the meadow, I covered the worst part with planks and plywood.

Yvonne had arranged the dining room table to hold plates and food for the upcoming brunch and had prepared two spanakopitas and wrapped about 60 dolmades and would bake them as the first guests began to arrive. She'd picked up some champagne and orange juice and would be serving mimosas as well. At 12:15 I left the house to run the first ferries with Ken in the *Huginn* and me in Margaret's boat, already on the Orcas side. Ruthie had called to say Andrea was sick so she was coming by herself. She was waiting with Nancy and Steve with Bev and Dave just arriving. I got them all loaded into the *Huginn*. Lynn had called earlier to say that she and Chris would be able to make the brunch after all and would be skipping their choir practice, and they were soon walking down the ramp so I directed them to Margaret's boat and told Chris he could be captain for the voyage to Crane. Only Ken, coming from a seed bank meeting in Eastsound was unaccounted for but within minutes he was on the dock and took his place at the *Huginn*'s wheel, heading for Crane with his load. Chris, Lynn, and I followed in Margaret's boat.

As Ken entered Pole Pass he held to the right side, too close to the reef below, I thought, but there wasn't anything to do about it right now. Once on the Crane dock, I cautioned him that it was prudent to stay in the middle of the channel. Ken and I left the group to walk to the house. Many had visited us one time or another and so knew the way, so we went back to Orcas for another load, the round trip taking about 20 minutes with loading and unloading. Though cool, it was a beautiful sunny day with a north wind that didn't much affect us, in the lee of Orcas Island. South, along the north edge of Shaw, a series of sailboats, moved east with full sails competing in the Shaw Island Winter Classic, an annual February circumnavigation of the island. The boats looked elegant and I imagined all those aboard enjoying the excellent sailing conditions — but I was happy not to be sailing today. It was too cold.

Pam and Craig and Joyce and Larry were on the Orcas dock but at the east end, away from the loading area. As Ken and I docked they rushed up to report that farther east a dog had chased a buck into the water and it was now heading toward Bell Island, a quarter of a mile away, its head well out of the water, dog paddling, I guess. Then we could see the dog, a golden retriever, about 100 feet offshore in pursuit, no doubt dog paddling, its head not as prominently out of the water. Ken left with his load and while I waited for Brian to come down the ramp, I walked to the east end of the dock, the bottom of the "U" and then around to the south side to get a good view and some photos of the buck, now perhaps two hundred yards away with the dog 100 yards offshore. With the water temperature about 48 degrees, cold enough to cause hypothermia in humans in ten or fifteen minutes, I couldn't understand what could keep both animals from drowning. Then Brian was at the top of the movable metal ramp on his camp stool resting from the walk down the 100-foot fixed wooden ramp from the parking lot. Soon he was on the dock next to Margaret's boat and I helped him get aboard. I saw that the dog had turned around, thinking better of continuing after the buck who probably was no longer visible and because it was beginning to get cold. Then I saw that the buck was no longer headed for Bell Island — which wouldn't have been a good place for it because it was so small — but was now west of Bell heading for Shaw Island. Because much of Shaw, Crane, and Orcas, and all the San Juan Islands, for that matter, are rocky and sometimes rise steeply out of the Salish Sea, getting ashore can be a big problem, except in the rare cases of beaches. The buck would have to find one. Brian wasn't worried about the buck. He reported he'd seen deer swim between Orcas and Jones, across President Channel. When I told Yvonne about the deer-dog story later she pointed out that after all deer live outside in cold temperatures and thrive. They could certainly handle cold water better than we could. But she also wondered whether the deer left "family" on Orcas.

Back on Crane, Tom and Liz had arrived at the community dock from their private dock on Crane and Don and Terri and their passenger Sheila had come from the Cayou Quay Marina. Everyone had arrived except for Clay and Karen, who because of her abstract art class wouldn't be able to get to the Orcas dock until 2:00. I'd make another trip to pick them up.

125: Plenty Room for Friends

Because it would have taken Brian quite a while to walk to our house, I put him in the Crane Fire and Rescue Vehicle and drove him almost to the studio deck. We entered the house to the warm sound of conversation, some people meeting one another for the first time. Yvonne had the iPad in hand, a small crowd around her, as she showed the kitchen project photo album I had posted on the family photo site. Others were going through the album on the notebook computer on the countertop. Seeing Tom and Liz, happy that they had been willing to come over after fearing that Tom thought I was angry at him, I took them on a tour of the kitchen, pointing out its features and telling them about the process.

After a while, I went back to Orcas to get Clay and Karen. Even with 23 people in the house, it wasn't packed but felt comfortably full of people — with enough places for almost everyone to sit. Yvonne took the spanakopita and dolmades out of the oven and we encouraged everyone to take a plate and fill it — with salad and bread Ruthie had picked up at Rose's bakery in Eastsound. Many people had brought wine and at Ruthie's encouragement, Yvonne began to open bottles and offer it to guests who were ready for more after finishing the mimosas. Brian said he didn't like spinach but thought the spanakopita was delicious. It was.

The buck, even if now out of the water, was cold. We were warm and happy to be together. Ruthie commented on how she would never again want to live in a city and especially a suburb. I commented that in the San Juan's, houses are far apart but people are close together. Maybe so.

One-hundred-twenty-six: A Day on the Couch

"Life can only be understood backwards; but it must be lived forwards." — Søren Kierkegaard

The kitchen project brunch had been a success, with a few "it was great" emails coming and more "thanks for bringing whatever" emails going out. But it had come at a cost; Yvonne's cold recovery was set back and she spent the day on the living room couch consulting her iPad — with an afghan tucked around her and the wood stove broadcasting comforting heat. The clouds had returned after several days of blue sky and it was cold and would get colder in the next few days — into the low 20s overnight.

In February four years before, after moving to Crane and then leaving for California for a while to visit Eric, Kristin, and Jackson, I had created a plan for transforming the garage into a studio, had the materials from Island Hardware and Supply delivered by barge, and gotten to work once the garage was emptied to a 10 x 20 tent/carport Yvonne had found at Costco and had loaded into the van.

The tent carton weighed at least 200 pounds so getting it down the Orcas side ramp, into the *Huginn,* out at the Crane dock, and then back home was almost too difficult for us, with the carton trying to fall on top of one or the other of us several times in route. We set the box about 100 feet from the house, near the existing tool shed and assembly required several hours but was straightforward. It's not a good idea to leave anything on the ground unprotected from the wet earth in the Pacific Northwest so since some of what we would move from the garage to the tent was valuable I made two tarps into a floor, hanging the edges from the horizontal tent bars so no moisture would flow on top of the tarp floor from outside. Not everything in the garage would fit in the tent so we stacked additional items on work tables that had been in the garage and covered them with sheet plastic. It didn't look good.

126: Early Morning Cogitation

The garage had a tongue and groove natural fir ceiling on fir beams set four feet apart and resting on a roof beam, just like the rest of the house, and one of the reasons we bought it, seeing immediately that we could increase the living area by repurposing the garage, with its vaulted ceiling, into space for Yvonne, guests, and storage.

The garage was about 25 feet deep and 20 feet wide with a 16-foot overhead door facing out to a concrete pad to the south and a hinged door facing the kitchen door about 12 feet away up a ramp and covered by eaves, with the outside wall of my office joining the garage and house. Getting to the studio from the kitchen would mean going out the kitchen door, down the ramp, and then through the studio door.

A pantry and a bedroom would be at the back of the studio, the walls separating the two rooms from each other and the open studio providing support for their ceilings and the loft floor above. The loft floor would be deeper than the two rooms underneath, cantilevering over the one-story back of the loft, the underside of the cantilever used to house can lighting. We had two wooden IKEA bunk beds and we'd split them into four grandchildren single beds in the loft. We'd replaced the garage door with a double french door with split windows on either side, the bottom section opening like an awning. The wall facing the house was insulated and sheet-rocked but the other walls were exposed 2 x 4 studs. The celling wouldn't require any treatment. Dean had installed a sink on the side toward the house near the door — with hot and cold water and we would make use of that. The garage had its own circuit box with a 40 amp breaker in the main box in the house. I'd be able to work indoors and the only structural work would be the wall across the middle of the room and the wall separating the guest room and pantry and the loft floor, a pretty simple project. I'd replace the one, fixed window on the west side with a sliding window and then add another sliding window to the guest bedroom.

Back in present time I had a new project, building an electronic publishing business that published enhanced versions of classic books and there was much to be done. Now sitting with Chris discussing publishing workflow, not far from where we had lived in Deer Harbor, with Lynn working in the kitchen, I noticed an osprey hovering, like a huge hummingbird, over the estuary, looking for fish, the forested hill behind where Bob and Megan had lived until moving to Eastsound two years earlier, and I had lost my train of thought in the world outside the window.

One-hundred-twenty-seven: Reconciliation

"To handle yourself, use your head; to handle others, use your heart." — Eleanor Roosevelt

Having much on my mind I paid little attention to my surroundings as I made my morning Crane circumambulation — except for the community water tank which had fallen from 13 feet to 11 feet over the last five days — about 5000 gallons. Either the undiscovered leak or leaks had gotten worse or Gary had scaled back the rate of pumping. Given that only three houses were occupied full time and only two more had visitors over the weekend (as far as I could tell) the actual water usage was probably less than 200 gallons per day but more than a 1000 were disappearing. I would write Gary an email and let him know about the falling tank level. The chlorine level in the system had fallen as well — from being in the acceptable range to almost unmeasurable. It wasn't about the water quality since it tests clean for coliform and other undesirable elements but the system is supposed to be chlorinated and Gary submits my monthly reports of daily readings to the Department of Health and perhaps they'd have a negative reaction. If the chlorine level didn't come up in a few days I'd let Gary know. He had said he would be on the island Sunday, the day of the kitchen brunch, but I hadn't seen his boat. An open item.

I had begun reading Brian Greene's *The HIdden Universe* on our way back from California in preparation for "New Science, New Religion", my talk to the UU group the fourth Sunday of the month and I was both trying to absorb Greene's report on contemporary cosmology, especially multi-verses (multiple universes) as well as mentally arrange the other ideas I'd gotten from my recent readings of Stuart Kauffman's (sometime Crane neighbor) *Reinventing the Sacred*, Bernard Haisch's, *The God Theory*, and Jesse Bering's, *The Belief Instinct*. And that thinking was commingled with organizational and software development thoughts about eNotated Classics as well as preparations I'd need to do for the Crane Board meeting coming up soon.

After spending the morning experimenting with a spell check module I wanted to incorporate into our book annotation software, Yvonne insisted that I go to the post office to mail out bills she'd paid (not online) and to pick up her Garden Club book she had lent to Diane to take to the meeting the previous Wednesday when Yvonne missed the meeting because she was sick — but when I'd gone back to the Deer Harbor Community Club that previous Wednesday to pick it up, I found no sign of it and Yvonne, wilted with illness, couldn't bring herself to call to find out what happened to it. This morning she had called and Mike said Diane had waited for me for two hours at the Community Club to hand it over and that I hadn't appeared, an apparent miscommunication. Mike would leave it at the club and I could get it when I picked up the mail at the Post Office.

127: Each Sunrise Unique

Margaret's boat was still at the Orcas dock — we hadn't brought it back to Crane after the Kitchen Project Brunch — and I had a suspicion I had forgotten to take the key out of the ignition and hidden it — so I stopped to check. I was right. I unzipped, unbuttoned, and unhooked part of the canvas cover so I could get in, pulled the key out of the ignition, and hid it. Then I noticed a strong odor of gasoline. I had switched tanks on Saturday replacing the primary one that was nearly empty and replacing it with the spare and then took what was now the spare with me when I took the *Huginn* to the Deer Harbor Marina to fill (partially fill — Yvonne said not to spend more than $75) its gas tank. Apparently I'd overfilled Margaret's spare five-gallon tank and it was to leaking out the cap. For pity sake! I put the spare tank into the *Huginn*'s open cockpit partly decanting Margaret's tank into one I keep for the chipper and a source for gasoline I mix with oil for my chain saw.

Tom's Bullfrog was at the Crane Orcas-side marina dock; likely he had gone to the Post Office, like many of us on a Tuesday after a Monday holiday. As I came up the ramp and around the corner of the big green shed that separates the parking lot from the water, I could see that Tom was checking the delivery locker we receive UPS and FedEx shipments in. Secured with a combination lock that the drivers and Crane Islanders know (at least those of us who expect deliveries) some packages sit in the locker for weeks or even months until the addressee returns to Crane for a weekend. Boxes for Martha and Cynthia were waiting patiently inside.

Tom greeted me enthusiastically, a change from the week before, and again expressed thanks that he and Liz had been invited to the brunch and went on to praise our work on the kitchen. I told him that I'd like his help in diagnosing the leak (leaks) in the water system because they were now too serious to ignore. As Water Chair he had done this in the past and I hadn't. He said he would be happy to but would soon be off to Sun Valley with Liz for two weeks to clean out her house there. Her Alzheimer's was worsening. Her three children wanted her to sell her house and move into assisted living near one of them, none near Ketchum or Crane but she didn't want to do that and Tom had suggested she stay with him at least through the summer — and that was what they were going to do. She loved Crane — its quiet, beauty, and freedom — and didn't want to be bound into some care facility. As far as I knew Tom and Liz, who had spent a good deal of time together but also alone over the last few years, were friends, not partners exactly, but each in their divorced states thoroughly enjoyed and valued one another.

Tom went on to say that he wanted to find a time to talk with me — that he had some things on his mind. I welcomed his overture and suggested we spend some time after he and Liz returned from Sun Valley. I told him I had a sense that he had unspoken concerns and that I very much wanted him to express them. I knew, but didn't say, that he felt I had unnecessarily criticized him for being obsessed with bad behavior he suspected but couldn't prove about his neighbor. And I didn't say that one of the reasons I had invited him and Liz to the brunch was to show him I had no ill feelings towards him. I liked him a great deal and he had done much for Crane. It was his obsession and the way it damaged the social fabric of Crane I didn't like. We would talk more in a few weeks. I held out my hand and he had taken it.

Along Deer Harbor Road Gene and Judy were returning home from their daily walk to the end of Deer Harbor road and as I approached the Post Office I waved to Chris and Lynn who then entered the parking lot and Chris and I talked about the spell check software I was working with and other business issues while Lynn waited patiently on this cold morning. The Crane mailbox had a foreclosure notice for one of the Crane Island Association members, a long drawn out process, ineffective in part because the member didn't live on Crane and hadn't set foot on the island for a year perhaps. I didn't touch the notice. It would have to go back to the lender.

Pulling out of the north end of the lot I saw Brian parked across Deer Harbor Road looking away, out across the Harbor, thinking perhaps about the cruising he had done years ago, twice to Tahiti, for instance, now no longer possible. Tom had confirmed that he and Brian had talked at the brunch about doing a cruising class, Tom thinking he could teach navigation and rules.

The missing Garden Club book was in a cloth bag hanging from the handle of the Deer Harbor Community Club back door. Mission accomplished.

Late in the afternoon, having some free time, James called and we talked about the weekend visit of Keith's parents and family to Los Angeles, a very busy three days and happily crowded as the three visitors stayed with the boys, as we had, in their one bedroom apartment — that also included Leo and Fyo, the Russian Blue kittens. As a neuroscience grad student, James was again grading undergraduate tests and had time left only for his lab work and none for study or writing journal articles, something one of his advisors was pressing him on. His other advisor, persecuted, including having his car firebombed, for doing addiction research on primates, had been the subject of a long and, we thought, balanced article.

Natasha, on the verge of beginning a process to find reviewers for the Slocum books reported that Morgan, Opal, and she had caught something from nephew Hunter and the kids had stayed home from school.

And where were Alan and Tessa, our Boulder friends? Last we heard they were on their way to Christchurch, in New Zealand, while at the same time an earthquake was laying the city low. Their email arrived in the afternoon. They were in the San Francisco airport when they heard about the earthquake but decided to go anyway. Their flight was to Auckland, not affected by the quake and they would fly from Auckland to Nelson and then rent a car to drive to Christchurch. Since the University was now closed temporarily, it wasn't clear whether or how Alan would proceed with his sabbatical project to organize the uncompleted research work of a colleague who had died a few years before.

One-hundred-twenty-eight: Boreas Blows Again

"Weather is a great metaphor for life – sometimes it's good, sometimes it's bad, and there's nothing much you can do about it but carry an umbrella." — *Terri Guillemets*

As the light rose, sitting in my chair near our cozy wood stove, to my left as I looked out our big living room windows, I saw an archetypal Pacific Northwest morning — low gray clouds riding not far above the forested dark green hills — both reflected in our gently rippling part of the Salish sea — a comforting scene and a change from the succession of sunny days we'd had recently. I returned to my writing, absorbed in making thoughts into sentences.

Yvonne emerged from the bedroom about 8:30 as she usually does and after we greeted one another and hugged , she made her coffee and breakfast toast and I disappeared back into my MacBook Pro. Later, when I looked up again and out the windows, I was shocked to see heavy snow falling on cedars, firs, alders, and willows, sticking to the deck and railings, covering the 6' x 14' skylight that runs along the peak of the living room ceiling and out of which we can usually see sky and firs — it was almost a white-out. Yvonne was amused at my surprise. The snow had been going on for some time, as it must have been to have accumulated so much.

The snow had been predicted but when it is it rarely amounts to anything with the temperature at or above freezing. But this was different. I had convinced myself that the cold weather was over and spring imminent — now in late February. It surely wouldn't snow again — but it had. The outside thermometer had fallen four degrees since I had checked it about 6:00 and Weather Underground was predicting much colder temperatures for the next few days. At least it wasn't very windy.

I spent the morning struggling with the spell check module I'd downloaded and experimented with the day before. It worked well except for one text area and I was trying to isolate the problem.

128: Foul Weather Outside

The next day Yvonne, driving our pickup with Sylvia as passenger, would take the ferry to Anacortes and then drive to a conservation facility near Burlington to pick up a load of bare root native plants that the Orcas Master Gardeners would sell that Saturday as a fundraiser and community service. With the weather outside frightful and because she was still snuffy and coughing and because I'd disconnected the F-150 battery so that it wouldn't discharge while we traveled to California, she asked me to reconnect the battery and bring the truck from the upper lot to the lower Crane parking lot on Orcas and to carry two Costco bags and three five gallon buckets, all related to the plant sale, putting one bag in the van and the other and buckets in the truck — and make sure the truck had a tarp since they'd need to use it to cover the plants. I wasn't eager to go out — I was comfortable inside but I put on my knit hat and Carhart jacket, grabbed the bags and buckets, and headed out into the frigid snowy world.

As I arrived at the community dock I saw that the tide was out so the movable ramp connecting the section fixed to the shore and the floating lower portion was very steep and everything was covered with snow. With both hands full, I couldn't hold onto the railing and as I started to descend the ramp I began to slide so I turned sideways as if I were side-sliding on skies. At one point I lost my balance and flashed on a scene of being pitched into the cold winter water and considered what I would do to keep from drowning. But I recovered and soon reached the floating dock. When I told Yvonne about the little adventure later she said she would have put a bag over each shoulder, and holding the buckets in one had would have had the other free to hold on to the rail. Of course. Why hadn't I thought of that.

On the Orcas side I put one bag in the van and carried the other bag and buckets across Deer Harbor Road and climbed the stairs to the upper lot. I'd left the *Huginn* tool kit on the front seat, took out the socket wrench I'd used to disconnect the battery three weeks before and used it to secure the cable connector to the positive terminal post and then drove to the Post Office, picked up the mail and walked across Deer Harbor Road to the ATM at the marina store to get Yvonne cash she'd need for her Anacortes foray and in Seattle over the weekend. Rene was behind the counter and gave me $19 in change for the Seattle Times. A perpetual loiterer, who never seemed to work, was leaning on the counter bending Rene's ear. Though a very friendly person, I suspected she would find his daily presence tiresome. I commented on the weather and Rene, adding her piece, told me that the wind would pick up and was predicted to blow in gusts to 60 mph overnight and through the next morning. That didn't sound very promising though the Crane and Orcas docks and our house are not very exposed to the northeast but it wouldn't be much fun on the Orcas north shore or maybe even in Eastsound, lying on a flat north-south isthmus with 2400' Mount Constitution on the east and hills on the west, a funnel for wind between the Straight of Georgia and the East Sound fjord. The regular, still leaning over the counter separating him from Rene asked me whether I had a chainsaw. I did. You must always carry it with you he told me several times, his implied thought that trees could fall across the roads at any time and I might need to be able to cut my way through them. I wished them well, put three quarters into the blue Islands' Sounder box, pulled out a paper and drove back to the Crane lot, leaving the pickup close to the road and then moved the van there as well so that in the event of more snow and then ice there would be no problem getting out of the lot. Two years before James helped me get the van out of the lower portion of the lower lot after ice had made it difficult to drive the van up to the road.

Gary's pickup entered the lot just then, the truck bed filled with 12 5 gal propane bottles and in the cab with Gary, Wilma, and their three dogs — now including an Australian shepherd puppy, Cooper. They were bringing the propane to Crane and would turn on all the propane heaters in the well houses so that in the event of power failure the pipes inside wouldn't freeze. Yvonne and I had spent a cold evening in November in a wild wind after a power failure going from well house to well house turning on the heaters. Gary wanted to be ahead of the curve this time. We talked briefly about the leak — he'd put more time on pump #5 and was eager to find the source of the leak but not today or in the next few days. I carried one propane tank down to the boat loading area and warned Gary and Wilma about the slippery ramps. I encouraged them to use the rescue vehicle on Crane to carry them and the propane bottles to the six well houses and they appreciated the offer. Would they park the vehicle in my yard in front of my Ranger sailboat and close to the yard power post? Yes, of course. And they did. Later, after dinner, I plugged in the heating pad attached to the 20-gallon water tank that was part of the rescue vehicle compressed air foam system to keep it from freezing.

Mid-afternoon Yvonne had a call from the San Juan Island Master Gardener in charge of picking up the bare root plants for their sale that coming weekend and she said the reports from the mainland were bad — more snow and icy roads. She was going to delay for a week. After a flurry of calls Yvonne arranged a delay for the Orcas group as well. She and Sylvia wouldn't have to take the ferry in the morning. Yvonne and I were both relieved. Taking up her knitting sitting in a chair like mine but facing out toward the water she knitted her first ever button hole into a glasses case she was making. The fire was warm. We had lots to do at home. We wouldn't have to deal with the cold, icy world out there the next day.

One-hundred-twenty-nine: First Draft

"The bamboo that bends is stronger than the oak that resists." — Japanese Proverb

I should have worn a warmer jacket. With the thermometer at 26.5 and the wind blowing I felt chilled as I checked the heater on the compressed foam water tank on its platform off the front bumper of the Fire and Rescue vehicle parked in our yard near the *Discovery*, our 20' Ranger daysailer on its trailer for the winter but I was sure I'd warm up as I made my circuit around the island. As it turned out I came home colder than when I started. The community water tank was still at 11 feet — it hadn't dropped since Gary had added more pumping time to compensate for a worsening leak in the system.

With snow on the ground, I could see traces of the comings and goings of island fauna. Deer had crossed Eagle Lane not far from the house. I also saw what looked like rabbit tracks — but I had never seen a rabbit on Crane and didn't want to. The West Sound area is overrun with rabbits and they've expanded their domain to the Deer Harbor area as well. Like the deer, they face no natural predators. The *Islands' Sounder* reported that deer were changing the ecology of the San Juans and the Gulf Islands by their selective grazing and one consequence was the dramatic reduction in bird life where the deer were numerous. As rabbits have become a problem one island imported foxes only to find that they had other undesirable effects. European rabbits have become especially problematic on San Juan Island where their extensive warrens cause soil and water problems.

A raccoon had crossed South Circle Road heading inland, another crossing North Circle Road going to the water and a third, near the dock also heading to the water. All the tracks could have been left by the same animal I suppose but more than one raccoon lives on Crane Island (I've seen many of different sizes). A mink had apparently climbed the hill above the concrete barge ramp on the north side of the island and had hopped along Circle Road — to what destination I couldn't tell because blowing snow had covered its trail. Birds weren't evident until I approached the dock and perhaps 30 or 40 black-capped chickadees bounced along the ground and flitted back and forth in the understory. Gary and Wilma and their dogs had left tracks as well as they replaced propane tanks in the six well houses and turned on the catalytic heaters as a backup to the electric heaters that would become useless should the power fail, not as likely as if we had heavy wet snow or higher winds, but certainly possible.

129: Morning Light Floods In

We'd consumed most of the firewood on the front porch so I brought two cart-fulls to the house from the one remaining stack of split wood, less than a cord, and I wondered whether it would be enough for the remainder of the heating season. Probably not. I had a cord or so of green, unsplit wood, the three logs I had retrieved from the community beach and the three trees Tim had cut, but they wouldn't burn well until they dried out. I knew of three deadfalls within a quarter mile that I could cut and cart back to the house but I wasn't enthusiastic at the prospect. Maybe the mild spring weather we expect will appear.

One goal for the day was to create a first draft — a complete ebook version of *The eNotated Two Years Before the Mast"* and send it to Chris for checking, with the thought that we could publish it to the Amazon Kindle catalog in a few days. To do that I'd have to create some simple way to handle the chapter notes the original publication contained — that would be completely separate from Chris' eNotations. The book text contained the chapter notes but not in a form that would create links in the text to the notes and then from the notes back to the text. I decided on a simple tagging system and used my software's search capability to find and change all the to-note and from-note text and then added a routine to the program to process the tags into anchors and links when building the HTML version of the book. The notes would be the last items in any chapter that contained them, part of the original book and not have anything to do with the eNotations. In one case I noticed that Chris had added an eNotation to Dana's (or his son's) chapter note. The process worked well and once I added additional sections to the database (Chris' introduction, help, and so on) as well as the sequence everything would be shown in, I could create a first draft MOBI file for Chris to review. By evening he'd reviewed his notes three times and sent me corrections. The final publishing steps wouldn't take long.

Because she was still a bit sick and because it was so cold, Yvonne decided to skip practice for Grace's Rock and Roll Choir — as she had the prior Thursday when she'd been sicker still. Because she had spinach, potatoes, and chicken she made a big pot of spinach soup and we ate it with toast from the bread she'd baked the day before and a mixed greens salad with pears, walnuts, and blue cheese dressing. Delicious, of course, but evoking a kind of joy from my body at being really well fed, its typical reaction to Yvonne's cooking.

One-hundred-thirty: Another Volunteer

"Collaboration allows us to know more than we are capable of knowing by ourselves." — Paul Solarz

Yvonne would take the 8:55 ferry, on her way to Seattle to attend the Northwest Flower and Garden Show with her friend Julie who would come over Snoqualmie Pass from Ellensburg in Central Washington, and stay with Jeni, giving her a chance to visit and catch up. We walked out of the house at 7:30 into 21-degree cold and a strong northeast wind. I'd worn my warmest down jacket so I wasn't cold — except my nose stung and my eyes watered. In Colorado, 21 degrees wouldn't have felt this cold, with its drier, thinner air, but the denser, more humid sea level air here would carry body heat away quickly.

The Canada goose couple paddled in the water among a group of Mergansers sheltered behind the rock that marks the south side of Pole Pass. Did they feel cold? Yvonne didn't think so — after all, they came from the arctic region. The forward deck of the *Huginn* was covered with crusted snow and the cockpit with ice. The three mooring lines (I usually used just two but added a third because of the wind) were frozen and very stiff though not difficult to untie because I used the simple parallel tie Brian had taught me, completely secure but easy to undo. Yvonne hopped out onto the Orcas dock a bit concerned about whether the van would start so I offered to walk up with her and stay until she knew all was in order. No need.

130: Kitchen Calm

    I'd been recording inside and outside temperatures as well as accumulated kilowatt usage twice a day with the thought that at some point I'd put the information in a spreadsheet and find the relationship between temperature and current draw with and without a wood stove supplement. I wanted to figure out exactly what I saved by spending all that time finding, cutting, splitting, and stacking firewood. That project would wait for another day but this morning I was struck by how much power the house had used from midnight to 5:45 a.m. — when the house temperature was 62 and the hot tub was still cooling down and not drawing power — 36.1 kilowatt hours, twice what it drew when the temperature had been 31. A ten-degree difference required twice the power, virtually all of it used for baseboard heat. By 9:00 p.m. we'd used 128.7 KWH but probably not much after that since by 10:00 the hot tub was coasting down to 90 from 102 and the house from 68 to 62. We had had a fire going from 6:00 a.m. until about 4:00 p.m. — otherwise the usage would have been much higher, though by how much I didn't know. In any case, our electric bill for the day was about $10.

At 9:30 I crossed again to Orcas to meet Barbara at the marina to introduce her to our eNotated Classics publishing idea she had expressed interest in to David. The marina store had only one small table and it was occupied by the same seemingly unemployed man who had given me advice about chainsaws the day before. Anticipating that possibility I thought we could probably sit in the resort lobby, surely empty now, so Barbara and I walked the length of the dock back to Deer Harbor road, crossed and walked uphill on Jack and Jill Lane, the Post Office on our right and the former store and Star Fish restaurant where James worked one summer as a dishwasher to earn money to buy a MacBook Pro after deciding he couldn't live with the Dell notebook computer we had given him to use his freshman year in Middlesex School in Concord. When James decided to replace his MacBook with a new model five years ago we bought the old one, and it had died a few months back. We had bought that second MacBook Pro when he replaced his with a newer model and started graduate school at UCLA. Yvonne had an iMac on her desk in her studio, the kind with the screen on a moveable arm attached to a cone-shaped base that was now at least seven years old but with equipped with the latest Mac operating system and it worked fine. I also used a six-year-old Averatec notebook still running XP for Windows applications I needed to run and once the old MacBook Pro died it became the kitchen counter computer — though sometimes competing with the iPad.

The desk attendant didn't object to our taking a table on the south wall of the lobby — flooded by blue sky sunshine. I told Barbara about where the idea for eNotation and eNotated Classics had come from and she understood immediately, as a former American Literature college teacher and literature lover. In graduate school, she had studied medieval literature and loved it. What book might she do from that period? Perhaps Mallory's "Le Morte d'Arthur," the most complete account of the Arthurian legends. I had 20 or more Arthur books and was attracted to the idea of her doing an eNotated Mallory but it would be a big job. Perhaps it would be a good idea to start with something shorter and more modern. She'd prepared a list of public domain novels she felt competent to eNotate and I immediately fixed on Willa Cather's *Death Comes for the Archbishop*, a favorite at our house in part because

Yvonne and I have spent so much time in New Mexico, for the Chimayo Pilgrimages especially but many other times as well. She would get a copy, read it again, mark it up, and create a plan for eNotating it, the kind of thing she would have done to teach it. She had been looking for something to do that made use of her skills and in which she had an interest. It was perfect. Having known Barbara enough to say hello or a short conversation over at least ten years I knew her, by reputation, to be hard-working, organized, and completely dependable. And now I had learned that she had taught American literature. She would be great. Since Barbara had a Nook, the Barnes & Noble competitor to the Kindle and because it required a different format, ePUB, an industry standard, rather than Amazon's MOBI, her participation in the project would provide motivation to create ePUB versions and to add our books to the B&N catalog.

As we walked out of the resort lobby we saw David in the Post Office parking lot and told him that we had a plan. He and Maxine were friends of Barbara and so he was pleased for several reasons. He said he'd been unable to load the *The eNotated Two Years Before the Mast* MOBI file on his Kindle to read and comment on before I uploaded it to Amazon, so I told him I could stop by the next day on my way to Eastsound to work at the library book sale.

Later, reporting in from Seattle, Yvonne said that Julie had decided not to come to Seattle Saturday for the day to attend the garden show — so Yvonne was disappointed. But Yvonne had met Jeni at a happy hour where Jeni was enjoying Friday evening with her Swedish Hospital colleagues and the next day she'd enjoy the exhibits and presentations at the show, something she'd done for many of the last ten years.

One-hundred-thirty-one: Books, Books

"One man's trash is another man's treasure." — Proverb

Snow again, blowing from the southeast but just a dusting. A 20-foot tree has fallen over, out of a grove of willow and fir that shelters our Ranger day sailer, *Discovery*. A good-sized dead limb has fallen across our driveway where it bends upward toward Eagle Lane. The top 10 feet, about eight inches in diameter, has fallen from the top of a three-masted maple a few feet from Circle Road between Jansen's and Westlund's. I'm surprised, as I've been in the past, to see how many dead trees or parts of dead trees are still standing, despite rot, wind, and wet snow. The tank remains at 11 feet.

My shift at the Friends of the Orcas Library Winter Book sale starts at noon, so about 11:15 I load the ten-gallon empty propane bottle into our dock cart and walk across Och's meadow to the community dock and as I approach the *Huginn*, I'm aware of the smell of gasoline coming from the cockpit where I'd temporarily stored Margaret's alternate five-gallon fuel tank I'd filled — overfilled apparently — a few days before. The gas was leaking out of the plastic insert that holds the steel feed pin as well as from around the fill cap. I cleaned up with a spill cloth but when I arrived at the Orcas dock some of the gas had gotten out of the cockpit through the self-baling valve coating the water behind the boat in a multi-colored sheen. That wouldn't do so I carried the tank up to the parking lot and left it near the storage shed out of the way.

Crescent Service would fill the propane tank while I volunteered at the Book Fair. Then I stopped at Office Cupboard and bought four square feet of bubble wrap for my talk to the Unitarian congregation the next day. The Orcas School lunch room was full of people and books. This time I would successfully resist the temptation to take home books I didn't need. I took my position as a cashier, something I'd done for a number of years and enjoyed, sometimes serving people I knew and always interested in seeing what people were buying. Pierette was president of the Friends and both of us served on the Library Board, she for four years and me for five, sometimes finding ourselves in contentious disagreement, especially over the budget, though that had never interfered with a kind of cordiality, since I was impressed at how much work she'd done for the Library over the years. She walked her talk.

131: Deer Harbor Community Club History Corner

She thought that the sale was going reasonably well, and I was glad to hear that since the Friends provided a not insignificant part of the annual Library income, from the winter and much larger summer Book Fairs, but, she continued, change was coming; this might be the last Book Fair. Why? A number of reasons. First, since the county had recently imposed recycling fees to cover general revenue shortfalls, island residents were donating — or dumping — more books and magazines at the Library — too many, in fact, than could be displayed and sold — so that half those denoted were still in the storage shed. And now that people were buying more and more eBooks they were beginning to clear out their paper home libraries, donating to the Friends. Wouldn't the buyer who shows up after the sale take all the books? No, not this time. The buyer would no longer take the whole load but was willing to pick through the leftovers. But that wouldn't help, right? No, it wouldn't. If the Friends had to pay to dispose of the books it would eat into the revenue they'd made. The community didn't want to pay to dispose of their books and so was passing them on to the Friends — assuming of course they were doing something worthwhile but with the new conditions they were in fact costing the Friends and thus the Library money. The Friends board would meet in a week and decide what to do — with the tons of remaining books and about the summer sale. A trend for the rest of the country?

When the checkout line cleared I joined the shoppers looking over tables of titles — fiction in one section, literature in another, children's books on two tables. I found Mitch Albom's *Tuesday's with Morrie* — that Yvonne had recommended I read for insight into well-received memoirs. Then I spied a nine-volume set of Emerson's essays, published in 1888. They were in reasonably good condition. I didn't need them; I already had a library of Emerson books — but how could I walk away? I found some children's books, and a James Hillman and a Stephen Jay Gould, and a few more, filling a box and then paying the late-in-the-sale price of $1. A bargain — for what I really didn't need and contributing to a problem sometime in the future — getting them off Crane to go wherever they're bound next, given the Friend's experience likely a dumpster. Maybe we could burn them in the wood stove?

One-hundred-thirty-two: Multiverses

"The universe is not only stranger than we imagine, it is stranger than we can imagine." — Arthur Eddington

Some weeks before I'd read someplace that Stephen Hawking had changed his mind about whether some kind of creator God might be necessary to explain why the universe existed at all or why it had characteristics so favorable to humans and life in general. God, as a First Cause, a way to fill the gap between nothing and all there is was no longer relevant or necessary, Hawking was saying. About the same time I'd seen an enthusiastic review of Brian Greene's new book, *The Hidden Reality: Parallel Universes and the Deep Laws of the Cosmos* and bought it for my Kindle thinking it might provide the background I needed to understand Hawking's shift — and since I had promised to do a talk at our UU service on February 27th, I was hopeful Hawking and Greene might provide me a topic. And they did. My topic: "Why did Stephen Hawking Close the Door on God?"

Greene's book focused mostly on multiverse theory and the reasoning and evidence in its favor. Five kinds of multiverse seemed especially relevant to my talk. What he called the Quilted Multiverse was a claim that if our universe is infinite, and there is now good reason to believe that it is because it is "flat," uniform in all directions, as an infinite universe would need to be rather than what would seem more likely, a little different in one direction versus another. One interesting implication of a flat universe is that sections sufficiently distant from one another are in fact independent, sub-universes. Since a sub-universe is finite, that is has a fixed number of particles, it's possible to compute how many different ways the sub-universe could be arranged, and since physicists have a pretty good idea how many particles our "universe" or sub-universe contains, it's possible to compute the odds that another sub-universe would be exactly like ours — and the odds, though large, are finite. That means that at least one other sub-universe is identical to ours in all respects — and more are almost identical and so on. Earth and all of us are duplicated someplace else living exactly the lives we're living here. Greene calls this the Quilted Multiverse because he thinks of each independent section of the larger universe as a square on an infinitely large quilt.

132: Technical Services Nerve Center

The Inflationary Multiverse is theory that the BIg Bang didn't create just one universe (or Quilted Multiverse) but many, perhaps an infinite number and continues to give rise to new ones as they precipitate out of the incredibly high energy ground created by the Big Bang like bubbles forming in Swiss cheese. Recent extremely accurate measurements of the Cosmic Microwave Background show a consistency indicative of a Multiverse that spawned our universe and numberless others. One implication is that some bubbles aren't completely precipitated and might go through another birth process — a cataclysm were that to happen to our quilted multiverse.

String Theory, a mathematical framework that unites Quantum and Relativistic physics (the very small and very large) isn't proven but becomes more promising by the day as physicists fill in the details. Strings, if they exist, are extremely small, and their frequencies of vibration give rise to elementary particles like hadrons (protons and neutrons). It turns out that string theory requires the universe to have eleven rather than the four dimensions we're aware of — the three spatial dimensions and time and one of the implications of these extra dimensions is that multiple universes, in different dimensions, can exist within one quilt section in one bubble universe, that is alternative universes, Branes, or Mbranes could be very close to us and we wouldn't have the foggiest idea they were there. Greene calls this the Brane Multiverse. The Large Hadron Collider, recently completed outside Geneva, is intended, in part, to detect a parallel universe, a Brane near ours. Under certain conditions, crashing two hadrons together will cause them to split and the resulting energy can be measured. If energy is lost in the process, that would be consistent with it leaving our Brane and showing up in another.

String theory implies that Branes can collide sometimes and when they do, the universe holding them will be destroyed but then reform and perhaps go through the development and destruction cycle again. This is the Colliding Branes and Cyclical Multiverse.

Finally, though the Inflationary Multiverse theory pictures each universe to be pretty much like all the rest, that is with galaxies, stars and so on, that assumes that the basic settings, apparently arbitrary constants, like the strength of the force binding nucleons into nuclei, are always the same but string theory allows them to vary so rather than a multiverse of similar universes, we have a multiverse of wildly different universes, some that will never form atoms, some that won't form galaxies, and some that are completely empty — universes of nothing — places where there is nothing rather than something. Greene calls this multiverse the String Landscape Multiverse.

Getting back to the Hawking question, it's now possible to see what he may have been thinking. The String Landscape Multiverse answers Leibniz's question (and our question) "Why is there something rather than nothing" by pointing out that some universes are in fact nothing, are empty. It answers the question "Why is our universe so special?" by pointing out that it only appears to be but is only the result of a random process, much in the way that while the evolution of the species looks engineered, it can be explained as the result of random events, some of which lead to the perpetuation of some patterns and others not. If the Multiverse contains every possible version of a universe, including empty universes then there is no need for God at all. Perhaps that is why Hawking changed his mind.

The UU group was surprisingly receptive to my presentation of Greene's book and its implications for at least naturalistic or Deistic religion. I used some props to help get across the ideas of the various multiverses: a piece of cardboard with a black grid and red circles on its intersections to represent a quilted multiverse, bubble wrap to represent the inflationary multiverse, cardboard cards to represent the Brane Multiverse, the cards crashing into one another to represent the Cyclical Multiverse and bubble wrap again for the String Landscape Multiverse, but this time with some bubbles clear (for universes not yet formed), some colored (with different colors representing different kinds of universes — having different basic settings), and some black (that is empty).

Will the world end in fire or ice? A brane collision or a further precipitation of our bubble would destroy it in fire — only to be reconstituted. In any case, since the space in our quilted multiverse (in an inflationary multiverse bubble and with branes in it) is expanding in all directions faster and faster, more and more of it will disappear as light won't be able to keep up with the expansion — so that eventually the night sky from earth would contain only our galaxy and then only the planets — ending not in ice as much as loneliness.

We talked a bit about some other ideas as well. If I understand Greene correctly, our universe looks infinite to us but with a finite duration — that is in-process. To an observer outside, it would look finite but eternal — that is complete — and could be viewed like a cradle-to-grave "photo album" of everything that happened (but was still happening inside it). That outside observer (if it were possible) could look at every universe in a one-quilted universe and compare differences — for instance seeing what happened if someone "chose" one thing rather than another. So perhaps the free will/determinism question disappears. We are both free and determined; free because every possible way we could live (a series of "choices") would be expressed in some universe but determined because for any particular universe within a quilted multiverse all outcomes are determined — that is that universe is already complete — not in process.

I mentioned but didn't talk about the Many Worlds or Quantum Multiverse, where different versions of a universe split apart whenever a quantum probability wave is resolved — allowing for all possible resolutions, or the Holographic Multiverse (which I do not understand), or the Simulacrum Multiverse (it's an illusion created by a higher intelligence), or the Ultimate Multiverse, all of the above. As Jane pointed out as she left, the Multiverse concept compared to one, special universe is very much like the heliocentric solar system idea compared to a geocentric solar system idea — both displace human beings — from being special to being a little piece of a very large whole.

I thought afterwards that the question really is whether there is one, special universe created for a unique purpose or whether there are an infinite number that express every possibility. I don't know how we can decide but the latter makes more sense to me.

Though I really didn't know what I was talking about, I had come to understand much more about multiverses and string theory (and quantum mechanics and relativity) and I enjoyed trying to share that with others — who were interested — and in applying these new ideas — which weren't just speculation but were grounded in a consistent way with the physics enterprise of the last century — to philosophical and theological questions that have preoccupied people for millennia — and offering science-based answers — though many apparently intractable questions remain — such as the nature of consciousness, why the world appears to be describable in mathematics, and whether the world can be best understood as a manifestation of mind — whether or not that mind has any notion of purpose.

A fun morning — with the group, a surprise to me, more interested in this topic than any other I'd spoken on. Since I had been reading Jesse Bering's *The Belief Instinct* about why it is we project purpose everywhere, even where it seems not to belong, for instance on the universe (especially given the Multiverse view), giving rise to certain ideas about God, astrology, exceptionalism, psychology, literary theory, and one's overall purpose in life, I asked whether they'd like to hear about it. Two Sundays were open in May. They were eager to hear more, this time from a different direction about what new science has to say about God and religion and how religion might change to accommodate these findings.

One-hundred-thirty-three: Oh, oh!

"The garden suggests there might be a place where we can meet nature halfway." — Michael Pollan

As I walked into the kitchen to greet Yvonne, at the counter enjoying her coffee and toast and reading yesterday's *Sunday Seattle Times*, she turned and said she needed to talk to me about something.

Oh, oh.

Something had eaten the tops off the emerging carrots and leeks in the west raised bed near the west garden gate — leading to and from the outbuildings area (rain shelter, two shops, tool shed, trash/recycle shed, storage tent, and 20' Ranger sailboat on its trailer and covered with two brown tarps). Someone had left the gate wide open. There didn't appear to be any other damage. She couldn't understand why the deer ate the leek — because they weren't supposed to. Argh!

Yvonne had gone to a great deal of trouble to protect her garden — bushes, small trees, flowers, two raised vegetable beds — by constructing a deer-proof fence (where the house itself didn't create an obstacle) made from strong and soft but nearly invisible black nylon 3" by 3" netting hung from 6' metal fence posts except at the five gates where the posts were wood. She'd created bamboo gates, each in a different design, stapled and then tied together, the gates hinged with waxed twine tied to the posts and the gates. Because the netting was very flexible, soft to the touch, it didn't hang straight across from post to post but dipped in a pleasing way. Since the netting was eight feet high but less was needed, she had wound the bottom of the netting around hooks placed all along the fence. It wouldn't be possible for the deer to push their way underneath. Of course in a way the fence was an illusion to the deer. Were they interested enough they could crash the gates open. On the other hand, because it was both very strong and very flexible, it wouldn't be easy for a deer to go through the fence. Strength wouldn't be adequate. The fence was soft, flexible, resilient, quiet, retiring — rather than like most deer fencing — hard, rigid, breakable, brash, and demanding.

On one occasion deer got into the garden through the fence — by chewing it. Yvonne had planted too close to the fence, it turned out, and the deer during their daily circuit through our lot had stopped to graze on the tasty beans just on the other side of the fence, pushing the netting toward the object of their desires and then feasting on it — not noticing or caring that they were chewing nylon as well. The result was a hole they could crawl through and they did, selectively decimating some of Yvonne's favorite plants, some quite expensive, including a beautiful Japanese maple. On another occasion, hearing a crash, I saw a buck just outside the northeastern termination of the fence where it's fastened to the house. The buck had hit the fence there, pulling it away from the house but not breaking the netting. Yvonne deduced that the buck had slipped through the bottom of the south gate facing the grass-covered driveway that joins Eagle Lane, several hundred feet away. She introduced a new gate practice: the tops of the gates would continue to have removable loops that held them to the post opposite their hinges, but bungee cords would now be used to tie the gate bottom to the post as well, making it impossible for deer to push their way through the bottoms of the gates. And it worked— provided the gates were closed and secured, what I had failed to do the day before. The one disadvantage was that it was a somewhat involved process to open and then close a gate — at least it seemed that way to me — with the result that I was somewhat reluctant to go out a gate: it was too much trouble and I was too lazy.

Yvonne's style with the fence and gates was to be understated, to create something effective and attractive but not over engineered or visually intrusive. When I designed the 12' by 12' rain shelter after a photo in Sunset Magazine, Yvonne had pointed out I made it strong but not massive and followed the same principle with our hers and his 16' by 12' shed-roof shops with sliding barn doors that would open half the front side. I used translucent polycarbonate roofing panels for the three structures, giving them a sense of lightness and bringing in ambient light so that it was easy to see when inside without requiring artificial lighting.

133: Big Sky Over the Salish Sea

We both prefer what's practical and light over what is, in our minds, excessive and unnecessary. Though the bamboo gates will have to be replaced at some point (though at this point are holding up very well), the fence netting should last a long time, as should the polycarbonate roofing.

One-hundred-thirty-four: Why do we project purpose?

"The purpose of life is not to be happy. It is to be useful, to be honorable, to be compassionate, to have it make some difference that you have lived and lived well." — *Ralph Waldo Emerson*

This morning three sea gulls soar in huge circles under high and dreary clouds, the interisland ferry held fast by Orcas Landing, Yvonne's chair, empty, facing Orcas, brown and gray skeins of yarn, and orange, green and white patterned cloth knitting tools pouch lying open, the iPad propped on its case at an angle, on the tan living room carpet. Where do the seagulls sleep at night? The Canada geese, the Mergansers, and Buffleheads come ashore I think; the cormorants roost on the ferry terminal pilings. One day cruising toward South Pender Island and the Bedwell Harbor Canadian Port of Entry, a single seagull raced eastward from Stuart Island in the direction of Bellingham, 30 miles away. Was that part of its daily routine? Why did it choose that moment to head out over the open water? Did it hear a call to dinner someplace we couldn't see?

Sunday, scores of healthy-looking young men and women, some dressed in colorful, warm sailing outfits, wet and dry suits, others in jeans and sweatshirts, in clusters, laughing, eating sandwiches, moving to and from the Orcas Island Yacht Club shelter and parking lot to the Club and county docks across Deer Harbor Road in West Sound, entering or leaving small sailboats, mainsails swelled in the cold northeast wind, jibs going up, coming down, a young woman jumping recklessly, confidently into her moored boat; boats, crew, and sails all one gliding creature on the water, tacking around course markers, coaches and officials in powered dinghies, observing, shouting. Immortal youth.

These intrepid sailors are members of the Northwest Intercollegiate Sailing Association, including students from Western Washington University in nearby Bellingham, the University of Puget Sound, University of Oregon, Portland State University, and the University of Washington and the event is the Northwest Team Race at West Sound, Orcas Island. I had seen the kids in their boats Saturday afternoon, a very cold, and very windy day and wondered who would have the nerve or lack of judgment to be out sailing on West Sound in small boats on February 26th.

134: Room for Lots of Books

They had used the West Sound Community Club building to warm up on Saturday but couldn't Sunday morning because the Unitarians (us — me giving a talk) had reserved the hall and they'd camped in Moran State Park on the east side of Orcas at the foot of Mt Constitution, along the shore of Cascade Lake. The report from two young men talking together in the parking lot: "It was a blast!" For me the two days of sailing would have been a hardship at best, fatal at worst. For this lively, smiling group it was life, intense, invigorating, and undoubtedly romantic in the best sense.

On the association blog Ash had said: "I'm so excited for this weekend, it should be a blast. A little chilly, but hey we're the northwest!"

Natasha had called in the afternoon seeking council about whether to rent the Ferry Street house in Shelton she and Noah managed and we owned together to a couple with two dogs, one a Chihuahua and the other an indeterminate breed whose back legs were more or less inoperable because of an accident two years before. The prior couple with two young children had moved out because they could no longer pay the rent and would live with his parents until they could find jobs. With almost new laminate flooring Noah had installed all through the house to replace ruined carpeting, I wasn't much worried about dog damage. Their references were positive. I told Natasha to use her judgment. And then we talked about eNotated Classics marketing and about the six inches of snow they'd had the previous week, with school called off, the whole family home and the kids out sledding then wet and cold and in for a warm-up and cocoa and then back outside, joyous.

I'd sent a summary of my Sunday talk to my usual mailing list, our family, my sisters, our friends in Boulder, and the Grey Beards in Deer Harbor (who were not meeting while Howard was with his daughter and family in France). James had responded quickly, reflecting on the implications of the findings of new cosmology, wondering whether it would depress people or whether they might deny it wholesale. My sister, Julie, wrote back that she would read my paper but had been a bit surprised that my title "Multiverse" wasn't in reference to some kind of poetry, her perennial love. Otherwise, silence.

Yvonne and I talked at dinner and she said again how she wasn't at all interested in questions about how the universe began. What's the point? How did that have anything to do with anything at all? And she was very interested in my topic for a May service — Why do we project purpose where it doesn't belong — on nature, on invisible undetectable entities, on history, on the stars — rather than just on people and maybe some animals? I told her how pleasantly surprised I'd been that the Unitarians had been so interested in "Beginnings" and I thought they'd be even more interested in the topic: the illusion of purpose and its cause.

One-hundred-thirty-five: More More

"Curiosity is the wick in the candle of learning." — William Arthur Ward

When I walked into the OPALCO conference room the group around the table looked up in surprise. Winnie said she didn't think I would try to cross from Crane the way the wind was blowing. No one wanted to be on the water this morning. I told the group it hadn't been that bad. Coming through Pole Pass with the wind opposing the current the waves were at most three high, trough to crest, more fun than a worry. The video teleconference was ready to begin — Orcas, San Juan, and Lopez all appearing on the big screen. By the time I got back and Yvonne had to leave for her DHCC Women's Auxiliary meeting, the wind had died and the sun was shining warmly — after two hours of good rain.

The OPALCO Board had given the MORE (Member Owned Renewable Energy) committee the green light and had approved its plan for using OPALCO member donations to help defray the costs of other members who were installing local green power generation attached to the OPALCO grid. The basic concept was to encourage the build-out of a local, distributed one-megawatt renewable energy generation capacity. For more than ten years OPALCO members (a San Juan County power distribution co-op) had volunteered to pay a surcharge so that OPALCO could buy green power through the Bonneville Power Administration, its power supplier. Bonneville had closed the program at the same time OPALCO had signed a long-term supply contract that forbade OPALCO from buying power elsewhere unless locally generated, something it had been doing for some time. The thought was that OPALCO members who in the past had been paying a surcharge to buy green power through Bonneville would likely be willing to continue to pay a higher bill to support local green power. The MORE steering committee was charged with creating a plan and submitting it to the OPALCO Board. After a year of

MORE meetings that had been accomplished. Living on Crane, a San Juan Islands out island and familiar to some members of the OPALCO Board because I had run for election to the Board the previous spring, I had been asked to join the MORE committee, managing to attend about half the meetings. The task now was to define what it was the permanent MORE committee would do to actually make the member-supported (voluntary) program successful in raising local green generation from about 200 kilowatts to 1 megawatt, a 500% increase.

135: Ready for the Grandkids

Leaving the meeting in the pouring rain, I went first to the Library and seeing Chris and Lynn there for their weekly volunteering stint, I passed along three books (two from Noah) related to book marketing, encouraging Chris to see what he could find that might be useful. If he could do research and look for tools and strategies, Natasha could use them in her marketing operation. He reported that he had successfully set up a Google ad-sense account with ads for certain Joshua Slocum searches that would be billed based on click-throughs. The experiment would tell us something about how many people search for Slocum, wanting to read him. I talked for a few minutes to Phil, the library director and we wondered together what the future held for the book sale given that disposing of the leftovers had become problematic. Don and Terri were at the counter checking out a *Barlett's Quotations* — I assumed was to help them with their sailing adventures/cookbook — and it was. They repeated their appreciation for the kitchen project party more than a week earlier, my encouragement of their writing effort and my suggestion to use italics for Terri's passages in the narrative to make it clear who was narrating. I suggested using block quote formatting and indenting the paragraphs on both sides as another alternative.

I was now running behind schedule. Yvonne had a Women's Auxiliary meeting in the afternoon and I needed to be back on Crane so she could take the *Huginn* and be ready for her ride from Marion. I called her from the Library, confirmed that I would be home before she needed to leave and then stopped at the bank to pick up signature forms so that Yvonne, Chris, and David could be signers on the account and then on to the Island Market to pick up the *Seattle Times* and *Islands' Sounder* for Yvonne before driving back to Deer Harbor and stopping at the Post Office to pick up the mail, today's to include a box from Amazon with *Jane Eyre*, *Frankenstein*, and Thompson's *Merchants of Culture* a sociologist's study of the trade publishing industry that had been reviewed in the *New York Review of Books* and which I thought might help me understand better how we should structure our nascent electronic publishing business.

At home and making myself a sandwich for lunch, I could see that the sugar ants that had crowded around the bait stations on the counter next to the refrigerator early in the morning were now gone. The ants had shown up in numbers the day before, starting their spring season. Tiny, perhaps 1/32" long, they looked for water and sugar, and when a scout found either they would set up a supply line with thousands of ants — walking across our countertops or floor. Though the ants are harmless, as far as I know, we didn't want them in our house any more than we wanted deer in our garden, raccoons in our garbage, or mink in our storage tent. Here the natural world was so powerful that it would overrun and destroy you if you didn't create boundaries and fight back. Later in the afternoon, Yvonne returned from Orcas, a Macy's shoe box in hand that she had picked up from the UPS delivery shed at the Crane parking lot on Orcas, sandals for our Chimayo trip, provided she decided to keep rather than return them.

One-hundred-thirty-six: Would Wood

"He who buys what he does not need, steals from himself." — *Swedish Proverb*

How much wood would a Cranian chop if a Cranian could chop wood? That's what I'd been trying to find out — well not exactly that — more like how much wood does it take to heat a house on Crane, specifically ours — given that the wood stove heat is intended to be the primary but not exclusive heat source, so I'd been tracking how many cartloads of firewood I'd burned, the average being about two loads per week, depending on the outside temperature, the wind, the quality (partly rotten didn't give much heat) and the type of wood (alder burning quickly and fir much more slowly). The practical question for today: how much longer will the current wood supply last?

I had estimated earlier a cart would contain about seven cubic feet of wood given that it was stacked above the sides. A cord of wood was 8' long by 4' wide by 4' high or 128 cubic feet and would last about nine weeks or two months. Assuming an eight-month heating season (October through May), with us a month traveling during that time and lower use at the beginning and end of the season, we'd use three and a half cords. Between what we had on hand in October and what I'd added that month, using our pickup truck, on the island for a while, I thought I had enough wood. But maybe not. We had a stack about 4' high by 10' long by 16" deep or about 50 cubic feet or a five-week supply at our current rate of consumption. With a week's supply on the porch (a bit less actually), we'd have a six-week supply — through mid-April. Since we'd be gone for part of April, the wood could last almost until the beginning of May. We'd almost certainly need more wood — or be willing to rely on electric heat — to get through the season. Several downed trees were asking to be cut up and brought back to the house but they were a quarter mile away and that would mean hauling the wood by cart (unless I brought our truck back on the island) but that would cost (coming and going) at least $250, so we'd want to keep it on Crane for a while, perhaps all summer but then we wouldn't have it to use on Orcas.

136: Yvonne's Office and Studio

It was early March and the daffodils, usually in flower by late January, weren't yet close to opening. So far it had been a cold winter with none of the mid-50-degree days common in years past. Looking at the actual statistics — degree days in January and February for 2010, the total was 1128 but for this winter 1480. It's easy to misremember — 2009 was 1540, 2008 1524, and 2007 1447 — so last winter was the exception, not this one. Compared to New York City, at 2891 total for January and February 2011 our climate was balmy, so who can complain?

I woke Yvonne at 7:00 since she would need to meet Sylvia at Orcas Landing to take our pickup on the 8:55 Anacortes ferry to pick up bare root plantings to be sold at the Orcas Master Gardener fundraising sale that Saturday. As I backed the *Huginn* to the end of the Orcas dock to drop Yvonne off, we both noticed a small, colorful duck 50 feet away. A Harlequin — very fancy with rust, black, and white feathers. Back on the Crane dock and happy to return to our island home, a palpable feeling of happiness Yvonne and I have every time we step on the dock, I was especially aware of the crystal clear water covering the beach. The Canada geese pair that calls the little harbor home were about 50 feet apart on the breakwater talking to each other. Last year they had brought five yellow goslings into the world. Walking across Och's meadow, I heard two other pairs talking with one another, loudly. Maybe the males were romancing the females. I had that sense from the three pairs — the fact that they were having conversations this way very unusual compared to the behavior I normally observe. Overhead the sky is clear, an opening to heaven, while in every direction clouds hide the blue. Over the mainland, twenty miles east, the clouds are black and threatening — where Yvonne and Sylvia will be going.

I'll pick up Yvonne in the evening since after coming back to Orcas she'll go to Grace's choir practice. By 4:30 I'm ravenous for dinner and heat up a bowl of chile Yvonne had made the day before and I put together a green salad and make myself a piece of toast with Yvonne's homemade bread.

One-hundred-thirty-seven: Sad News

"Friendship is born at that moment when one person says to another, 'What! You too? I thought I was the only one.'" — C.S. Lewis

The mail included a small envelope from Margaret, our next door neighbor who spends some of her time when not on the island teaching anthropology and folklore classes at Ohio State and writing scholarly articles, with an emphasis on women's folklore in Persian speaking-areas and some of her time traveling to places like Kabul to record folk tales and women's narratives, and I felt some apprehension as I pulled it out of our Post Office box in Deer Harbor. Why would she send us a paper note rather than an email? I felt like I was holding a telegram with bad news but put it into the sack with the other mail, including a box of books from Amazon, expecting Yvonne to open Margaret's letter as she did virtually all the mail, including checks and bills, her bailiwick, ever since early in our life together she became appalled at the way I managed (or failed to manage) our family finances up to her standards, as she had done with the laundry after being very upset with the way I crammed damp clean clothes into baskets, leaving them permanently wrinkled (probably) and she was even more upset when her sweater ended up five sizes too small.

Margaret's athletic 66-year-old brother and only sibling had suffered a massive heart attack while riding his bike near his house in Atlanta and in spite of getting almost immediate help could not be saved, dying two days later without regaining consciousness. She'd be delayed returning to Crane for the summer and probably wouldn't arrive until sometime in early May. Yvonne and I felt terrible and Yvonne replied by email with a note of sympathy. Margaret's parents, from Seattle, had bought the property on Crane about 40 years ago, camping there summers with Iris and Dean, the next lot over, doing the same, both couples eventually building in the '80s. Like some other Cranian's Margaret had known Crane for a good bit of her life, loving it deeply and understanding its nature better than we did, relative newcomers after four years. Her plan was to retire from teaching and live full-time on Crane within the next few years. We looked forward to having her generous and interesting company nearby.

137: Studio, West Side

Margaret had taught Yvonne how to crab and they sometimes went out together to drop or pick up pots and Margaret introduced Yvonne to her technique for removing crabs from their shells by holding their legs while saying "Blessings to the Goddess of the Sea" and then catching the front of their carapace on a rock in a downward arc. I don't eat crab, too creepy, but Yvonne has been able to serve it fresh often to guests and keep a supply in the freezer.

Natasha reported that four of the eight sail bloggers had expressed interest in reviewing *The eNotated Sailing Alone Around the World*, and she'd sent them Kindle copies through Amazon. She'd see what happened with these four before she went on to contact more potential reviewers of the Slocum/Thomerson book and would use her time to look for review prospects for *The eNotated Two Years Before the Mast*, Dana's classic memoir on the life of the common seaman in the first part of the 19th century. Since the book related to California history and was more about the culture of sailing ships rather than solo yachting, the potential reviewer population overlapped but was not identical to the Slocum audience. And because the book was written more than a half-century before Slocum's and the sailing ship and process much more complicated, eNotations were if anything more appropriate, even necessary to understand Dana's adventure. The book had been submitted to Amazon but the company had put a hold on it claiming that it was in the public domain and therefore didn't deserve the revenue split for original copyrighted works. We'd had this problem with the third Slocum book so I again explained to Amazon the value we were adding, in this case more than 800 explanatory eNotations, and I got an email back suggesting that I resubmit the book. Now listed in the catalog, Amazon hadn't made it available for sale.

Natasha commented on the multi-universe write-up I'd done, reporting that Noah had been doing reading in the same area, cosmology and theoretical physics, and even though neither of us knew what the other had been reading, we were somehow in cahoots. A long email from Noah explained why he was doing the research — background for novel he was planning that would take place in Bellingham in the 90's and feature a male protagonist fascinated by a mysterious young woman who would appear and disappear at will. He'd read an earlier Brian Greene book, *The Elegant Universe* and was now thinking maybe he needed to look at *The Hidden Reality*. We'd talk soon about the topic and perhaps could have an extended discussion when Noah and family came to visit in early April, with a trip with all of us to Victoria on nearby Vancouver Island.

Yvonne, Sylvia, and other Orcas Master Gardeners completed preparations for the bare root sale — a fundraiser scheduled for the prior weekend but delayed because of bad weather — especially the unseasonable cold. When Yvonne got home in the afternoon she said she felt beat up by the wind on the Orcas and Crane docks — that made it feel unsafe to walk. Some of the day I spent analyzing the association's books — to understand and be able to report to the Board what the prospects were for completing the fiscal year — another five months — on budget and in doing so found some items in the fiscal year budget that needed to be recategorized and talked with the bookkeeper about it.

One-hundred-thirty-eight: Details, Details

"The most important thing in communication is hearing what isn't said." — Peter Drucker

Yvonne, in a black shift dress and black tights, looking very nice, was on her way to Seattle for Kelly's baby shower, the little boy not due until June but Tim and Kelly would be leaving Seattle because Tim, a software engineer with Google, was being transferred in April to Paris. She'd see Jen and have dinner with brother Ron and find out how his acupuncture practice startup was doing. Back on Crane walking south on the dock I noticed a pair of Common Golden Eye ducks to my left that had just abandoned the beach, the female with a rust-colored head and a salt and pepper body making a dive into the shallow water and the male, very elegant with white cheeks on a black head, a black back with white side chevrons becoming to a white belly.

Jason and Dan knocked on the back door just before 9:00 and took their shoes off before taking a seat at the dining room table. Pat came in the front door about five minutes later. Using the association's tabletop conference phone I called the conference call service Martha had arranged. Dave, Blair, and Martha were already online and chatting. Tim and Kate were missing. I offered my guests coffee or tea and banana bread but they demurred though picking up bread slices on the way out after the meeting. I didn't actually have any coffee but Yvonne had set up the coffee maker and showed me the button to push.

Crane Island Association had completed seven months of its fiscal year and as treasurer I had spent a full day going through the financial reports supplied by the bookkeeper in Friday Harbor to see how we were doing in non-discretionary spending, that is expenses imposed from outside over which we have no control and I wanted to provide a followup report on income that I had previously reported as close to budget except for one member who had been making time payments that had now dried up — with the bank having taken over the property. My best guess was that we would be within $1000 of projected income anyway — income, in my view being the most sensitive element of our finances — dependent almost solely on dues and service fees collected annually in the fall — with interest on our reserves at current money market and CD rates almost negligible. Property taxes had come in on budget, the Department of Natural Resources leases against our docks actually under budget — as were our four insurance policies. Bookkeeping/Accounting projected for the rest of the year would take us a bit over budget — the bottom line being that looking strictly at income (lower) and non-discretionary expenses (lower) we would come up about $750 short — a negligible difference in an $82,000 budget. I asked all committee heads to report their expectations for spending in their areas by the next meeting (I would look into the water area) so that I could project budget versus actual for the year across all accounts — so that we could modify our spending for the remainder of the year should that be necessary.

The most interesting part of the meeting was the discussion around policy. The Board had adopted a variety of policies over the year that supplemented or clarified the association's CC&Rs but they weren't available in one place, were inconsistent, and the membership had differing notions as to what they were. Dave had researched and collected past policies and then asked for recommendations. We'd gotten through water and had adopted a new consolidated set of policies, some of which I'd written based on my experience with the water system, what made sense, and what was missing. The most problematic area though was docks and that was today's topic. Having been dock steward for two years I also had some ideas about where existing policy didn't work and where some new ones ought to be put in place. Docks are a limited resource and very expensive. If all members, their guests, and their contractors used the docks without any guiding policies, the members might come to blows or cast one another's boats adrift. Some members have boats that are longer than our 23-foot summer limit. Should we tell them they can't use the docks? Some have their own docks but occasionally use one or both of the community docks but never moor overnight. Should they pay a service fee? How many boats per member should be allowed? Should full-time residents have priority over occasional visitors to the island? The biggest bone of contention was how moorage charges should be calculated. One approach would be to charge as commercial marinas do with daily, monthly, and annual rates — but it wasn't workable since members simply would not track their usage that closely and there was no one else to do it. The existing policy was that if a member (or guest) used either dock in a month they would have to pay a moorage fee for the whole month. Since some members didn't agree with that policy they unilaterally prorated their fees or failed to report their usage because, having their own dock, they'd used the community docks for an hour or two once in a while.

138: Midmorning Drama

Though several members offered moorage fee plans that might have made more sense than the all-or-nothing whole-month-at-a-time plan, the rest of us felt that the suggested plans were too complicated for members to use or that they involved some new kind of fee the members would balk at so we ended up agreeing on a modification to the current policy saying that anytime a boat is moored overnight, unless because of an emergency, the member owes for the whole month. It was a spirited and thoughtful discussion, part of a successful democratic process.

One-hundred-thiry-nine: Eagle Walking

"Discovery consists of seeing what everybody has seen and thinking what nobody has thought." — Jonathan Swift

At about 8:30, Nick, a stranger called to say he had found Yvonne's driver's license on the street in downtown Seattle the night before and he would be putting it in the mail the next day. I thanked him and then called Yvonne's cell phone, assuming she'd be relieved to hear the news but could only leave a voice mail.

The community water tank was holding steady at 12 feet. Birds were now in abundance on Crane. Two flickers perched high in a dead fir at the community dock. Robins chirping joyfully under a blue sky, the rising sun pushing its way around scattered clouds behind Blakely Island, warming me through my Carhart jacket, the thick air abundant with promise. Spring is here — even though the daffodils lag. They'll come along soon.

Even though they're wet and muddy, it's time to pick up the planks I put down on the meadow path two weeks ago for our Kitchen Project Brunch. It's heavy work since the route back to the abandoned lumber area behind a grove of willows and firs — where the stored planks have already begun their rapid return to the earth — is mostly uphill. Then I think about how, in dry Colorado, disintegration can take a century.

Yvonne would be at the Orcas dock about 11:30, having gotten an early start leaving Jeni's. Turning left into the Crane marina area from Pole Pass, Yvonne pointed out a large bird perched on a huge log, a lingering remnant of the log boom that had broken up in a wild storm thirty years ago, now high on the beach to the west. The bird was a bald eagle. I brought the *Huginn* to our usual parking spot on the dock just behind Margaret's boat and handed Yvonne the binoculars we kept aboard. The eagle, about 100 feet away, turned to look at us but with no inclination to flee. Was it guarding a salmon it had pulled from the water? Yvonne passed the glasses to me and I watched the eagle turn, lean forward and then stalk along the log raising its legs high, its talons huge in proportion to its white feathered legs. Scowling out of yellow eyes under an overhanging brow, the grounded raptor gave me the chills. Was it ill? Had it been injured? I reminded Yvonne of how an attendant at the transfer station had been seriously injured while rescuing an injured eagle even though he was wearing long heavy leather gloves. I returned to the dock with our camera and took a series of pictures. The eagle had moved only a few feet. I'd check back later to see whether we should call animal rescue.

139: What Is the Eagle Thinking?

Well past mid-afternoon, Yvonne and I took off for a round-the-island walk, stopping at Ilse's house, in the process of being remodeled, but with the carpenters absent for the weekend, it invited our inspection. I showed Yvonne where the bathroom would be, floor-to-ceiling windows looking out on a deck and woods with water visible through them, and a composting toilet to prolong the life of the old septic system. She'd been surprised at the ambient pleasantness of the composting toilet she'd enjoyed at Morningstar Farm almost a year ago.

Back at the community beach we saw no sign of the eagle, so we scrambled down a moss-covered rock face along a mink trail that connected the western and southern beaches, separated by a large rock outcropping, with a fork in the trail heading off into the woods to an unknown destination. Walking along the top of the huge beached log we saw no sign that the eagle had perched on it but otter scat peppered the trunk here and there. We had lived on the island for four years and had never walked on this part of the beach even though we'd looked at it thousands of times.

One section of the beach was thickly covered with bleaching clam and a few oyster shells. Why were they here? I recalled how we'd seen a collection like this on the Morro Bay dunes when walking there with son Eric and his family — though they may well have had different origins. Then I noticed that where erosion had opened the dark black soil above the beach a thin under layer was composed of white shell fragments. Shells had been collecting here for time out of mind, put there by one Salish group or another at summer camps over millennia, or by birds, or currents.

As we sat across the kitchen counter Yvonne told me how the license had been lost during the process of cleaning up after Kelly's baby shower and that Jeni had immediately printed out a temporary license from the Washington State Department of Transportation web site and ordered a replacement that would arrive in a few weeks. Neither one of us knew that was even possible.

The shower was a great success with Kelly especially appreciative of the "lovey" and shoulder burping pads Yvonne had made. Natasha and Opal were in attendance, Opal initially shy but then drawn together with two other girls her age by child gravity, the trio soon whooping and running through the foyer of Jeni's apartment building where the shower was being held. Noah and Morgan were in the building gym playing basketball and would leave later for Crystal Mountain to ski on Sunday. Ron's acupuncture practice was beginning to pick up and he was happy. Some of the group ended up having sushi at Umi's but Yvonne, like me, hasn't been able to acquire a taste for what others in our family are enthusiastic about.

Yvonne was reporting to me Sunday on what had happened in Seattle on Saturday. Sunday evening I called Noah and heard that the skiing had been terrific, the area enjoying four feet of new snow and the conditions as good as Colorado's best. After trying snowboarding, Morgan was committed to skiing, at least for now, and had made his way down a double black diamond for the first time, slowly of course, but without worrying about it. Noah had completed about 40 pages of his new novel and was researching multi-verses — and the history of science — for that purpose. And then while Yvonne and I had settled down in my office after dinner with a Kristin Scott Thomas film of female passion and male oppression, Natasha called to say that the first review, five stars, had come in on the eNotated Slocum book, understanding the value of the eNotation concept and appreciating the quality of Chris' work. Excellent!

One-hundred-forty: It Works!

"The beauty of the world has no boundaries, and neither does the power of observation." — *Ralph Waldo Emerson*

Sunday evening we'd had a call from Natasha saying that a blogger, Rick Spillman she'd sent a complimentary *The eNotated Sailing Alone Around the World* had read the book and written a five-start review for his blog, praising Slocum's work as a literary classic — not just a sailing yarn, explaining the eNotation concept, describing how Chris put it to work in an appropriate and useful way — with examples, and encouraged his followers to get the book — with a link to the Amazon Kindle catalog — and then posted the review into the Amazon catalog as well. Chris quickly added a link from the eNotated Classics site to Spillman's review. We were all very pleased.

What was especially striking to me was that Spillman had immediately understood the concept of eNotation (words and passages as links — not one or two character, tiny, footnote indicators — with links back to the text from the eNotation) and how appropriate it was for a 19th century sailing book). He also pointed to the paragraph and eNotation identifiers and how they provide a way for one reader to refer another to a specific location in the book, no matter what device either one is using to read the book. A stranger, with no connection to us had confirmed what we suspected or hoped for — that we knew what readers needed and how to provide it. I had been worried about whether anyone but us would get it. Spillman did and others will. It works!

Shortly after sunrise streaming solar rays found their way between a handful of clouds on the horizon creating a widening carpet of golden light unrolling to the west toward Crane Island, a ferry crossing the fiery strip from Orcas Landing to Shaw disappeared from view behind a headland. Later as Yvonne did her yoga stretching and I sat by the fire, my observant wife reported she had seen a Blue Heron wading in our cove, occasionally finding a treat with its long bill poked into the water and then raising it high to swallow. Big birds that appear ungainly at times, can seem extraordinarily calm, detached, focused — with their own sense of time — eons, not seconds or years — classy observers of a frantic, worried, world — except when they squawk — subtle in their approaches and landings. Usually solitary, they sometimes convene, a score or more, to trade stories, I suppose, about the silly world they make their way through.

140: Golden Morning

Skip Stickney, brother of my high school friend, Mike, had written me through Facebook from Mike's in Denver and I wrote back with the eNotated Classics site link and our family website link and asked whether Mike would attend the Willowbrook High School 50th reunion in August. No. I hadn't corresponded with Mike or seen him for four years. Google had replied to Yvonne's plea to figure out why she could no longer use her account name and password to sign on by asking more questions — technical enough that she had no idea what they were talking about. I had stayed with Rock Island, in the San Juans, as an email provider in part because I wanted someone local I could call with any problems. Yvonne had been too frustrated with their on-line email package (which I didn't use) and had redirected all her contacts to Gmail but now it was broken. Not a good thing

Tuesday Chris and I would meet with Jens and I decided I had time to prepare a new version of the eNotation software for him, simplifying its use as part of our change in policy to focus the eNotators on writing and delegating assembly of the ebooks to us. Now with spell-checking, serviceable but not great, the eNotator software could act as a reliable, somewhat transparent tool to create eNotations, so I sent it off to Chris, who was celebrating his birthday, to try out and report any bugs. We'd supply this new version of the software (or a newer one) to Stephen, who I hadn't heard from in several weeks, Margie, who also had disappeared from view, and Barbara, about whom I had high hopes.

One-hundred-forty-one: What Do People Want?

"Feedback is the breakfast of champions." — Ken Blanchard

Not so cold today but raining off and on, the wind blowing fitfully from the southeast, we take both the *Huginn* and Margaret's boat to the Orcas dock and then Yvonne and I ride together to Sylvia and Gordon's to retrieve our pickup after its use for the Master Gardener's bare root plant sale over the weekend. Turning into their driveway a half mile from Enchanted Forest Road we pass Ed LeCocq's property, the scene of a fire ten years ago that destroyed his under-construction house. The first few years in Deer Harbor we would hire Ed to cut our lawn with his field mower — until I bought a string mower that did well in high grass and even with blackberry sprouts. Yvonne would visit a bit with Sylvia and then stop at the lumber yard to look for deer fencing to put up around the flower bed below the east deck, facing the water, a home for daffodils, daylilies, and lavender — all yet to bloom — and all deer resistant — except when the deer don't know about it. Yvonne reported later that the 100-foot rolls were too expensive ($100) but that an Internet search led to an order for a lighter-weight version for $20.

I arrived at Enzo's first, getting a cup of tea and positioning myself on the window seat at a corner of the long table, to the right, just inside the door. A young woman was at the piano, banging out something I didn't recognize but sounded like a hymn, most of the smaller tables occupied by an Orcas cross-section — young to old, struggling to well-fixed. Chris came in a few minutes later, followed shortly after by Jens. While Chris went to get coffee for Jens and tea for himself, Jens sat down at the head of the table, to my right, and when Chris returned he sat across from me. Jens had enjoyed Maui but found it crowded and as the time approached to leave he did so without hesitation. He had finished a draft of the eNotations and additional sections for *The eNo-*

tated *Metamorphosis* and was looking for guidance about their appropriateness for what we conceived of as our market.

The evening before and finishing it early in the morning, I'd read what amounted to a draft of the book — with Kafka's text peppered with links to Jen's eNotations. It was my third or fourth read of this strange story, and I found Jen's notes very useful in providing perspective and pointing out patterns in the progression of the story — and his Kafka timeline, biography, and bibliography created a context for the novella that deepened my reading without trying to suggest a solution to the riddle of what Kafka "meant," a quest Jens believed would never succeed and which would actually detract from appreciating Kafka's text. I agreed.

The idea was to provide value to serious readers without distracting them into interpretation. Some of what Jens had supplied filled out Kafka and his turn-of-the-century life in Prague. He wasn't a hermit, he kept up with and was interested in popular culture, had a busy social life, did well and was serious about his day job at a workers' compensation insurance company where he was instrumental in instituting reforms that reduced workers' job injuries, and when reading his stories to friends often broke up in laughter at the comedic effects he had intended. Jens would review and add to his eNotations, finishing in a week or two while I looked into the rights situation with the illustrations he wanted to include, with the joint intention that we'd have a book draft we would then circulate among a small group to proofread as well as suggest changes or additions to Jens' eNotations and other writings. Then before our coffee shop meeting broke up, I installed the latest version of the eNotator software on his Mac and showed him how it worked, pointing out the spell checker and the simplified user interface.

About half-way through the meeting Yvonne had come in, reporting that the left front tire on the van had been low and she'd had to refill the tire at Crescent Service and that she would take the pickup and I would figure out what to do about the tire. Even though I arrived at Crescent Beach service just east of Eastsound at noon, they took the van inside and had the tire fixed in about fifteen minutes, pointing out that according to a tag on the window and looking at the odometer, the van was due for an oil change — something they did and would be happy to do for me and did I want to make an appointment? Since we had no plans to leave the island (I normally had the oil changed off-island) in the next four weeks, I would make an appointment but sometime later.

143: Clouds and Calm Seas

Driving back to Deer Harbor along Crow Valley Road, with the bulk of Turtleback Mountain rising steeply to 1500 feet and the tranquility of the pastures and hayfields on my left crowded by forest with massive Mt Constitution in the background, I felt very relaxed, on vacation emotionally for a little while at least, after a very busy four months of all kinds of work and deadlines. I could pause and actually be retired. It felt good — but of course wouldn't for very long as relaxation morphed into boredom.

I'd skipped my Crane circuit walk in the morning because I had to finish getting ready for our *Metamorphosis* meeting, so I took it late in the afternoon, pleased that the tank was holding at 12 feet. Coming up Circle Road at the north end of the airstrip I saw two men coming my direction from a house that had been vacant for years, one of Jim Jannard's Crane holdings that he'd included in a $5 million offering that had had no takers even when times were flush before the 2008 crash. When the two came closer I recognized Wally Gudgell, Orcas's heavy hitter realtor and then he introduced himself and Greg White an Orcas surveyor and gave me his card. Was Jim putting his properties back on the market. Yes. In the same way — as one package? No, the holding would be broken up and sold in the same groupings as they were originally purchased, in some cases a house on a lot or a house, guest house, and pasture — three lots — Rachel and Marilyn's farm, and they'd be sold at the price he paid for them 16 years ago. At that point Wally and Greg headed west to look at another Jannard property.

That evening I wrote a note to Martha to distribute to the Board and to Gary directly. These sales could affect Crane in a variety of ways over the next few years — not the least of which might be higher water demand coming from houses that had been vacant for a long time.

One-hundred-forty-two: Alternate Realities

"Trust is the glue of life. It's the most essential ingredient in effective communication. It's the foundational principle that holds all relationships." — Stephen Covey

Howard wouldn't return from France and visiting his daughter and her family until Saturday, so, because he's the host of our Wednesday morning get-together's, the Greybeards, as he calls it, we'd skip meeting for the third time in a row, except that Brian, who enjoyed our company, couldn't abide another miss and so called around the night before to say he'd host and could we come.? David and I could; Chris couldn't, soon on his way to Tucson with Lynn to attend to her father and his situation.

Another windy and rainy morning with choppy water coming through Pole Pass and white caps on West Sound a half mile east and the *Huginn* being driven to the west after I got out to tie the mooring lines at the Orcas dock. Today, again, I was wearing my big yellow and black raincoat, trying to keep dry in the blowing rain. Inland the wind was hardly noticeable and at Brian's, facing northwest and in the lee of the wind, the only sign of it was the whitecaps beginning about a half mile off Orcas and beating against Flattop's cliffs. A rainbow appeared, its southwest leg entering President Channel and then faded. Brian's cat sat patiently outside the patio door, David pointing out that it had all four feet together in order to keep warm — though it was already 46. Stretching out with front feet high on the glass, the cat revealed a big belly, clearly a creature of almost continuous comfort.

The day before, on our way to Eastsound, Yvonne to visit with Sylvia and me to pick up our F-150 at Sylvia's after its use for the Master Gardener's bare root sale Saturday and then meet with Jens and Chris at Enzo's to discuss the eNotated version of Kafka's *Metamorphosis*, we had talked about alternate realities, from my side the one portrayed in Kafka's story and from Yvonne the outsider's view of New Zealand that had come from emails Alan and Tessa had sent over the last few days reporting on their tourist activities, pursued in lieu of Alan's research organization project work in Christchurch because the city was still recovering from the recent earthquakes and the university building that housed the computer with the data wasn't now and perhaps never would be available. One interesting report was how public education is financed, poorer areas receiving more support, and richer asked but not required to pay more.

142: How Many Books Are Enough?

What Yvonne gleaned from the emails was that people in New Zealand had a different take on the world, much more inclined to see advantages in cooperation and having a sense of the common good and a culture and morality to support that world view. Certainly there was no lack of anxiety in New Zealand but the sense was that it wasn't pervasive and continuous and not directed at the government or other groups. The sense of society at large generated confidence not fear, a sense of shared abundance rather than scarcity, a society where people weren't at one another's throats but trusted each other. Having watched "Inside Job" the night before, Yvonne, who hadn't read much about the tight connection between Wall Street, government, and academia was now more critical of and disappointed in the direction American culture had been taking for some time. She'd been thinking about the effect of being in the richest, most powerful country in the world for which there is an expectation that everyone else's business is America's and to the contrast with a small country at the edge of the world that has no illusions or interest in trying to change the world and whose preoccupation is with its own needs and successes.

Brian and David had each spent extended time in New Zealand, Brian about a year total in two visits, one as a Professor of Forestry from Oregon State and once as a tourist, having sailed there with his wife from Orcas. David and Maxine had visited more recently for a month. David had a story about how a friend flying to New Zealand to make arrangements to import fruits and vegetables made all the arrangements in route — with his seat-mate who happened to be in the business and they had operated on that handshake, without any contract, for decades. Brian was impressed at how quickly sheep ranching had been reduced because of market decline and cattle introduced. Both acknowledged that New Zealand seems 20 or 30 years behind the US but in a good way.

Without stretching the comparison too far, both New Zealand and Crane Island share small-town, sink-or-swim-together mentalities, where disregard for the greater good is morally repugnant and people continue to be concerned, in these less anonymous settings, with their neighbors' approval.

In the afternoon sun, I watched a cormorant perched on Mike's mooring buoy 50 feet off Margaret's point stretch its wings to dry them in the light 54-degree southeast breeze.

Yvonne reached Cresi, her grandniece, after dinner at her uncle's where she'd been staying and they talked about the college application process Yvonne was determined to help her with, since both her parents, distracted by their illnesses and struggles with addictions, were unable to. A junior with good grades and determination to stay out of the trouble her older sister had fallen into, our monthly financial contribution to her well-being was making all the difference. Her mother, Gina, somewhere in western Washington she said, had lost the use of her kidneys, and lived by dialysis. Cresi was engaged with life and wanted to succeed; maybe we could help.

One-hundred-forty-three: A Roof Over Our Heads

"Experience is simply the name we give our mistakes." — Oscar Wilde

Approaching Ilse's driveway, I could see that half the new gray metal roofing had been installed over the new blue water seal material. A few days before, on a Sunday, when Yvonne and I walked Circle Road together, we'd given ourselves a tour of the construction project, the free standing bathroom that would have a composting toilet, the new loft that had been added where the roof had been raised over the entryway, how a living area had been turned into a covered deck. Yvonne liked what see saw, quickly identifying the location of the kitchen — which I assumed was at the other end of the house. Closer now to the Esary Roofing & Siding truck and trailer backed into the driveway, I could see someone moving about, on the other side of the truck, near the driver's door and as I walked by and said hello I could see that it was a young man who had spent the night, camping (there was no heat in the house — which had been reduced to its frame and outside walls). I saw no sign of the carpenters who weekdays I thought stayed in Ilse's teepee several lots away and close to the community dock and beach and where we had seen the grounded eagle earlier in the week.

Our house has six skylights, including one very large one, about fourteen feet by six that runs along the peak of the vaulted ceiling in the living room, with a massive fir supporting roof beam underneath, the beam supporting smaller beams on four-foot centers that run at a 90-degree angle to it down and outside the house under the eaves, with two layers of fir tongue and grove topped by insulation and then plywood, roofing felt, and finally asphalt shingles on top that keep the rain out or are supposed to.

Beginning about two years ago one of the smaller skylights, in the guest bathroom, began to leak intermittently. Perhaps it was because I had pressure-washed the roof to remove moss — an issue in the Pacific Northwest, especially where roofs are shaded. One neglected building on Crane has moss at least six inches thick; it's not good for the roof. I'd applied zinc powder, which is supposed to kill the moss but it was already too thick in spots so I decided a mechanical rather than chemical solution was called for and I spent about 16 hours over several days, with my pressure washer at the peak of the roof, supplied with water by a hose and power from a long extension cord, inching, literally, back and forth over the five connected roofs that cover the house and studio, knocking the moss off, along with some of the mineral covering on the shingles that protects the underlying asphalt from damaging ultraviolet light (though we have much much less of it here compared with Colorado, for instance). And I ended up using more than a 1000 gallons of water for non-domestic purposes, something we hesitate to do on Crane and only in the wet season, November through May.

Perhaps because of my enthusiastic and unprofessional pressure washing the skylight in the guest bathroom began to leak intermittently, not a lot, just drips in a sustained rain, but the drips carried with them bits of dust and dirt that littered the sink below and I knew over time leaks could compromise the wood it kept damp. When we toured the house before buying it I asked Dean, the owner-builder, about roof leaks, and especially around skylights. He'd acknowledged that they'd had some but they'd been fixed. A legacy of that experience was a can of roofing tar so on a sunny day I took it up on the roof and with an old paint brush slathered the uphill side of the leaking skylight with the gooey black substance and used a hose I'd dragged up on the roof to test my work. No change. The skylight dripped into the bathroom below. It was as if the pitch itself leaked. I then tried adding sheet metal flashing, tucking it under the shingles above, applying plenty of tar underneath, and since it turned up at a 90-degree angle, expected to see no more leaks. Water can't flow through sheet metal. It made no difference. The leaks persisted. I needed to find out where the leaks were coming from. A general solution wasn't working. I brought an extension ladder from behind Yvonne's shop and set it up in the bathroom, extending it up the wall to just under the skylight's wooden frame and trim about fourteen feet above the floor and removed all the trim so I would be able to see exactly where the water was flowing along the edge of the skylight and then climbed up on the roof and turned on the hose and then went back to the bathroom to observe. Aha! The water was coming from the upper left corner. I now knew where to apply tar, and so pulled off the useless new flashing and put the tar on thick all around the corner area where the skylight rose above the roof about six inches. Job done. I turned on the hose and then climbed down, going into the house and into the bathroom — prior to running a self-congratulatory lap. Argh! the dripping had started again, perhaps worse than before.

143: High Water and Waves Had Displaced Our Pocket Beach Ramp

Brawn and tar didn't solve the problem. The fact that the leak appeared at the corner didn't mean that's where the water was getting in. I knew it could enter at one point, travel along something and then show up someplace else so I spent the next hour wetting the roof above the skylight at one spot and then asking Yvonne to report whether she saw drips, then wetting another spot, and so on. That test showed that the water was entering some place next to the up-roof four-foot long side of the skylight. I just needed to know exactly where. I found some food coloring in Yvonne's cooking supplies, got permission to use a little, and arranged the tar into three separate areas, put a little water into each and a different color in each: green, blue, and yellow. And lo and behold, the drips in the bathroom turned yellow, so I applied an extra thick layer of tar in the area that had held the yellow water and reran the experiment. Now the drips were blue. More tar, more colored drip trials and then I was back to yellow and then green — but I couldn't be sure the green was pure green or a mixture of blue and yellow. After two hours I gave up. I was applying logic but the roof and drips didn't care — and that's why software is so much more tractable than the physical world.

I was way beyond my level of competence. Someone, I can't remember who, had recommended Esary Roofing — on the mainland — and one of their estimators came out in a few days, no problem since he was on Orcas once a week. I pointed out the bathroom skylight problem and another skylight in the eves over the back deck that had begun to leak. He could have someone out in a few weeks; the cost, about $1000 and the leaks were soon fixed. I didn't watch how it was done. I couldn't make myself.

One-hundred-forty-four: Waking to a Tsunami

"We do not inherit the earth from our ancestors; we borrow it from our children." — Native American Proverb

The bedside phone rang and after some effort in the dark, Yvonne switched on her reading light and picked up the call. It was 5:26 a.m. and I had been doing my slow deep breathing for the last twenty minutes or so. Yvonne had been asleep, snoring lightly in a delicate and charming way. Who would be calling this early? A wrong number? Trouble? It was Margaret calling from Columbus to warn us about the tsunami, the result of the massive earthquake off northeastern Japan, and headed for the Washington coast and that might hit the San Juans by 8:00 a.m. She was worried about Lou, the only Crane resident who spent more time on the island than we did, rarely traveling beyond Orcas and though not frail, not strong either. For the past year or so Lou would leave the Orcas dock cart at the bottom ramp rather than push it back up the ramp to leave it in its appointed place under the storage shed at the parking lot and out of the weather when he brought back his groceries and clean laundry from Eastsound. Yvonne finished the call and went back to sleep. I finished my deep breathing, got up, recorded the time, accumulated kilowatt usage for the new day and the inside and outside temperatures, made oatmeal and heavily buttered toast, poured a big glass of non-from-concentrate grapefruit juice, checked my email and then pulled up weather.com to see what it had to say about the Japanese quake, the tsunami, and whether we should be worried about Lou. I couldn't imagine any noticeable effect here since we were far from the ocean and anything entering the Straight of Juan de Fuca at Cape Flattery would be mitigated as it spread out into the Salish Sea.

The pictures and video on weather.com, the first place I went for natural disaster reporting, then the New York Times, and then the Seattle Times were shocking, even bizarre, like nothing I'd ever seen, even in elaborate special effects. Natural disasters confined to natural surroundings or lightly-settled areas seem natural but this was wholesale destruction of an elaborate human construct, a modern city with sophisticated infrastructure built to withstand earthquakes, and it did, but not the 23-foot wall of water that washed over it shortly after the quake. How could it? Alan and Tessa were now in Christchurch or nearby, an area that had suffered from a 6.4 magnitude earthquake. The earthquake off the coast of Honshu, at 9, was more than a 1000 times more powerful.

Nancy, a member of Yvonne's book group, on vacation with Steve, was on the north coast of Kaui, reporting by email during their night that they'd been evacuated to higher ground before 2 a.m. and that sirens were sounding every hour. In a later report, she described how her cousin had, with Steve's help, taken his boat out into deeper water until the tsunami passed and wasn't allowed back into the harbor until after 11:00 a.m. The tsunami wave, close to two feet on the Washington coast had little effect though some areas were briefly evacuated.

At the Deer Harbor Community Club monthly potluck that evening Gene and I talked about the low risk of tsunami damage for the Deer Harbor area and agreed that even if something massive came through the Straight of Juan de Fuca, Whidbey Island would likely be hit hardest, with Port Angeles and Port Townsend on the south side and Victoria and outer sides San Juan and Lopez island on the north most susceptible to damage and serving as barriers to the inside of the San Juan Islands, with Deer Harbor and Crane Island just about in the center. Even a quake to the east, if it raised a tsunami in the Salish Sea (Puget Sound on the south and the Straight of Georgia on the north), wouldn't be likely to penetrate the ring of islands around us. A new eruption of Mt. Rainier, were it to cause severe mudslides that entered Puget Sound could cause severe damage at the south end but probably not to the San Juan archipelago. A severe local earthquake would be a problem for structures and utilities but not because of waves. We'd had earthquake insurance on our Deer Harbor property, perched on the side of a hill, but I'd chosen not to get it for Crane Island, where the house sits on rock in a relatively flat area and is only one story high.

144: Our Destination in Chimayo

Gene and I went on to talk about pilgrimages — Dave had returned our book on sacred places and I had it in my hand — trading stories about Santiago de Compostela — he and Judy having walked parts of it in the Pyrenees and a friend who had walked most of it. I told Gene how our friend Ann had also done much of the walk and that Yvonne and I would be seeing her and Dave, Alan and Tessa, and Barb and Dean in a few weeks in Chimayo where we would do our 19th annual walk, a shared scared time for the eight of us and thousands of other pilgrims.

Yvonne had made an Irish stew for the potluck: cabbage, ham, potatoes, and onion, and the small group remaining cleaned the large pyrex pan. Kate had some questions about the "multiverse" after listening to my UU talk two weeks before and I worried that what I'd said was being understood in too "popular" a way. I'd wanted to explain why Stephen Hawking and other cosmologist/theoretical physicists thought a God was no longer necessary to fill in the creation gap but the reaction to my telling was as if it was science fiction. Terri talked with me about HAARP, the US government's High-Frequency Active Auroral Research Program in Alaska, and told me it might be implicated in the Japan earthquake, perhaps through a kind of conspiracy. She later asked Yvonne about my multiverse talk and whether it covered time travel, a subject that interested her since she'd read an Orcas author who described how a pilot and plane from World War II landed on an aircraft carrier in 1968. Hmmm.

One-hundred-forty-five: Thirty-one Years of Bliss

"And in the end, the love you take is equal to the love you make." — Paul McCartney

The tank was holding steady at 12 feet. Tom and Liz had returned from Ketchum appearing on the Orcas dock about 1:30 as I prepared to head back to Crane after picking up the mail. Tom confirmed that he would show me how to do leak detection by alternately isolating sections of the Circle Road loop, important since we were leaking as much as 1000 gallons a day and so far Gary was occupied with other projects. Arriving on Crane, a juvenile raven, perhaps the one I had seen the day before flapping to hover over Yvonne's water feature outside the garden fence and then dropping down out of sight while I continued my conversation with GoDaddy technical support, sat in a dead tree 30 feet away today croaking a message to an unseen friend in a dialect I hadn't heard before.

During my morning island circuit, I cleared a six-inch diameter dead fir limb from Circle Road near Dick's inland cabin, the site of a large deadfall across the road in late summer last year that I had cut up and taken home, long since burned. Just below the north end of the airstrip on the north side of Circle Road toward the concrete barge ramp, something had torn apart a seagull. White down and light gray feathers in a three-foot circle created a stark contrast with the muted browns and dark grays of the gravel, earth, and composting leaves, with little flesh and few bones remaining. A spot of pink I assumed to be flesh on closer inspection turned out to be intestine. An eagle, probably, had plucked and eviscerated its gull victim, perhaps carrying the corpse to its nest or perhaps a raccoon had carried off what the eagle had left behind.

145: Sound of Music

The day before, Natasha, on a whim, had written Andrei Codrescu, au and NPR commentator about our Slocum books and offered to send him a copy. A Kindle fan, he was interested and had been considering doing a book of annotations, perhaps on Frankenstein, initiating a literary new genre. Since I had read two of his books, *The Disappearance of the Outside*, a critique of Western culture, and *Casanova in Bohemia*, an entertaining historical novel that he promoted in a talk in Boulder I'd seen, I felt entitled to pick up the email thread Natasha had begun, explaining what we were doing — and since *Frankenstein* had already been reserved, offering *Dracula* instead. He responded quickly, praising our concept but acknowledging that he didn't feel qualified to do the research needed. His annotations would be personal responses to what the text evoked, thoughts he was now recording with his Kindle as marginal notes — as he and others were doing; they were not intended to be objective or explication of the primary text but he looked forward to reading

Slocum. A New York Times writer had also expressed interest in Slocum and Natasha had sent her a Kindle copy. Planting seeds.

James called about 2:30. Winter quarter exams at UCLA would be next week and he'd be very busy as a TA but would be released from this particular obligation for the spring quarter and was looking forward to completing the revised submission of an article on an aspect of addiction he expected to be published. Yvonne reported that she'd confirmed the Crane visit dates with Keith's parents and I told him a little about Jonah Lehrer's *Proust Was a Neuroscientist*, a book I found more interesting in its approach than I had expected. He and Keith were planning to roast a chicken for dinner — and as we observed later, the boys were good in the kitchen in a way that Yvonne and I couldn't be. Yvonne was a good cook but I wasn't interested in or capable of cooking anything more complicated than oatmeal or poached eggs.

Though the 15th was our 31st wedding anniversary, we'd celebrate it this evening with a date so about 5:00 crossed to Orcas and headed for Eastsound, its winter sleep still uninterrupted by the tourists who whose appearance was in proportion to the temperature and amount of sunshine. A quick stop at Island Market, mostly deserted, and then to Allium, the restaurant that succeeded Christina's and we had yet to visit for happy hour, Yvonne, in her frugality, thinking she might enjoy some wine while we ate appetizers and became sufficiently satiated without spending much money. My carrot soup was excellent, the best I'd ever had but the rice paper-wrapped salmon Yvonne ordered wasn't. We'd eaten at Christina's several times over the years and had enjoyed the sparse, recycled furniture decorating but this evening we were in the bar area, nearly empty and it felt lonely and precious. We'd need more food but Yvonne didn't want to stay and suggested we go downstairs to the Madrona Grill, once housing the island's auto repair shop, with wooden exposed trusses and a vaulted wood ceiling and plank floor — rough construction you might expect to see in a garage built in the 1920s, but today as a grill warm and inviting and we were quickly seated at a table looking out into the darkness of East Sound, the water not visible but felt. More people, more noise, with a basketball game on a big screen, unpretentious but welcoming, a bleu cheese salad for me and prawns for my date, who said her second glass of wine was an improvement on the first she'd had on the floor above.

Reminiscences, especially of our travels, some just us and some with family, very happy to have found each other in Washington D.C., both divorced, with children, looking for better partners, she working at a travel agency after migrating from Seattle to seek her fortune and me visiting the agency to install travel system software, nearly 33 years before, love at first sight for me after an unhappy time dating after a collapsed marriage.

The reports of the demise of the SeaView Theater were apparently exaggerated and *The King's Speech* had filled the house and drew a long line for popcorn, Orcas Islanders loving and appreciating good films and not willing to wait for their appearance through Netflix, were making a $10 ($7 for seniors) investment in quality popular culture and at the film's end applauded both it and their good judgment. Though we had thought either *The Social Network* or *The Kids are All Right* might have been more interesting, this Oscar winner was excellent as well — small but well done and enough going on to make it satisfying.

After mooring the *Huginn* on Crane, the dock illuminated by our LCD headlamps, we walked up the ramp and home, commenting on how much we loved the island and our life on it and marveling that somehow, with our kids, we had found our way to each other, added a fourth kid, and now lived in a place we had a hard time wanting to leave even to get groceries. But, as we had talked about at dinner — maybe we were in a comfortable, pleasant rut, though one without any sense of confinement or desire to do anything differently, never the sense we'd had until these last four years.

One-hundred-forty-six: Recovery of Lost Time

"Time flies over us, but leaves its shadow behind." — *Nathaniel Hawthorne*

We'd managed to set the bedroom clock ahead for Daylight Savings before we went to bed after coming home from our anniversary date night in Eastsound, so we weren't late leaving Crane for the bi-monthly Unitarian Universalist Fellowship meeting in West Sound on what turned out to be a very windy morning. Crossing to Orcas with the bundt cake Yvonne had made and with a big thermos of coffee and another of hot water for tea was bouncy on the chop coming from the southeast and a few times a bucket of the Salish Sea covered the windshield and then was cleared by *Huginn's* wipers.

A very small group today: a new couple from Palo Alto who had been coming to Orcas for years but now considered themselves residents, with a house in Eagle Lake on the far side of the horseshoe that makes Orcas, at least 40 minutes away — and this on a small island with no traffic; a quiet young man who appeared occasionally and who Yvonne suspected lived in a packing crate and who was served by the Food Bank; Babs, who with Peter was one of the founders of the group eleven years before; Margot, who organized the music when I had had responsibility for the services for six years before handing it over to Suzanne who wasn't present today; Jane, who told me after the service that she'd bought Brian Greene's *The Hidden Reality* after I'd discussed it two weeks before, adding that when she'd ordered it at Darvill's Bookstore in Eastsound the clerk had asked whether she was a UU since others had been in to order it as well; Megan, who told me that Bob was adjusting to life in the Friday Harbor convalescent home; Kathy, who would give the day's talk, "The Goddess Paradigm Shift," and her husband, Ray, who worked at the NAPA store and who I consulted about getting a battery switch for our pickup truck (he said they had what I was looking for in stock).

146: Golden Daffodils in the Sunshine

Now at its ebb after services in past years that attracted upwards of 50 people at times on an island with 5000 residents, the group could no longer afford to advertise and soon wouldn't be able to pay the rent on a meeting place. Nanette, the original organizer and promoter had moved to Bellingham five years before. Many of the other regulars had moved away or died or had quit attending after I retired from being a pseudo-minister. When the services had been advertised and attractive, people had come and were interested but not, as it turned out, enough to actually do any work to make the services happen. Today there were no orders of service, the service was ad hoc, created as it went along, and the talk was very short, like an oral high school book report. David, I discovered was no longer treasurer and Peter had picked it up. Chris hadn't done the emails for more than a year, Suzanne was doing that, and not having direction or encouragement from Suzanne, I hadn't brought the website current in many months. Yvonne and I enjoyed and appreciated the group but it had fallen below some threshold so that it could no longer satisfy us or probably anyone else really. We didn't expect the group to continue past the current season and we would probably be unwilling to put much time or effort into it. It had become a ghost of its former self and there was no reason to believe those past times could be recovered.

The prior summer Yvonne had gone through our family photo albums for 1978 through 2002 (when we migrated to digital photography and had posted thousands of pictures to a family website), keeping only those memorable and of decent quality and then picking out a hundred or so for me to include in a biographical video I put together of Yvonne for her 60th extended birthday party the family gathered for in eastern Washington and western Idaho, where Yvonne was born and her mother, Opal, had grown up and was buried. We had talked about scanning all the pictures, hundreds and hundreds, and had done nothing about that to date. Now Yvonne had more time, having reduced her volunteer load, and she wanted to get started. Terrific! After Yvonne cleared the dining room table and put down a protective cover, I took my $60 Canon MX320 multi-function printer/scanner out of my office and put it on the dining room table, then downloaded the drivers and software from the Canon site to our six-year-old Averatec notebook computer running Windows XP (the computer we keep on the kitchen counter for internet and email access and which I use to run the Kindle book generation software) and Yvonne was soon underway scanning 1978 (not many pictures — the year we put our families together) and 1979. I'd done scanning for Yvonne's video with a tiny, faster scanner but the results were unsatisfactory for creating an archive. The Canon turned out to be faster than I thought it would be, fast enough for Yvonne not to become frustrated, and in an hour she'd done almost 80 and then quit for the day.

We saved the scans to disk into a folder labeled for that period and I'd then load them into iPhoto on my Mac PowerBook Pro as a back up (and which itself would be backed up by the Mac's Time Machine software onto an external hard drive). Though the scanner did a good job set at 300 dpi, the originals were of much lower quality than even the early generations of digital cameras and some had faded, now with color balances out of whack. Having them in digital form could make some improvements possible and I might try to find the negatives and scan them when it was really important, since I had a Minolta slide and negative scanner I'd gotten about six years before that did a good job (with clean, good condition slides and negatives). And we had hundreds of hours of VHS, 8mm, and DAT video and 8mm film, from 1978 and later of our family — not to mention the photos and film Yvonne and I brought to our marriage and later inherited. I had a vague plan but the gist of it was to put all these sources into digital form and make them available in a library to the family and to use for future video projects, online albums, and special-purpose photo books, very ambitious — but with Yvonne's scanning we were underway and perhaps could capture this part of the past in a way that would be accessible and usable in a practical way.

One-hundred-forty-seven: Survival

"The time to repair the roof is when the sun is shining." — *John F. Kennedy*

The tank was still at 12 feet — an indication that Gary had set the pumping to exactly replenish the amount of water used by the three active households and the persistent undiagnosed leak that had appeared suddenly in October and accounted for as much as 1000 gallons per day compared to the 200 gallons going through meters. This week would be too busy but I'd arrange with Tom for his help finding the leak next week and along the way teaching me how to do it. About six weeks before tire tracks had shown up from what had to be a wide axel heavy truck — much wider than a typical car or pickup truck certainly. It had to have come from off-island and since the tracks appeared all the way around Circle Road and down the Eagle Lane (our road) and Rocky Road spurs, it must have been up to something that involved multiple houses. I assumed it was a propane truck making deliveries. There had been at least two other visits since then it looked like to me, the truck having come by barge, topping up homeowner's tanks and knowing which ones probably needed attention, I assume from watching the accumulation of degree days, and then using per degree day usage in the past.

Since we heat with electricity and wood and our only propane use is the range cook-top (with electric oven) fed from two 10-gallon propane tanks with a "Y" switch between them (and a spare tank just in case) and since the tanks are easy enough to take to Crescent Service in Eastsound for a refill whenever needed we have no need for propane delivery. What was disturbing to me about the truck and its deliveries, given my strong proprietary feelings that the island belonged to Yvonne and me — which of course it really didn't — was the apparent carelessness of the driver. The tire tracks didn't stay on the road but wandered into the side ditches that keep water off the roads. The truck was being driven off the heavy gravel road bed onto wet soil with no foundation. Was the driver going too fast? Didn't he care? He wasn't driving like a professional. In one spot, next to Dick and Nancy's waterfront house, the road had actually subsided with water collecting during rains and with this truck driving off the road and damaging the ditch which was now not properly draining. I wrote Pat and Jason about the potential Circle Road subsidence problem and then called San Juan Propane in Eastsound to find out whether they were the culprit. They weren't. They'd only been on Crane February 18th and the tracks I was seeing were more recent. Eric, one of their drivers said they were always very careful especially since "tagging" a water line a few years ago. So who was it? Maybe not a propane truck.

With the situation in Japan extremely serious after the earthquakes and tsunami, thousands killed or missing, hundreds of thousands without power and water and several reactors on the verge of meltdown, Yvonne and I spent some time talking about our emergency preparedness, about which we'd done little real thinking or preparation, except for short term problems, for which we felt we were in reasonable shape. We could cook (we had at least six months of propane for the range) and heat the house (an indefinitely large supply of firewood on the island), we had access to at least 25,000 gallons of potable water in the community tank and 250 in the hot tub, and we could recommission the outhouse if we couldn't run the pump for the septic system. We had a month's food supply on hand but limited emergency lighting, except for two windup LED flashlights that could serve in a pinch.

But what about severe damage to the Puget Sound infrastructure as has happened in northern Japan? Because we're first responders on the island we have both San Juan County emergency system pagers and two-way radios. It would be reasonable to assume that the larger community and the government would do something to help, though that might take some time. The Deer Harbor Community Club building is designated an emergency shelter and has a propane generator with a reasonably large capacity tank. The Deer Harbor community and Orcas and the other islands would organize themselves in whatever way was needed — I was absolutely confident about that. Thousands of boats, many large sailboats, could transport people wherever water allowed it.

147: Gary Carries Ruby and Two Pooches

Though depleted, the islands and surrounding water were the home of or could be for many potential sources of food, cattle for instance, and salmon, crab, deer, rabbits, extensive orchards, and what could be planted, like potatoes, chard, berries, and other crops that could do well here. Orcas was developing a community seed bank that, in the future at least, could serve the island. Chickens were being raised here and there and that could be expanded. In the past, the islands provided most of its own food. That could be done again, I think, for a limited period anyway. The climate was moderate enough that it was possible to get along without much heat, and air conditioning was never necessary. We have a sailboat, a dingy, and four kayaks and if necessary could crab from the dingy, getting to where we needed to be — a quarter of a mile away for the best crab grounds. The kind of emergency that would require us to fall back on 19th century and earlier technology would be a grave one but the islands could survive the loss of the elaborate infrastructure Japan, the US, and other countries depend on better than urban and much better than suburban areas.

Of course were the worst to happen all bets would be off since the US more than Japan might be susceptible to falling into social chaos, with armed groups protecting themselves on the one hand and marauding groups on the other and all bets would be off. Not a happy thought.

One-hundred-forty-eight: Flower Show — First Act

"The earth laughs in flowers." — Ralph Waldo Emerson

Five daffodils of maybe 30 have bloomed in the rockery below the deck outside the dinning and living area windows and the heather is underway but weeks away from full bloom. The day lilies have yet to appear and that's a good thing because though documented as deer resistant in Yvonne's horticulture books, the island's illiterate deer population doesn't know and last summer made the lilies suffer. Once Yvonne gets this area fenced the health of plants in the rockery, so far exposed to rapacious deer, should improve.

In the afternoon a raven swooped past the rockery area several times, its partner watching from a fir on Margaret's point. One day an eagle had landed near the rockery but that was to inspect a white, wooden, full-size seagull figure with outstretched wings fastened to a log that Iris and Dean left behind when they moved out of the house. But the raven didn't care about the seagull figure; it was looking for something else. What? Yvonne confirmed that the other day after making halibut for dinner she had disposed of the bones and skin in the normal way — by throwing them in the water — except that sometimes it doesn't get that far. The raven had seen something fishy — that's what it wanted to check out.

The three raised beds off the studio deck and inside the deer fence on the south side of the house are still mostly quiet, waiting for seeds or transplants but the three blueberry bushes Yvonne planted together in a large pot so they could cross-pollinate are leafing out. Deer tracks stand out in the soft soil of the eastern raised bed — a cutting garden area, left there a few weeks back when I forgot to close the western gate overnight and the deer discovered the oversight in the early morning — but they didn't eat the emerging lupin and for that I am thankful. A small lilac next to the studio deck and below the higher south house deck — from which the hot tub is accessible — is beginning to leaf out and the much older and larger red current is well on the way to leaves and flowers.

A large Douglas fir presides over but does not shade the front yard — bounded by a deer fence on the north (and this time of year enhanced with bamboo for wind protection from the Salish Sea not thirty feet away), on the east and south (with stretches of dense evergreen salal) and deer fence on the west. The north, front garden is the focal point for anyone approaching the house from the path across Och's meadow, becoming visible as the visitor comes through the dense barrier of trees and bushes between the properties and is the area on which Yvonne has lavished most of her attention. She gave me a tour of what had, now was, and would flower shortly.

I had seen primroses all winter and now they had mostly faded away. Three Bleeding Heart, an herbaceous perennial, under the drip line of the covered walkway that leads to the front door, were beginning to leaf and might begin to bloom in April and would carry on into the high summer. Winter weeds had popped up here and there, one price Pacific Northwest gardeners pay to have four-season gardens — but they weren't hard to pull as Yvonne demonstrated to me — because the soil is moist. She'd sprinkled slug bait into a rectangular planter to keep the pests out since they loved the ligularia that would later be succeeded by begonias. Baby daffodils, miniatures of the real thing, were now in flower among and around the hellebore, a wonderful Northwest winter flowering plant, here some in pink, others purple or green, the happiest in the garden, Yvonne told me. The variegated sedges, bunched grasses, showed new growth, luxuriating in the damp under the roof drip line. The winter daphne had lost most of its leaves but big buds were on the verge of unrolling into new leaves. Reticulata iris, an early bloomer, weren't this spring, but remembering them from last year I looked forward to their appearance. The five Japanese maples, all different, were in bud, and awarded Yvonne's "Very, very wonderful" designation. The bamboo clump, in the corner near the door and picked out very carefully by Yvonne grew only one or two new stalks per year and so would not take over the yard anytime soon. Tulip leaves were everywhere but no stalks yet. Though beautiful in their colorful diversity, their season is much shorter than the less varied but more sturdy daffodils. Two different cryptomerias were turning green again after going brown gold in the fall and over the winter and the twenty-year-old but mismanaged butterfly bush Yvonne had pruned to improve it was showing green and gray new growth. The witch hazels were trying their best to recover from deer browsing but struggling and Yvonne told me about how badly deer can set plants back when they go after new growth the plants depend on to prosper in the new season. A hellebore that Yvonne had brought inside the fence after it had been attacked by deer who were supposed to know better also struggled to recover but might not — ever.

148: Miniture Irises

Star magnolia were at the pussy willow stage, their fuzzy buds would mutate into flowers in a few weeks. Sarcococca, a Himalayan fragrant grass was doing well, but pansies and crocuses in a pot on a pillar were also deer victims, probably from when I left the gate open. The heather was in full bloom, a deep rose, and will last well into the fall. Purple crocuses were everywhere and the restios, another grass, was healthy but the pieris, a flowering shrub, had suffered deer attack. And there was the Archosanti bell we had found at a garage sale years ago. I had met Paolo Soleri, its founder, at Northern Illinois University in 1969 when I taught Philosophy there.

One-hundred-forty-nine: My Antonia

"A society grows great when people plant trees whose shade they know they shall never sit in." — Greek Proverb

For the first time in three weeks the Greybeards were again convening in Howard's "Honeymoon Cottage," at the south end of his fenced garden, missing Chris on his way back from a weekend in LA with Lynn who was going on to Tuscon for family matters — and Bob, of course, who Megan reported at the UU service Sunday was finally adjusting to the idea he was now living in the Friday Harbor convalescent home and had given up, at least for now, any expectation that he'd be "coming home" any time soon. His home was now in Friday Harbor.

Howard reported observing hard times in England but good times in France. Britain appeared to be dismantling what had in the past been "socialist" elements of its economy and unemployment was widespread and its infrastructure in disrepair. France, on the other hand, was vibrant, the people optimistic, and public construction projects in full tilt. Howard said that the French simply wouldn't put up with what the English would. We talked for a time about the contrast between the US-UK and France-Germany understanding of their social contracts; one being focused on freedom and the other on equality. In the US many people seem willing to sacrifice their practical well-being for the illusion of freedom to own guns, choose their doctors, and become incredibly rich. In Europe people are willing to sacrifice unlimited choice for the illusion of equality — to get medical care, retirement care, generally to have things taken care of by a beneficent government. The US and the UK seemed to be heading in the direction of a very wealthy elite, a small class of well-paid professionals, and a large lower class. Europe, on the other hand, was continuing to narrow the gap between poor and rich at least in the services they got. In France, waiting tables was a career and could support a life and perhaps family. In the US waiting tables was a throwaway job, temporary until the real thing came along.

149: Orcas Library Kids and Books

A review of the possible consequences of a tsunami yielded the same conclusions I'd come to; not a threat and general agreement about the potential resilience of island life should it have to retreat to 19th-century technology should that be required. And then general opprobrium about the financial wizards who do what's legal but not, in our opinion, moral.

A nice day finally, not much wind, with an island of blue sky several miles wide directly over Crane Island, an artifact of the Olympic Mountains rain shadow, giving the San Juans a significantly drier and sunnier climate than Seattle or Vancouver. As Natasha quoted Opal saying of Harstine Island, we were having "sun showers." I was in Margaret's boat today and Yvonne would take the *Huginn*, each of us with different schedules. The Canada goose pair waddled down to the beach and entered the water as I came through the break in the split rail fence that separated Och's meadow and our path across it from the community dock area and parking at Pole Pass. The buffleheads were off to the the left, well away from the dock area and two mergansers took flight from the shallow water to the right, with rapidly beating wings flying just over the top of the rocky breakwater that protected our little harbor from the prevailing southeasterly winds. Just through Pole Pass a harbor seal surfaced to the right watching me for thirty seconds as I headed east toward the Crane dock on Orcas, at one point lifting it's back flippers out of the water to show me and then disappearing into the depths of the Salish Sea looking for tasty salmon perhaps. An eagle circled over the Caldwell Point — Bell Island passage, perhaps also on the lookout for salmon and then turned north, flapping its way into the interior of Orcas Island. Twenty feet off the Orcas dock a cormorant, only head and neck visible looked back and forth trying to decide what to do given my approach — fly or dive and decided the depths the safer bet. Later when I returned a blue heron gently landed on the outer breakwater section of the dock, its long neck folded into an "S," with a large bright yellow beak and two small, very stylish feathers off the back of its otherwise smooth feathered head and then taking a good look at me and becoming alarmed, pushed itself easily back up into the air and continued east.

When I walked into the Library Barbara was already in the lobby. Not finding a table we could sit around in the general reading area we appropriated the table in the children's area, that part of the Library unoccupied midday on a Wednesday and talked about what Barbara had seen in her re-rereading of Cather's *My Antonia*, a story of immigrant life on the Nebraska Prairie that she admired again. We talked about themes: east/west, immigrants/locals, time and remembrance, fecundity/sterility, cynical sophistication vs earnest directness, the depth and strength of Antonia overcoming being jilted and left pregnant to lead a rich life, the dangers and satisfactions of early prairie life (I was reminded of the wonderful times James and I had reading Laura Ingalls Wilder's *Little House* series). We went through the eNotation agreement (what we each promised each other) and she signed it, and I took her through an outline of the entire process to publication. I'd spent the day before reconciling the Gutenberg version to a definitive printed version, re-paragraphing to the first edition and then loading the text into a database. I explained the eNotation software and we agreed I'd come to her house on Monday, install the software and give her a lesson. In the meanwhile she'd write up a description of what she planned to do with the book, a kind of lesson plan so that we'd start with the same expectations. On the way back to Deer Harbor and the Crane dock I stopped at NAPA and with Ray's help bought a battery switch for the pickup and installed it while parked at NAPA. I'd now be able to easily switch off the battery when I wouldn't be using it for a while and so wouldn't have to worry about the battery discharging when not in use. And I bought a dehumidifier kit (dissolving BBs in a basket over a collecting pan) to leave in the F150 to capture the moisture that seemed to fog the windows when parked.

At dinner Yvonne reported on what had been an unusually interesting program at the Garden Club meeting on genetically modified food by a Washington State professor who spent a good deal of time at the extension service in Mt. Vernon. Since Wall Street had gotten into commodities the price of wheat had increased enormously forcing small bakers out of business. At the same time some consumers, locovores (locally grown and eaten food — the stuff of farmers' markets), encouraged by writers like Michael Pollan, were becoming interested in the source of their foods, first animal products but now the wheat in their bread. Because wheat, unlike corn, remained an open field, not highly regulated and the gene stock not patented and owned by multinational agribusinesses, it was still possible to create and sell hybrid wheat seeds. A teenage girl had developed three especially interesting strains appropriate for the northwest for a science fair project and they were now in use by small farmers who were using new, small mills, to supply small bakers in Washington State, going around the edges of agribusiness to support a local high-quality food chain. Ken had talked about this development at the potluck Friday night in conjunction with the Orcas Seed Bank coop and not quite understanding then now saw the pattern — which tied back to the prospect for survival in dire times as well. Ken was now experimenting with wheat and perhaps others would on Orcas. Perhaps not practical, local wheat growing, the production of the staff of life, here in the islands, is a fascinating idea. Yvonne knows of a mainland bakery that does a million loaves of hand-formed bread a year and uses local grains. We'll have to visit. Rose's Bakery on Orcas also creates beautiful, and expensive bread, the unsold loaves benefitting the Food Bank, though I don't know the provenance of the wheat they contain. How was the wheat grown and the bread baked by Antonia and other Bohemian immigrants to the Nebraskan prairie, necessarily locavore, different from today's emerging locavore cultures?

One-hundred-fifty: Specimen Day

"You miss 100% of the shots you don't take." — Wayne Gretzky

Awake just after 5:00, deep breathing until 5:35, out of bed, laying a fire in the wood stove, made real oatmeal and ate homemade bread toast, and real grapefruit juice — while checking emails, the weather, the New York Times online, Slate, Huffington Post, The Daily Beast, and Google's FastFlip to check on what's happening with technology.

I had been thinking about the problem I'd had with my family website hosting service and realized their renewal email was in error, had talked about domain name renewal when it should have talked about hosting, so, worried that they might dump my website into a big bit bucket, sent a Help request to their accounting department to do a hosting renewal — coming up in two days.

I'd done our taxes but not mailed them yet and had been thinking about the right tax treatment for the replacement roof Natasha had arranged for one of our two rental houses we co-owned with Noah and Natasha who did much of the management. The roof had leaked badly on our tenants and we'd had it repaired twice but the problem returned each time as the roofer had warned so we followed his recommendation and had the roof replaced — which we wouldn't have done except for this intractable problem. Checking the IRS and other sites I concluded we could expense rather than depreciate the cost and wrote Natasha who replied that she'd already sent in their taxes and had not thought of expensing the roof.

By the time Yvonne came out of the bedroom, about 8:15 I'd finished my journal entry from the day before and took a shower — but noticing that the five-gallon bucket we fill until the water turns warm — was almost full and carried it out to the hot tub, Yvonne amused at the site of an old naked guy shuffling through the living room carrying a big orange bucket.

150: Firewood and Kindling on the Front Porch

Checking my email again I had a notice from the *New York Times* that they were going to begin charging for access to the paper on all but a cursory basis. Yvonne and I had talked about this change and agreed that we valued the paper enough that we would pay the fee, $260 per year, telling each other that it was fair and necessary to support the *Times*.

I printed out the last week's journal entries and put them under the stack Yvonne kept on the living room coffee table to read when she had nothing else to do and then read the first part of an article in the *New Yorker* by Daniel Mendelsohn about the 19th century German writer Theodor Fontane and made a mental note about looking into him. Then I remembered I'd forgotten to forward Jason the note I'd sent Elise about receiving another installment payment from Becky toward her Crane Island dues(unexpected). I filed our UBS monthly statement and then wrote Tom asking whether he'd be willing to work with me on the following Tuesday to try to find the source of the leak in the island water system. While on the subject of water I wrote Gary a long email reporting that the tank level was approaching overflow and next steps for surveying Crane owners about their water systems and the implications for our new cross-connect policy, when he would finish the two hydrants that had been under construction for almost a year, what it would cost to install tank float switches so the tank could stay full but not overflow, what water expenses he expected for the rest of the fiscal year, and when we should start putting valves and pressure test ports at the water main and at the road for hydrants on member property — the weakest elements of our system.

Then I got to thinking about my meeting the day before with Barbara and how hard it was for me to describe and for her to understand what I imagined we could do together to create a first-class eNotated *My Antonia* and wrote up what a table of contents might look like, which elements she would write as eNotations, which she'd write as standalone or near standalone documents with a word processor, which I'd supply and which would be automatically created by the book building software I'd written. The note seemed so helpful I sent a copy off to Stephen who was working on *Frankenstein* but still somewhat unclear about where he/we were going with it.

I was working my way through a stack of mail I had put aside and saw the note from Keybank about renewing the Crane safe deposit box, something as treasurer I should pay attention to. I had no information about it, where it was or what was in it, so I wrote Tom. He said there were two, one in Friday Harbor and one in Eastsound but didn't know what was inside or who had a key but that Dan might know. Dan wrote back that he had turned his one key over to Jason so I wrote Jason. Dan thought the boxes might contain deeds — for Association Property and/or the nature preserve the association had set aside some years back and which operated as an independent entity for which Yvonne was the Chair — but had no information about it.

An early lunch, peanut butter, strawberry jelly, cheddar cheese, and butter on toast, with warm rice milk, and sesame corn chips — my favorite — while reading more about the crisis in Japan, especially the uncertainty surrounding the nuclear power plants. A terrible situation for the Japanese people.

Our reservation for my 50th high school reunion, Willowbrook, in Villa Park, west of Chicago, was due soon. I wanted Yvonne to send it in with a check — and she would but wanted to talk about which part we'd attend. Only the Saturday night dinner-dance at a local country club. We have to do some planning about what else to do in Chicago and whether to try to see some infrequently visited relatives. Our eBook company wanted to add signers to our bank account — wanted all of us to have access — so I'd gotten signer forms at the bank and gave Yvonne one to fill out — and I'd take the rest to the business meeting the next day for Chris and Dave to complete.

Crane Island has an airstrip and so has to have airport liability insurance. The renewal was coming up and the agent had sent me a survey form I needed to complete and return. I found the form Mike had filled out for the last renewal and copied his answers, made a copy and put the form in the supplied envelope and put it in the outgoing mail pile Yvonne would drop at the Post Office when she left to go to Rock 'n Roll choir practice.

I opened and filed the No Wake Zone bank statement, for which I acted as treasurer; the balance, $21.99. That wouldn't go far. Steve was supposed to be working on a fundraising mailing to the Pole Pass area residents — but it hadn't happened and it would soon be time to do maintenance on the buoys and add some more. But I didn't need any more work and wasn't inclined to bother him about it.

Among its investment vehicles, Crane Island subscribes to Legacy Treasury Direct, a very safe way to get what is now a minuscule return and the expiration date was approaching so I followed the directions on the form they'd sent and renewed for another six months.

Because we'd be having our monthly business meeting the next day, I needed to prepare an agenda, create, and organize documents for the meeting and email the package to David and Chris and to Natasha, on Harstine Island, more than 100 miles away, an interested observer. As corporate secretary David was in charge of archiving important documents, like contracts, so I found the agreements we now had with three editors and would give him one of each. We had joined the Chamber of Commerce but I hadn't yet provided them with a logo and blurb they needed to add us to their online listing of Orcas businesses so I found Chris' picture of a Kindle on a book and created a graphic of "eNotated Classics," wrote a blurb and created a document out of the three elements to have a discussion around and would attach it to the email I sent everyone. I'd bring along the account signer forms they'd need to drop at the bank.

I wanted to include sales and royalty reports in the agenda/report and so retrieved the month-to-date figures from our account on Kindle Digital Publishing (13, 7 of which were inside) as well as the January and February royalty reports as spreadsheet format file attachments. I had wanted everyone to have access to the KDP account but Amazon had no way to provide that; each account belongs to one person and is the same account that person uses for Amazon shopping, and so has credit card and other personal and business-irrelevant information in it — so we'd have to get by with me providing reports on a regular basis. I would also attach the standard workflow/book project process I'd been working on as an outgrowth of the experience of doing four books and we'd need to talk about quality assurance, one area we didn't have a good answer for. David had proofed Dana's book but we needed more of a system. I included a summary report of what I'd been doing to improve the software and the good idea Jens had regarding topics — annotations covering the same theme and collected together so they could be read together — namely, that the eNotator write an essay on each topic, leaving space for and referencing the annotations for that topic, that is the eNotator would cite him/herself. And I listed the near-term enhancements I thought important for the software, including being able to create ePub (the industry standard) as well as MOBI (Kindle) format electronic books.

Supporting our eNotators was also an issue and would evolve over time. For now the simplification of the user interface and up-to-date online help was an improvement and I'd also changed the way the program was built so that there would be a different version of the program for each book/author — the program and book having the same name. Each eNotator would get a kit of matching parts and Chris and I would each have those kits as well so that we could, if necessary, duplicate what the user was doing. And then once the book was completed the kit — with software, database, and output HTML and XML files, as well as the MOBI and ePUB format files would go into an archive. Natasha and Chris had each written reports; Natasha on what she'd done and learned looking for reviewers and Chris on the various elements he had in place and was updating (website, blogs, Facebook, Google Adwords, and so on).

And we had some open questions to consider: should we go to DRM for Metamorphosis; should we consider Print-on-Demand as well as electronic; should we expand our distribution to Barnes & Noble and other large channels and/or consider small, specialty channels; should we consider doing classic annotations where the annotations are primary and the original text secondary, where the annotator is well known and already has a following — as I'd be discussing with Andrei Codrescu by email.

Before I took her over to Orcas so she could go to her choir practice (they'd have a recital next week at the Orcas Center), Yvonne asked me to "save" the scanned images she'd made. She's started in 1978 and had been working on the project several days now and I'd been doing saves by year, making copies for my Mac and importing them into iPhoto. She's finished 1987 now, 125 images for that year. We had boxes of slides I'd have to look at and scan at some point as well.

Back at the house I brought two dock carts full of firewood to the porch. We had a week's supply left in the pile — that had disappeared faster than I'd anticipated. I'd have to cut and transport wood from a quarter mile away by dock cart — or just use electric heat until June.

Because I hadn't heard anything from our family website hosting service and because our subscription would expire in two days I called their service department and though the helpful young man on the other end couldn't do anything more than put a note in the record — accounting would need to take care of it — I felt relieved at his assurances that nothing would happen to the tens of thousands of pictures I'd posted to the site over the last eight years.

Dinner, leftover cauliflower, pasta, and gorgonzola cheese; green peas; and toast while I watched network news about the problems in Japan. Picking up Yvonne later by the light of a nearly full moon I found out that the nature preserve had its own safe deposit box, she had an inventory of its contents, and the key. So the Crane Island Association had only one box and Jason had the key. The fog lifts. I'm determined to organize the accounting material, including the safe deposit box, and create an inventory of everything that is important that must persist through board and treasurer changes.

A little John Stewart, Stephen Cobert, *The Office*, (usually it's a Netflix film — the night before *Never Let Me Go*, a striking adaptation of Ishiguro's troubling novel) the hot tub in the silver moonlight, and cozy in bed, more of Lehrer's "Proust Was a Neuroscientist," the section on music, with Yvonne working on a book that follows the lives of six North Koreans. Good night.

One-hundred-fifty-one: Skylight Leak Detection

"Problems are opportunities in work clothes." — Henry J. Kaiser

As usual the Buffleheads were to the left off the end of the community dock and the fewer Mergansers to the right and all took flight as I approached. Three Canada geese floated near the breakwater with no plans for the morning as far as I could tell. The big bushy willow at the head of the dock, with an old bicycle seeming to wait for its owner to come back and claim it hid overhead among the branches that had yet to show signs of spring. David, Chris, and I were convening our monthly business meeting — to review, to decide, and to assign tasks and overall were pleased, perhaps delusionally, about the progress we'd made over the last four weeks.

Back home and after lunch I called Gary on his cell phone. He and Tom were in the vicinity of well house #1. He'd left a copy of the state Department of Health cross-connect survey template I could use to contact association members about their water systems on the front seat of the Fire and Rescue vehicle parked near the community dock and I would pick it up later. He and Tom would soon be on their way to well house #4 where they had begun leak testing and I caught up with them there about 30 minutes later.

I'd spent half a day near well house #4, at the intersection of Circle Road and Rocky Road, both nothing more than cow paths without the cows, cutting up a fir that had been pushed over by the wind and bringing the sections home in the bed of my pickup which I had on the island then, the wood all burned up now, split week by week over the fall and fed to the wood stove in the living room.

151: Central Skylight

The island water system is roughly in the shape of a circle with four two-inch lines following the four spur roads that come off Circle Road. Six wells and one 30,000 gallon tank are connected to the main circle, a four-inch PVC line. At each point a well line joins the main, that is makes a "T," a gate valve sits across each end of the top of the T allowing the main to be closed in either or both directions around the circle or even, with both closed, to isolate the well from the rest of the system. Because the system is a circle, closing just one valve on the main doesn't stop water from reaching every point in the system; it only means that water has to flow in two different directions around the circle to reach points on either side of the shut valve.

The tank can also be isolated from the system. One valve keeps water from flowing up to or down from the tank. (One line is used to feed into and draw from the tank.) The tank line also enters the main at a T — with valves at either side of the top so that the flow from the tank can be restricted from going either or both directions from the tank. A number of other valves are placed strategically around the circle so that flow can be stopped at any point or sections isolated from one another. Finally, each spur has a valve and a meter for measuring flow down the spur. Leak detection is basically a logical operation of isolating smaller and smaller sections of the system by using appropriate valves until the leak is discovered.

Gary had brought Wilma, his wife, and Edie, one of their two daughters recently back from two years in Vietnam teaching English and now to start college, as well as Wilma's canine companion and Gary's new puppy, both Australian shepherds. They'd shut all the spur valves and the main valve at well house #2 and isolated the tank and then at the intersection of Circle and Eagle Lane alternately closing valves that directed water to the north half of the island and then the south half after pressurizing the system from well #6 and then watching its pressure gauge. No drop in pressure from the north half but a measurable loss in the south half over a few minutes. They were at well #4 now to repeat the same process, this time with smaller sections of the south half of the circle. Gary explained the process to me as we walked to a valve to the west that we could close to divide the south half into two sections. We'd use well #4 to pressurize what would now be a southeast quadrant. I explained to Gary and Tom my theory that the leak, which had appeared in October came from a hydrant on the south side of the island and most likely where there'd been construction activity, right where we were now checking.

The pressure test did in fact show a leak in the southeast quadrant so the valves at either side of the "T" were used alternately to reduce the testing area to one-eighth of the system. Defying expectations pressure dropped when each eighth was tested. Did that mean two leaks? Gary and Tom then closed both sides of the T, thus isolating well #4 from the system and then used the well pump to pressurize the fifty feet of line between the well house and the T — and the pressure dropped very quickly, both Gary and Tom able to hear water running underground at a frost-free hose bib sticking out of the ground near the well house used to take water samples. Though maybe not the only leak, we'd found a significant leak area. Was it the frost-free? Gary thought it probably was but couldn't be sure until he dug it up. Chlorine was injected into the water coming from underground which then spent some time in what amounted to an underground tank so that the chlorine could come into contact with all the water and kill any microbes. The frost-free was attached to the outflow from the tank which then led to the T at the road. There could be a leak in the tank, mostly likely where the ten-inch pipe turns back on itself coming back toward the well house and the frost-free. Both he and Tom had seen that kind of problem before, elsewhere and it was much more difficult to fix than a frost-free.

Gary thought what made most sense was to turn off well #4 and keep it isolated from the system and then see whether there was unexplained water loss to the system over the next few days. Lou, Tom and LIz, and Yvonne and I used 200 gallons among us. The system had been losing about a 1000 gallons a day on top of measured use. If the problem at well #4 was the cause, the tank level would drop very little over several days even with no pumps running. Given that the tank was at 13 feet and would overflow at 13 1/2 feet and with the leak probably now isolated from the system, it made sense to discontinue all pumping and check the tank level on Sunday. What fun we had!

One-hundred-fifty-two: Whidbey Island

"The best journeys answer questions that in the beginning you didn't even think to ask." — *Jeff Johnson*

Yvonne needed to be at the Coupeville High School on Whidbey Island for a 10:45 presentation Saturday morning on rock and concrete wall building at the Master Gardener meeting there, so we'd take the 8:55 ferry, putting us in Anacortes a bit before 11:00 and we'd try to make the 30-odd mile drive to make the start of the class. As it turned out, we didn't arrive until 10:52 but since the class was late getting started Yvonne didn't miss anything important.

Whidbey is about 50 miles long and eight at the widest, the south end, Clinton, just above Mukelteo and Everett where Boeing manufactures 747s in a huge building that eyewitnesses tell me has its own climate, including clouds, at times. The north end of Whidbey Island is separated from Fidalgo Island, where Anacortes and the San Juan Ferry are located, by Deception Pass, a narrow canyon through which strong currents carry tides in two round trips every day. For most boats, the only safe time to be in Deception Pass is at slack tide, the short period when the current stops and prepares to flow the other direction.

Oak Harbor, ten miles south of Deception Pass and located on the north side of Penn's Cove, a major indentation to the island from the east, is the major town on the island and home to a naval air base that is sometimes the source of big noise when Growler fighter pilots practice their touch and gos. Coupeville, a historic district, is on the south side of Penn's Cove and where, in 1984 we made a contingent offer on a house that was accepted but which we had to give up when our house in Boulder didn't sell or even see any offers in more than six months on the market. Today we had several goals in mind: Yvonne wanted to attend the Master Gardener meeting; we wanted to do something other than stay at home and work, work, work; we wanted to get to know Whidbey better; and we wanted to see the house we had tried to buy longer ago than our youngest son was old.

After dropping Yvonne at the Coupeville High School I drove back north to Oak Harbor, stopping first at a Les Schwab tire store to have the tires for our two wheelbarrows repaired. They both leaked and my attempt to fix the tube on one was unsuccessful. I needed expert help. Yvonne had also complained that the brakes made a noise she was worried about when she touched the pedal, something I hadn't noticed. I helped myself to the hot popcorn these helpful stores provide and tried to read some of Codrescu's *Posthuman Dada* book he'd strongly encouraged me to read in several emails, especially one I'd received that morning but quickly found myself reading the Wikipedia entry on Dadism on my iPad and then since it was near noon and I was hungry helped myself to the chicken salad sandwich Yvonne had made for me — concerned as usual that I might starve before she could feed me in person. And then the wheelbarrow tires were complete — two new tubeless models rather than an attempt to put new tubes in old tires (one that I knew was at least 30 years old), so I drove a few blocks north to a Jiffy Lube, a service I frequent religiously wherever we are when the van has put on another 3000 miles and then to a Shell station with a car wash that had been recommended at Jiffy Lube. Yvonne liked her car, the van, to be clean inside and out. Jiffy Lube had vacuumed the floors and cleaned the windows so a car wash would just about do the trick. Then back south a few blocks to Starbuck's for a hot chocolate (because I'd had my caffeine ration at the Orcas Hotel while Yvonne and I waited for the Anacortes ferry that morning) and an hour to work on the eNotator software since I'd noticed that one aspect of the spellcheck I'd installed wasn't working right. And then into Coupeville for a look and then back to Coupeville High School to pick Yvonne up at 3:35 when she would be let out of school.

After our first visit in 1984 when we were touring the island with our oldest three kids and Yvonne's mother Opal, Yvonne and I came back in 2002 in Gumption, a Camano Troll, pocket trawler, mooring at the public dock, walking around the small historic waterfront and having a meal before going farther south and spending the night at the Langley marina on Whidbey. Yvonne and I drove past the one-block waterfront to see whether we might want to eat dinner there. Nothing spoke to us.

152: Whidbey Super Moon

We checked into the Anchorage Inn, a B&B Yvonne had found on the internet, two blocks above the waterfront, a modern version of a Victorian mansion, that had the least expensive room acceptable to Yvonne in the little town and then we headed south to Langley, not far from Clinton, the Whidbey end of the ferry from Mukilteo, on the mainland, a passage we'd been through twice together and me two more times, once when I brought our sailboat, Simrishamn north from Lake Union in Seattle and once when I took Gumption to Lake Union to put her up for sale.

Coupeville is in an historic district that spreads out from the town to the agricultural areas south of it and both are held in a kind of stasis, little changed from what we had seen more than 25 years before. There is a kind of charm in the outdoor museum quality of it but also a sense of paralysis. Langley, on the other hand, is vibrant and more attractive, with a focus on shopping and a few galleries. Yvonne found Star's, a clothing and grocery store with, she explained to me, a nice selection of uncommon contemporary styles. After being kicked out at the 6:00 closing time we walked across the street to Village Pizza, perched on the palisade high above the Saratoga Passage below, Camano Island a few miles straight across and Everett farther way, where we'd stayed at the yacht club marina on our way back from Olympia and Harstine Island eight years before. Behind Everett and Snohomish and the other towns west of the mountains lay the Cascades, a wide jagged line of floating faded white, broadening here and narrowing there, reaching higher, falling lower, the same blue above and below.

We managed to eat only half of the half Sicilian-style pizza, splitting a Caesar salad, Yvonne enjoying her chardonnay served in a 6-ounce juice glass filled to the top. The food was good, the ambience lively, and the staff attentive. We'd go there again. On the way back north to Coupeville we turned west off the main road to drive into a development below Whidbey's characteristic cliffs on a wide flat beach into which canals had been dredged, allowing some of the houses to have their own docks. Coming back to the highway the perigee moon rose over Greenbank Farm, huge and golden and I parked near the stop sign and ran across the road in the dark with my camera to take pictures of a "supermoon," an event that last occurred eighteen years ago.

One-hundred-fifty-three: Forest Road

"The road goes ever on and on, down from the door where it began. Now far ahead the road has gone, and I must follow if I can." — J.R.R. Tolkien

At breakfast around the big dining room table we shared with a couple and their 10 year old daughter, a gray haired couple from north of Bothel and still working (she a master gardener visiting Whidbey for the meeting), and a gray-haired single man from Oregon, conversation went from where we had come from to why we were in Coupeville, to what route we'd take to get home — the problem being that the Mukilteo side of the Clinton ferry was closed over the weekend for repair so the Clinton ferry was departing Edmonds instead, doubling the amount of time the mainland-Clinton sailing required and thus halving the number of trips. With the Clinton-Mukilteo route always being problematic for Sunday returns, the reduced service might mean four-hour waits. I described the impact of losing the Orcas Ferry landing for a few weeks when the dock had been plowed into by a runaway ferry ten years before. People on foot but no vehicles could come and go except by barge. Fortunately for us we already held flight reservations from the Eastsound airport because we were headed back to Colorado for several weeks and didn't return (and then by air) until the ferry dock had been put back in service. The breakfast, banana pancakes and a bowl of fruit, pleased everyone. We were soon on our way south to Greenbank farm.

Originally a historic island dairy farm that became a loganberry farm and was purchased by Chateau Ste. Michelle who then wanted to convert it to a huge housing development, the community managed to buy it in the mid 90's and convert it into a park, living history farm-museum, community center, and studios and galleries. Yvonne's interest was the large demonstration garden the local Master Gardener chapter had created there. Still cold at the 10:00 a.m. opening time and windy, we stayed long enough to get a sense of the property and walk through the demonstration garden — which won Yvonne's approval. She had tried without success to interest the Orcas group in a more modest project but had found little interest from the group in making a commitment to a garden project — having more interest in providing gardening advice from a table in a booth at the Orcas summer Saturday Farmers' Market. We were beginning to see how Whidbey could be a satisfying family day trip.

153: Lighthouse at Fort Casey

Farther south we drove through Freeland, stopping at the Nichols Brothers Boat Builder site at the foot of Holmes Harbor. Behind the high fence we could see the aluminum superstructure of a new ferry intended originally to twin with the new ferry they'd built running the Keystone-Port Townsend route to the Washington Peninsula but the international financial crisis and Washington State budget shortfalls had intervened and the new ferry would serve the San Juans instead, deeply disappointing the Whidbey Islander's who had significant economic interests in the route to Port Townsend, gateway to the Peninsula and the Pacific be well-served.

Starting north again we drove into the driveway of the Whidbey Unitarian Universalist Church parking lot, too late to be able to attend the service but curious about the size of the group. At least 50 cars, every other one a Prius, filled the lot, like the building, only a few years old. With an island population of 70,000, fourteen times that of Orcas while only three times the size, it made sense that a UU group of perhaps 200 could thrive. Then on to the Keystone Ferry terminal and nearby Fort Casey and its lighthouse. Chetzemoka, the new ferry and twin to the one we saw under construction at the Nichols Brothers in Freeland, was just leaving for Port Townsend and I managed to take a few pictures before it got too far away. We enjoyed seeing the finished article and a ferry that looked considerably different from what we were used to — with mostly solid sides around the car decks rather than the open design of other Washington ferries.

Fort Casey is a large state park and once one of three forts that protected Admiralty Inlet and thus Seattle and Tacoma from enemy ships entering from the Straight of Juan de Fuca and the Pacific at its outer end. The Forts became obsolete with the advent of air power during the First World War, little by little losing their staffing and finally being sold to Washington State for a park and the housing to Seattle Pacific University for a conference center. Fort Worden across the Straight at Port Townsend had gone through a similar transformation, now also a park and conference center Noah and family had spent time at a few years back when he was working on his Creative Writing MFA.

Farther north, a mile or so beyond Coupeville we turned west on Libbey Road to see if we could find Point Partridge, a beach we'd visited in 1984 when we'd made an offer on a nearby house. Except that it wasn't Point Partridge in the Fort Ebey State Park, it was Libbey Beach a bit further north and that wasn't really the point anyway, Yvonne explained; it was to find the house we tried to buy and see what it looked like today. Yvonne wanted to know whether we had been nuts at the time or whether we could have made a life that would have made sense and satisfied us even though we had looked at the house only once before making an offer on it and committing to moving from Boulder to Whidbey Island, not entirely implausible at the time because I had sold my first business (insurance software) and had started a second, an insurance technology newsletter that could be done anywhere. It would have been a practical problem for Noah though whose mother would continue to live in Boulder so ultimately it was a good thing the purchase fell through.

153B: Whidbey House We Made an Offer on in 1984

I had remembered how to get in but had only the vaguest idea where to find the house in this densely forested area — but Yvonne, surprising me since my sense of direction is generally much better, guided me to the right road and driveway. Trying to decide what to do next, we were hailed by a resident who had just finished a mountain bike ride in the nearby park. After a short conversation, it was clear that Yvonne had found the house and he invited us up the driveway for a tour of the grounds. The house had been expanded, a two-car garage added and more of the lot cleared, the lawn intensely green with spring growth. They'd added more fruit trees and moved and expanded the vegetable garden. Having bought the house in 2002 from the wife of the couple that had bought it out from under us in 1985, the new owner, a refugee real estate lawyer from the Bay area, his wife, a graphic designer, and their two sons, growing up on Whidbey, had thrived on the island and in their pretty house in the woods. How had Yvonne found the house after having seen it only once? Because for months back in Boulder she'd visualized living in the house, working in the garden, walking down the driveway and then two blocks to the beach — facing the Straight of Juan de Fuca with Lopez, San Juan, Orcas, Blakely, and Cypress Islands clearly visible 30 to 40 miles away to the north and west, the Straight leading to the infinity of the Pacific and to the west and south the dramatic snow-covered Olympics, rising 6,000 feet from sea level and forming a moisture barrier that made our Crane Island climate considerably drier and sunnier than locations only 10 miles away.

Then back across Deception Pass and east to Burlington and a more prosaic world that provided resources like Costco. Back in Anacortes and the ferry line, we agreed we'd had a great time and would find time to take the Keystone-Port Townsend ferry to the Peninsula and points west. Eric called after dinner and he and Yvonne had a long conversation, Eric giving a detailed description of their trip to China Peak in the Sierra's, Jackson's growing skill with skis and Maddie, not yet three, adapting quickly to this new activity. And Eric talked about seeing his boyhood friends in the Colorado mountains, skiing together, as they had for twenty years, bachelors for the weekend but all married, most with children or trying, and now heading for the later part of the 30s, definitely feeling old. If they only knew.

One-hundred-fifty-four: On Circle Road

"In the presence of nature, a wild delight runs through the man, in spite of real sorrows." — Ralph Waldo Emerson

All I could think about was whether we had in fact found the leak in the water system Friday at well house #4. The proof was in the tank level. As I understood it, Gary would turn off all pumping and the system would coast. If we no longer had a 1000 gallon per day leak and given daily usage in three households of 200 gallons or less, the tank level would drop slowly, much less than a foot a week and almost imperceptible day by day. If we hadn't isolated the leak the tank would drop a foot in two days. I wanted to see what had happened — so once it was light enough to see I put on my raincoat and new Muck shoes, found the big black umbrella and was on my way. No wind today — just a gentle northwest wind and 45 degrees. Beautiful.

The tank is on a hill, probably 50 feet above the community center and well house #1 and on the other side of Circle Road. The tank levels are painted on its concrete tank wall in two-foot increments starting at six feet and going to fourteen. At thirteen and a half feet the tank will overflow. At seven and a half feet no water will flow out unless the bottom valve is opened but our policy is to do that only in an emergency. The bottom seven and a half feet are intended as a system fire reserve — about 17,500 gallons. A six-inch black square is fastened by a cable to a float in the tank and as the tank level changes moves up and down on the outside tank wall, its position relative to the painted lines indicating the level of the water inside. When the float rises inside the tank, the black square falls outside the tank. The more water in the tank the lower the square on the outside of the tank. Our convention is to take readings from the bottom of the square.

When I first assumed my duties as understudy to Tom I would walk up the hill to take tank readings until Wilma showed me a place on the road, 100 feet south of the community center where the tank, lines, and black square could be seen. That's where I was headed. The tank level stood at about thirteen feet, where it had been Friday afternoon. We had in fact found the serious leak. We were likely back down to not more than 100 gallons a day of unaccounted water usage. Hooray!

Walking on to well house #4, where the Rocky Road spur heads east and then north, I could see that a small tracked vehicle had traveled back and forth and had picked up a scoop of gravel from the supply near the well house — but the area around the frost free and the underground chlorine mixing tank had not been touched. Gary had been back to do work on the system but it must have been at lot 16, where the valve in front of the water meter no longer closed properly.

154: Deer Near Community Dock (2011 November)

Another quarter mile along the road, now at the southwestern corner of the island, I saw a large bird fly just above the road out of my sight. It looked like a heron but was smaller and had different markings than a Blue Heron and I'd never seen one inside the island. They worked the shoreline, at the edge of the water as it retreated or returned with the tides. Not long ago Yvonne watched a Blue Heron positioned on the rocks where our cove enters the Salish Sea, searching the shallow water and from time to time plucking something from it, raising its head and swallowing — small crabs probably. It's a pleasure to watch these big birds go about their daily work, quietly, methodically, and successfully.

    I hoped that the bird I'd seen for an instant had landed again on the road and that I could see it if I walked after it, quietly of course and without scaring it — and there it was, striding slowly down the middle of the road, a grass-covered hump between the graveled tracks. I stopped still. It had taken no notice of me so I continued to follow it. Not a Blue Heron, that was clear, but a close relative, a brown mottled coat, a black cap and white cheeks. Checking my Audubon later at home, I decided I had stalked an American bittern, shy, seldom seen marsh waders. Here and there the big bird would stop and pick something from the gravel or grassy verge. At one point it left the road and walked through the brush, hopping up on a rotting trunk. I was surprised. How could it take flight where it wouldn't have space to unfold its wings, probably a span of three and a half feet? Then it was back on the road, walking slowly, in no rush, and either not aware that I was 50 feet behind it or not caring. Perhaps I wasn't recognizable as anything dangerous. With an umbrella my silhouette wasn't human — and I didn't move whenever the bittern turned its head enough that it could probably see me if it looked.

    But I was due at Barbara's soon. I was halfway around the island and I wanted to follow my routine and go forward — but that would mean disturbing the bittern who occupied the road and walked very slowly. It should have its chance to make its living, to its breakfast as I'd had mine, to live with a minimum of disturbance here on Crane Island, which is what Yvonne and I sought as well. I considered cutting across the center of the island through the nature preserve, an entry path nearby at well house #3 but suspected that I'd encounter pooled water so I backtracked around Circle Road, turning off at Eagle Lane and was soon walking down our driveway and saw Yvonne turn on the lights in the studio where she'd be doing some work this morning. I set the umbrella on the deck under the eves and opened the studio door to tell her briefly of my encounter at the other end of the island. We'd talk later.

My meeting with Barbara went well — her house overlooking the south end of Jones Island, a state park across President Channel from Orcas. A technician was overhauling her security system. She had written a plan about how she intended to approach *My Antonia* and caught on to the annotation software right away. At the Post Office I ran into Bob Lundeen, history buff and island benefactor and when he asked what I was doing to keep out of trouble on Crane told him about of eNotation project — and he was interested. Tom appeared in the Crane parking lot from the dock as I pulled in and we talked about the water system. He confirmed that Gary had fixed the valve at lot 18 on Saturday and that the system was no longer leaking as it had. We wouldn't need to get together Tuesday to leak detect. A dinner of stir fry leftovers — very good — dinner conversation with my dear companion and a call to Noah (and Natasha). They'd been to the big Y pool in Hokquiam Saturday, had a wonderful time and came home tired. We'd see them in two weeks. Great!

One-hundred-fifty-five: Soap Opera

"Betrayal is the only truth that sticks." — Arthur Miller

Though the day was mild, sunny, and calm I spent almost all of it sitting on the living room floor, my back against the couch, and legs under the coffee table — with my MacBook Pro on the table and though I couldn't get outside the shining Salish Sea was right outside the windows in front on me, filtered by the madrone, juniper, and fir that partially hide the house from the water.

Jens had sent me all his work — the database containing his annotations to *The Metamorphosis*, MS Word files with essays, introduction, and other material, and about 50 image files he might want to add to his text. My role now was to assemble all the material into a draft electronic book that we could jointly examine and decide what to change — in form or content. The word-processing documents would have to be converted into a format compatible with the way we stored text — plain — with formatting codes and other tags that told the program how create the HTML text that the Kindle book-generating software expected. I'd done the conversions by hand in the past and the process was tedious and often introduced errors — so I wanted to automate it and spent the morning writing and testing a routine that would — and then imported all his new text into supplementary pages to the book and entered information into the database that told the assembly program the sequence the sections should take in the output files and how the table of contents should be structured. I did a test book build and it looked pretty good. A few changes to the text and I'd be done with that part.

Because there were so many illustration files (not all would be used) with some duplicate and triplicate versions, because some of the illustrations were much too large for display in an ebook, and finally because some of the file names violated Web file naming conventions, I spent hours adjusting the tags Jens had inserted in the text to indicate where an illustration should appear, renaming some of the files, and reducing the size of some. By dinner time, though not complete, the book — as a website draft — was recognizable and pretty much what Jens was looking for. A bit more work and I'd send him a draft that would be the starting point for discussing ideas for improvements to make before publishing.

155: Yvonne at the Electric Piano

In the evening, Jens responded to my email about the status of the draft and as a by-the-way said that he would be sitting in the newly forming Dante's *Inferno* class taught by Richard, a former friend with whom I started the annotated ebook company. I hadn't told Jens about Richard before but thought he needed to know — especially because Jens wondered in his email whether Richard might be a candidate to do eNotations for us. Actually, he wouldn't. The day before, Yvonne, searching the Amazon Kindle catalog had found three of Richard's Austen books there, books he had worked on with me and one of which we had published the previous June — *Emma (in Context)* — but he had suddenly and explicably asked me to pull the book from the catalog and informed David, Chris, and I — to our astonishment — that he was leaving the project, taking his books with him, and wanted as much of his investment money back as was possible. I complied with his requests, sadly but without argument, but on the condition that though we acknowledged his ownership of the words he had written, he would acknowledge that all the other intellectual property — software, processes, business plans, and so on — belonged to the corporation and that he was obligated to honor the confidentiality agreement he and the rest of us had signed when forming the corporation. But now — after withdrawing — without explaining himself and without attempting to negotiate any changes in our operation or principles before doing so — he was now in business as a competitor — seemingly imitating the format we had evolved and the business plan I had written. What should I say to Jens? Here it is:

Jens,

I know Richard Fadem very well. I took many of his classes and he spent a great deal of time with Yvonne and me. We listened to his endless stories of disappointing love affairs, fed him regularly, included him in family gatherings, and once I spent a day with him when he was suicidal. He and I talked books and ideas and I enjoyed our time together very much. I think he's a gifted teacher.

About two years ago after I got my Kindle and reading *Ulysses*, I formed the idea of doing a new kind of annotated book and began to look into how I'd approach it, having some understanding because I'd successfully built an electronic publishing company before. One evening when Richard was at dinner at our house I suggested that he and I go into business together — with me working on the business and technology and he doing some annotated books to get things going. I proceeded to work on a business plan, something I'd done many times in the past. Both David and Chris were interested and became stockholders in the company, Classics Unbound, and the four of us worked together.

On June 9th last year we published an annotated *Emma* and shortly thereafter Richard wrote me an email saying he wanted me to withdraw the book from the Amazon Kindle catalog immediately and that he no longer wanted anything to do with Classics Unbound — without any explanation. I was very disappointed both because it was a blow to the project I'd put at least 1000 hours into and because Yvonne and I considered him to be a good friend. I simply couldn't understand.

Last week he went public with what he'd been doing since he withdrew: he's gone into competition with us and has a site called bookdoors.com with several annotated Austen novels for sale on Amazon. Given what his site looks like and knowing what technical services cost, it's clear to me that Richard and perhaps an investor have spent a great deal of money to showcase his writing — and taking the most generous view of things I'd say that Richard believed we weren't adequate to his vision of what the project should be; he wanted presentation to take precedence over practicality. Or, if I take a more cynical view, I'd say that he and a silent partner wanted the business for themselves before we ever published Emma.

Whatever his reasons — which I'm certain make sense to him — Richard is a competitor on the one hand and deeply disappointing as a friend and human being on the other. Richard has a history of betraying people — usually women — but I never thought it would happen to us. He's a gifted teacher and a flawed human being — and so am I in my way but I don't betray my friends.

So — I don't think he's a good prospect for us. If you'd like, I'd be happy to tell you more about all of this. Orcas, as you'll find, has many stories.

John

One-hundred-fifty-six: Fire Danger

"We don't rise to the level of our expectations; we fall to the level of our training." — Archilochus

Yvonne spent nearly the whole day outdoors in the sunshine and fresh air, first putting a deer fence around her water-side rockery garden — with golden daffodils, flowering heather, and emerging day lilies — along the way asking if she could use a 12' 1 x 2 from my wood stash and then whether she could use my jig saw to cut it — and then in the front garden, pulling weeds, laying beach gravel (mixed with shell fragments from Dave and Caroline's beach at the other end of the island we carried here in the pickup last fall), mixing in fresh topsoil, and generally tending the plants she loves and knows by name — while I spent the whole day indoors in the stale air, going through a thousand steps to bring all the pieces of Jens' *Metamorphosis* together to create a first draft we'd use to plan changes and proofread.

Well, not quite the whole day. The greybeards met for tea at Howard's, only Chris absent, bringing Lynn back from SeaTac on her return from Tucson and aged parent tending. Howard wanted to talk about the featured article in today's *Islands' Sounder* — about how a level three sex offender wouldn't be allowed to live in San Juan county — the question being why level three offenders — defined as those likely to repeat — are let out of prison at all. Of course, it's a result of Washington State legislation. The discussion wasn't light.

At dinner I suggested to Yvonne that we take a walk around the island after dinner (having skipped my morning constitutional) and she agreed — the sky still blue and sunny though the sun had spent the afternoon sliding over to the other side of the island so it could slip into the Salish Sea for the night. As we walked up Eagle Lane toward Circle Road we saw Josh and Ethan, the carpenters who had been working on Ilze's house, who were taking an evening break. We talked about the vehicle or vehicles that had driven carelessly, on the verge in places, and when I asked them whether it could have been the roofing company that had installed the new metal roof two weeks earlier they assured me it couldn't have been.

156: Fire Danger Averted

I showed Yvonne where you could read the tank level from Circle Road — now just under 12 feet — more evidence that we'd located the major leak — and then the 40 square foot area we'd have to search for the source of the leak — and how we used the valves in the system to successively isolate smaller and smaller sections and then use to temporarily remove a section from the system. When we got to the far end of the island I showed her where

I'd trailed the American bittern for fifteen minutes — though trailed suggests movement and there was very little.

When we crested Circle Road at the north end of the airstrip we saw that some one had been clearing brush, cutting trees, and generally cleaning up around a house that had been vacant for sixteen years but would soon be put on the market — along with other parcels owned by Jim Jannard, who rumor had it tried to buy the whole island piecemeal but was thwarted once the rest of the owners understood what was going on.

And then we saw that an eight-foot burn pile was still burning — with no attendant in sight, no water supply nearby, no tools, a disaster waiting to happen. A sudden wind could carry sparks into a big nearby pile of cedar and fir boughs. If ignited it could threaten the whole island. We looked for water, found a hose but the water had been turned off. Several hundred yards east we walked up Ilze's driveway to ask Josh and Ethan what they knew about the fire. They had heard and seen men working on the property during the day but they we're sure the workers had left for the day. We walked home and I called Tom to let him know about the unattended fire and then the realtor representing the owner of the property. He didn't know anything about work on Crane but said he would check and within minutes Rocky called, the supervisor of the clean-up projects on Jim's properties. He was surprised to hear about a fire left burning and was skeptical — and because it was now dark not eager to come by boat from his house on West Sound at least a mile away. I wasn't sure when we hung up what he was going to do. Tom called back and said he and Liz would bring the fire engine to the fire site. I told him I'd bring the Fire and Rescue vehicle with its foam system. Yvonne, not eager to go out again turned on "The Daily Show."

Tom and LIz, in the fire truck, showed up at lot 50 not long after I arrived and Rocky walked up the hill from the house's dock next to the island's concrete barge ramp 100 feet below. He wasn't impressed with the fire — expecting I suppose a blazing inferno — and was, as he later admitted, grumpy from having to interrupt his evening and boat in the dark, though later acknowledged that the fire, glowing red and deep in very hot coals and ashes, could have spread to the grass or a large pile of cedar and fir boughs close by.

Tom pulled about 250 feet of hose from the fire truck and he and I tried to get the pump working but couldn't. Rocky tried and had no success and then suggested that Tom drive the truck to a little rise about 50 feet from the fire and perhaps 5 feet higher and use gravity to empty the tank onto the fire — but for whatever reason the water only trickled out. Josh and Ethan were now on the site, having seen the rescue vehicle drive by Ilze's house and Josh volunteered to go through the documented process to disengage the engine from the drive shaft and engage it to the water pump and after struggling for a while managed to engage the pump and Liz and Tom quickly flooded the fire area with water. The fire was out — the symptom treated — but the problem remained — how can Crane homeowners protect themselves from one another? Owners hire contractors and the contractors hire laborers and the laborers are ignorant about Crane, about its rules, about fire danger, about the fragility of its water system, and may not even care. They do as they please — damaging the roads, modifying the water system, and burning carelessly — and practically speaking — it's not clear we can do anything about it other than clean up the mess later.

One-hundred-fifty-seven: The Sound of Music

"Music expresses that which cannot be put into words and that which cannot remain silent." — Victor Hugo

At 10:00 a.m. the makeshift fire fighting team of the night before met at the Community Center, half of which is the garage for our fire truck and emergency equipment. The hoses had been laid out to dry and we fed them to Ethan and Jason to fold and put back in their racks above the truck's water tank. Rocky drove the fire truck to the nearby overhead water fill hose and he and Tom topped up the tank in what seemed like a few seconds. Tom then showed me how to drain this overhead fill mechanism so that water wouldn't be left inside and freeze — not a problem now since we didn't expect serious cold. One conclusion Tom drew from the exercise was that the pumper should have a foam system to make it more effective — a question for the board since the operating budget had no line item for a new foam system. While we talked I watched a fuzzy black bird with white strokes pick away at a rotted stump — very busy and not worried about me — a downy woodpecker — it turns out.

By mid-afternoon I was sufficiently satisfied with the draft *eNotated Metamorphosis* I'd been working on for the last three days to email the MOBI file to Jens — that he could then read in his Kindle or on his Mac with the Kindle software. I also loaded the book to the web as a collection of inter-linked pages he could look through as well, the advantage of having it online being that he could open the book in his browser, expand the browser to the whole screen and then reduce the size of the type — thus making it possible to see a great deal of text in one glance — and easily check links and formatting.

Yvonne was already at the *Huginn* when I left the house, a little late as usual, to cross to Orcas for our trip to Eastsound. Her recital practice was scheduled for 5:00 and she had to stop at Island Market first to buy what she needed for hosting her brother Ron, who would speak at the Unitarian service Sunday on the Five Elements philosophy and its application to Chinese Medicine, as well as a couple he had become friends with in Seattle and who would be coming with him for the weekend.

157: Choir Dress Rehearsal

I left Yvonne at the Market and went to Islanders' Bank to move things along in the process of adding Yvonne, David, and Chris as signers on the Classics Unbound, Inc. bank account — the most important purpose being to give David access to online banking so he could review the statements for accounting purposes. That took nearly 20 minutes and I wondered how the bank could be profitable servicing accounts like ours with a current balance of less than $800. But that's their problem.

We arrived at Orcas Center, the home of most island music and theater performances as well as many meetings, noticed the art exhibit in the lobby, and entered the main, 200 seat, auditorium. The center has two other venues, the Black Box, a smaller space that can be set up for theater in the round, and an attractive meeting/dining/dancing area adjacent to the kitchen. Grace, dressed in black, like her choir was down in front talking to two choir members. I set up in the last row and found a wall receptacle to plug my video camera into because I wasn't sure that it was fully charged and didn't want to run out of juice during the performance. Grace took the group, "Rock on the Rock Choir", fourteen women and five men, through their four pieces: a South African a capella song, *Senzinina*, then *Falling Slowly* from the film *Once*, *Blue Moon* and *All You Need Is Love* and then brought the youth choir *Cats* on for their two numbers. Great fun! Prior concerts had been at the Lower Tavern on open mic night and conversational and television noise made the singing difficult to hear. The summer concert on the Orcas Island Stage on the Green, an outdoor venue that's home to the Saturday Farmers' Market and the August Friends of the Library Book Sale, was more successful but the Orcas Center was much superior if only because of the better acoustics.

By 6:00 the hall was half-full, not bad for a recital, and Grace introduced herself to the audience and brought the Cats on stage. Then one of the girls, graceful and wispy — who was taking private lessons with Grace — did a credible job with *Memory*, followed by another solo and two duets. Then, the main attraction, the Rock on the Rock Choir coming down both auditorium aisles and then up on stage doing *Senzinina*. Afterwards, fifteen of us reassembled at the Outlook Inn bar on the waterfront to celebrate the success of the recital. No mistakes. We visited with Angie and Robert, drummer, and I met Kimaya, late of Munich, who had done a *Blue Moon* solo. The onion soup was tasty and Caesar salad adequate and Yvonne and I shared both, having had some cheese and crackers before the recital. A friendly, noisy evening. All the way home Yvonne had talked about being part of the choir when *Les Mis* was done at the Orcas Center, the next play on their schedule. Both Yvonne and Angie felt *Mamma Mia* should also be considered and they'd already cast themselves — generously explaining to Grace that she, at 35 or so, could play the 18-year-old daughter. Yvonne felt her musical career was near its peak. It was time to be part of something big. Coming back to Crane about 10:00 the *Huginn* glided over the still water, and though overcast, the reflected light from the twenty or so houses on the Spring Point hillside visible through Pole Pass made it unnecessary to use the spotlight. A warm-up in the hot tub on the deck and a little reading — lights shut and eyes shut.

One-hundred-fifty-eight: Fire, Fire

"Be prepared and be honest." — John Wooden

Very early I opened an email from Tom that was intended to report our fire experience to the larger group but couldn't access the contents so I wrote my own report and sent if off to Jason, Dan, Tom, and Gary.

The tank was holding steady at close to 12'. The leak at well house #4 continued to be considered the cause of the 30,000 gallons that had gone missing from the system each month. I was especially eager to see what had happened at lot 50 since the last I heard from Rocky was that they were going to connect to the meter on the west side of Becky's driveway so they could bring water to the burn pile site. They had indeed been at work the day before and had used their backhoe to put a big gash across the driveway but I saw no sign that they had found the line they were looking for.

As I misunderstood from Tom, neither the house, the site of the burn pile, or the lot with sheds on it next door, to be offered for sale together, had water because when new meters had been put in on the west side of Becky's driveway they hadn't been reattached perhaps because the Crane Island Association hadn't helped locate them so I emailed Gary and Tom asking for help so I could pass useful information on to Rocky who had been so helpful the day before.

Jens had read through the *Metamorphosis* draft and had a number of questions and suggestions that we talked through during our 45-minute phone call. Like us he was sensitive to the problems readers might have knowing whether they were reading Kafka or Jens, even though we'd formatted Kafka text justified (even left and right margins) and Jens' writing as ragged right. Perhaps we should use a different typeface for his writing or a gray background. We'd need to think about this some more. Overall though, we agreed we were in good shape with the book and down to what amounted to a punch list, a small number of items to be fixed.

Jason, responding to my report, asked why we hadn't used foam and I wrote back explaining that we thought it inappropriate for the type of fire and anyway had gotten the pumper going. A response from Gary explained what I had forgotten — the meter for Lot 50 was 70 yards west of the meter for lot 51A. Rocky's crew was looking in the wrong place. All they needed to do was turn on the water at the road — so I rushed down to the site and found that two workers had dug a trench up the west side of Becky's driveway. They explained that they were intercepting the line where it entered the lot — which they had found 75 feet up the driveway and would put in a temporary line from the meter to that point so they'd have water at the house. I tried to explain they didn't need to go to all that trouble because the house had a line from the meter on Circle Road and they referred me to Chris, their boss on site who they said was talking with Tom. Tom? He was already here.

I found Tom and Chris near the house meter and Chris explained that though they had turned on the valve no water came out at the house and they didn't know why. So they needed water from the other meter and that's why they were doing the trenching. Oh! They'd have water; they could do their burning safely.

Later I found an email from Dan suggesting that Tom, Rocky, and the rest of us may have gotten a little confused two nights before when we kept struggling with the pumper; we should have used the rescue vehicle foam system. I'd already explained this to Jason earlier and he understood our thinking. Now Dan was saying we had made a mistake but were excused because we had been too excited by the emergency to think clearly. I wasn't going to let that pass so I wrote him back explaining that the foam system wouldn't have put this fire out, it would have been foolish to squander the one certain firefighting system we had on something that wasn't an emergency, and that we hadn't been in a hysterical state — why should we be — at the time. Later Jason told me my explanation made perfect sense: in this case the foam should have been held as a backup and last resort rather than first response.

I went home and had lunch and after too many days with too little sleep I couldn't keep my eyes open. Yvonne was at the Deer Harbor Community Club for the Friday afternoon knitting group. I lay down on the couch and was soon asleep.

158: Crane Island Fire Department

I'd put the phone near the couch hoping that if I did that no one would call. I'd been asleep long enough to be startled at the ringing and for some time couldn't understand that it was Jason on the other end and that he was upset that Chris and his team had built a big, blazing burn pile at lot 50 and were feeding it with a backhoe. What to do? They did not have a burn permit. They probably had water now. But the fire that Jason had seen when he landed his plane on the airstrip, bringing his family to Crane for the weekend, was much too large and when asked about a burn permit, someone working for Chris had told Jason they didn't need one on out islands. I gave Jason Rocky's number and then called Paul, the Fire Marshall, interrupting him in the middle of a meeting. Paul was definitive: tell them the fire had to be out in 30 minutes or he would come to Crane and cite the crew involved — and that I should call him back in half an hour to tell him what happened.

I walked to the dock area, opened the hood of the fire and rescue vehicle to turn on the battery switch, started the engine and drove the quarter mile to the airstrip and the site of the blazing burn pile. Chris said they had a burn permit but not with them. I told him the Fire Marshall said they had no burn permit and the fire was to be out in 30 minutes or he would come to Crane and cite them. He said he'd call his boss. I drove downhill to Jason's and as we talked through the situation his phone rang. It was Rocky. When I told him about the Fire Marshall's edict he suggested that I get the fire engine and put out the fire. I explained that it was not the job of Crane residents to clean up after contractors' crews — but that I would do it this time — even though we'd done it just two nights before. By the time I got back up the hill Chris and his team had already buried the fire. I wouldn't need to bring the fire engine. I was relieved.

Back home I called Rocky to tell him the fire was out but his daughter explained that the crew didn't work for Rocky but for John Thompson of Earthworks, a company that competed with the two other, larger excavating companies on Orcas and which Gary later told me had been bankrolled by Jim Jannard, the property owner. Oh! I'd been after Rocky, who I now understood was a caretaker. I should have been talking to John Thompson. I reached his wife and she was apologetic. They'd take care of everything. They wanted to do it right. A bit later the Fire Marshall called to tell me John Thompson had just come in to get a burn permit and they explained to him that burn pile rules were stricter for the out islands, not looser. He thanked me for paying attention to a situation that could have been dangerous. I wrote up an email bringing everyone to date.

Shortly after dinner I crossed to Orcas and drove to the ferry landing; Ron and his friends Matt and Jami would arrive at 8:10 to spend the weekend, Ron to be the featured speaker at the Unitarian service Sunday morning — his topic — Acupuncture and the Five Element Philosophy, of great interest to him as a Taosist sympathizer. Back home and after some conversation I had to go to bed. I was tired.

One-hundred-fifty-nine: Bob Looks Good

"You can't stop the waves, but you can learn to surf." — Jon Kabat-Zinn

Our guests appeared in the kitchen before 9:00 having slept well in the Crane quiet and Yvonne had hot drop biscuits and coffee ready. Matt, a professional cook, fixed some poached eggs for us and we talked about Crane and what to do with the day, cloudy but not cold with little wind. I gave Ron the phone number of the Friday Harbor convalescent center and he soon reported that Bob would be happy to see us — Ron told him sometime after noon.

As we were leaving for a walk around the island, Matt noticed that our ramp to the beach had slipped off its perch, the high end having slid three feet down the bank and the bottom end out onto the beach, the high end held by a rope around a stump to keep in from sliding all the way to the beach. High wind, tides, and waves with the help of floating logs had dislodged the ramp in the late fall and though I had looked at it nearly every day I had no clear idea how I would remount this very heavy 8" x 12" by 10' cedar plank. Matt said he wanted to put it back where it belonged so he and I and soon Ron were on the beach and soon had the plank/ramp more or less back in position. Matt retied the rope at the head of the ramp to a tree higher on the bank creating less slack and minimizing the possibility that high water and floating debris would knock it down again. As I had decided over the winter that wouldn't be a good long-term solution. What we needed was a ramp or stairs that we could raise above the wave line on some kind of hinge or axel or entirely remove for the winter — which would mean a much lighter design.

Our island tour for first-time visitors included the fire station/community center, the Becker's barn, the airstrip, Clark's cabin, the osprey nest, and Rachel and Marilyn's little farm with its sod roofed house, vacant for ten years, but soon to go on the market and the second area that the burn pile crew would address, now I hoped more carefully and legally. Lou and his miniature dachshund, Rollie, came down the path as we were leaving the site, out for a walk, Rollie going gray in the muzzle, the Rollie of flying-out-the-second-story-window-in-pursuit-of-a-dragon-fly fame. Lou told us about the old days here at the farm, the big vegetable garden with two rows devoted to him, the honor system for paying for vegetables and eggs, the barn the "girls" raised with the help of neighbors, the beauty of the place in the past — before it had been ignored by the new owner — who had bought up many Crane properties — gossip had it, to buy the whole island piecemeal, something that proved impossible and about which we all supposed he had pouted about ever since, paying his annual dues but leaving the houses vacant and the lots unkempt. Now he had a crew doing clean up and was listing the properties, with implications for the water system, real estate values, and life on Crane we couldn't yet foresee.

Passing Skip's we noticed that he was now thinning the trees in the lot next door he had bought recently as he had done with his main property, giving it a park-like appearance, civilized, suburban almost, and much different from the rest of the island where homes and cabins sat in small clearings amidst dense, sometimes impassible woods. Was the character of the island changing, money leading to estate life rather than cottage life?

As we climbed the hill at the north end of the airstrip we saw a group of six and talked with Brooks's daughter about the house on lot 50, that it was for sale and my sense was that she was trying to interest her companions in buying it. Then Jason and his family appeared in their Gator and he commented that the property was listed for about $650,000, maybe a bargain since Jannard had had its dock repaired recently but the house wasn't very interesting and didn't have a view of the water, only the airstrip, though perhaps a house could be built farther north with a view of Deer Harbor.

A quick lunch of sandwiches and we were on our way to Friday Harbor, our first trip there in the *Huginn* since November when the engine had thrown a rod and we had been stranded off Shaw Island until towed to the West Sound Marina where Ian installed a rebuilt engine that so far I was very happy with. With Matt and Jami sitting in the removable seats in the cockpit and Ron and Yvonne and I in the cabin the boat was stern heavy and didn't handle as well as we bounced across the southeast wind waves to the county seat about six miles away. Before we left for the return trip I read the Volvo owner's manual and came to understand better how to use the trim system that was part of the outdrive. In the past I'd relied on the port and starboard trim tabs to trim the boat but as I was now coming to understand they were intended for adjusting the left/right lean of the boat and the outdrive had to do with raising and lowering the bow, something possible with the trim tabs but not as effective apparently in certain conditions — which I confirmed on the way back to Crane — my adjustments making the ride much more pleasant to Yvonne who I could see was very worried on the way over.

159.1: Visiting Bob in Friday Harbor

Matt and Jami would explore Friday Harbor; Ron, Yvonne, and I would walk the six blocks to the convalescent home to see Bob. We'd meet back at the *Huginn* at 3:00. We found Bob in a wheelchair in the common area choosing books to read from a shelf filled weekly with books from the Friday Harbor public library and when Bob had made his fourth choice I wheeled him into the adjacent atrium where four other residents were spending their Saturday afternoon. Bob looked good and as we soon found his mind was clear and he reported that he was having more success becoming strong enough to walk — with the help of a talented and demanding therapist. He said he felt as if he had recently awoken from a two-year period during which his brain hadn't worked properly and about which he had few memories. His neurologist couldn't explain it or guarantee that he wouldn't again fall into that twilight zone but he was grateful to be back and we were grateful that he was. Ron had met Bob in San Diego when Bob had visited there to work with his sons, who lived there, on a Boys to Men project sponsored by a Warriors group and they were both surprised that Bob was our neighbor in Deer Harbor. Yvonne and I left so that Ron could do an acupuncture treatment on Bob and after she found some yarn to buy came next door to the bookstore where I was lurking and we walked back to the boat at the county dock moored ahead of the Sheriff's boat. While we waited for the others I put a new line on one of the fenders, the old one having become frayed from rubbing against the bull rail at the Crane dock. Our return trip was smoother from a control point of view but rougher as we crossed waves coming from behind us. This time we approached Crane from the south, traveling through Wasp Passage between Crane on the north and Shaw on the south, our passengers now having a chance to see the southern and eastern sides of Crane where on the way out had seen the north and west sides. The tide was low enough to expose Temple's rocks, invisible at high tide about 200 yards east of Tom's place and the site of one or two boating accidents each year, some serious enough to demolish the boats though we hadn't heard of any fatalities yet.

    Matt and Ron cooked Thai chicken with rice and asparagus and Yvonne served a cherry tort for dessert. All delicious. At Yvonne's urging we watched the video I'd made for Crane's 50th-anniversary celebration that I'd shown at the party last August to a group of about 150 and used as a fundraiser to defray some of the costs of the party. Even though I'd seen it at least five times and was aware of all the things I should have done differently — it wasn't bad and the audience I think truly enjoyed it. Matt and Jami were getting the Crane Treatment and wouldn't soon forget our island or the San Juans, an area they had never visited before but I suspected would again.

One-hundred-sixty: The Five Elements

"The more I know, the more I realize I know nothing." — Socrates

Saturday had been a pretty day, mostly sunny and little wind. Today wasn't as promising: gray and blustery. In short order our guests consumed Yvonne's chilaquiles, which I think she learned to cook from Ann in Boulder, made in a fry pan and using crumbled corn chips, something new and delicious for Jami and Matt. Saturday and today I watched Matt's attentiveness to Jami — to her comfort and needs — both were affectionate to one another — and from time to time he complimented her — which I could see she appreciated, perhaps especially because her pregnancy had caused her face to break out — and perhaps because she was carrying his child.

Ron reported to me later that they considered one another soul mates and were grateful they had found one another. Both were about 30; Matt had a five year old son in California. He had just quit his job as a cook for Sodexo, a frustrated cook in that catering environment, Jami wasn't working, and both were active in the garden of the seven-acre rural property where they lived on the north edge of the Seattle suburbs. They wanted more out of life than they felt possible in the lives they had been leading, both attracted to the idea of locally grown, healthy food, a lower impact on the environment and what is sometimes referred to as a green life. Ron had warned them that once they came to the San Juans, they wouldn't want to leave and that had happened. They were already beginning to talk about how they could move up here, the cost of property and taxes and other details. We knew other young couples who had figured out how to live in the islands but it wasn't easy to make a living in an economy dependent on construction and tourism, both depressed since the 2008 crash.

Ron, Yvonne, Matt, Jami at airstrip

Ron's talk drew a group of 20 to the Unitarian Universalist service at the community club building in West Sound, more than my multiverse talk had a few weeks earlier. I acted as moderator, having prepared order of service sheets to hand out that morning. In our opening words section Ron talked about his formal credentials as a licensed Doctor of Oriental Medicine and potential primary health care provider and his informal identity as a Taoist Sage and healer. Many candles stood in the sand-filled ceramic dish Ruthie had sculpted years ago by the time everyone with something to say had come up, lit a candle, and shared their joy or sorrow. Given that Megan wasn't present, I felt free to talk about our visit with Bob and how good he seemed compared to what I had seen over the last two years. Matt and Jami came into the service a bit late having been walking around outside, perhaps going out on the county dock just across Deer Harbor Road sharing a vision of what their life — with their new child — might be on Orcas Island.

Ron's talk, "Five Element Theory and the World View of the Taoist Sage" engaged the audience and a half dozen surrounded him after the talk peppering him with questions. Suzanne wanted to know how to obtain treatment from him. During his opening words Ron had quoted Lao Tze in the *Tao Te Ching* in which he describes the Tao and being a sage by what it is not. Ron stressed the unity of all things, the principle that what's inside and outside are the same, diagnosis as recognition of what is out of balance with someone and the treatment to bring the person back to a balanced state. It seemed to me the Five Elements was an elaborate set of interlocking metaphors that was rich and flexible enough to serve almost any purpose, not true in the sense of reporting reality but useful enough to have stood the test of time in China, Ron said, for the last 4000 years.

We had driven our pickup to the service and afterward headed home. We'd given Ron the key to the van so that they could go for a hike, see Eastsound or whatever and then walk on the ferry later, leaving the van in the lot for us to pick up on Tuesday. The front porch had only a few sticks of firewood left and only a weeks' supply, perhaps two, was stacked outside in the splitting area. Though I had other wood I could split, it was green and wouldn't burn well. We had two choices: conserve the little wood we had left for special purposes — when we had guests for instance or lost power; or I could cut more from windfalls a quarter mile away and cart the wood home and split it. Since I wasn't eager to spend the time right now to cut, cart, and split wood, it seemed prudent to conserve what we had and Yvonne agreed. I adjusted the thermostats to heat the main living areas of the house to 70 during the day from 68. At this time of year, with the overnight temperatures in the low 40s overnight and the low 50s during the day, turning the thermostat up wouldn't make much difference — but not having a fire would. The fire carried the house all day, with the electric heat rarely coming on. And perhaps more significantly, the radiant glow of the stove made the house cosy and that didn't happen with baseboard heat, so 70 degrees from the stove and 70 from the baseboard heaters were very different and it was an open question whether we would be happy without the pleasure of the stove.

Yvonne and I both noticed the big bird flying back and forth over the low trees on the water side of our house. It wasn't an eagle because it had a brown tail. Then it turned and I could see its head — red. It was a turkey buzzard looking for a shoreline meal. In the late afternoon, after we'd each enjoyed naps on the two living room couches, Yvonne talked about how much she loved the flashing red light at Pole Pass. What about it? When I wake up in the middle of the night, she said, I can look out the window and see it flashing and I know I'm on Crane near Pole Pass, my home, and not someplace else in the world I don't want to be.

One-hundred-sixty-one: Green Fuse

"Every action has its pleasures and its price." — Socrates

Since our dry, split wood inventory was almost gone — perhaps three carts full left — and since it's important to keep a supply on hand to cope with a power outage or to stoke a cheery fire for guests — and because I wasn't eager to cut and cart wood from a quarter mile away — and am very busy — I decided it was time for a strategy change — no more fires for a while. So this Monday morning was the first in five months without a fire to warm the house after overnight cooling — and I didn't like it — so I adjusted the thermostats to bring the house temperature to 70 degrees from the 68 base we've had since October. But that wasn't satisfactory, at least at first. Heating the air in a room doesn't have the same perceived effect as having a radiant source that heats the air but also heats you directly. By later in the day not having a fire in the stove mattered less and Yvonne agreed reluctantly to this new heating strategy.

Our electric bill — heat, hot water, oven, appliances, light, hot tub for February 15th through March 15th was $223 — while last year for the same period it was $189 — even after being very conscientious about heating daily with wood — more so than last year. How is that possible? This winter has been considerably colder, below normal, than last winter, above normal. With daily temperatures now ranging from the low 40s to the low 50s, a more modest amount of power would be required than would have been in January and February so a wood fire would have less benefit — from the point of view of holding down or reducing the electric bill.

A mostly sunny day with a little wind — that found me computer-bound all day while Yvonne did more work in her garden, spreading more topsoil where her green friends weren't thriving. An after-dinner walk around the island with Yvonne revealed that huge buds are appearing on the ends of large leaf maple branches and the ocean spray is beginning to leaf out. The alder had been flowering for more than a month but now green is showing. In Colorado, warm sun following a May snow or rain lit a green fuse in the trees and grass and flowers. Here the fuse burns — slowly and steadily — so that while spring starts earlier Colorado almost catches up by the time Crane's deous trees are fully leafed.

161: Lou Falb Out and About

The workers at lot 50 have apparently finished their clean up, the grounds groomed and a small pile of ash all that remains of piles of tree trimmings. Though we didn't walk down to Lot 40 to see if they'd transferred their operation there I assumed they had. After dinner we called Keith in California, James' partner, to wish him a happy birthday, singing, for the first time for him, Ja, må hon leva!, the traditional Swedish birthday celebration song.

The slogging today was about pictures — integrating pictures for the eNotated version of *The Metamorphosis* that Jens had picked out look attractive and a natural part of his annotations on the Kindle and in the Kindle software on other devices. Too big and the pictures break the text so that the reader is left guessing whether there's more for the specific eNotation being viewed on another page. So I tried reducing the display size of the pictures to large thumbnails and that made the pages more attractive but the picture detail was lost. Fortunately on the Kindle if a picture is displayed smaller than its actual size a little hand appears over it and the reader can click on it to have it expand to take up the whole display but this blow-up feature isn't available in the same way on other devices so a larger version of the picture has to be made available someplace else. I tried using the thumbnail as a link to the picture (JPEG) file itself but the Kindle software doesn't support using pictures in a page to link to pictures on their own; the pictures have to be imbedded in another page in larger form, so I decided I'd need to add an images section to the book, like the plates section one sometimes sees in a paper book and use the caption as the link from smaller to larger. To experiment with the images section I coded the HTML by hand but that was very tedious so I wrote routines to do it automatically but that had its own challenges. In order to display an image in a different size and have it look right, you need to tell the computer the height and width it should use and they must be proportional to the size of the original or the picture will look distorted, like a 4 x 3 television picture displayed in widescreen format. Calculating the dimensions of an image would generally mean opening it with a graphics program, noting the original dimension, deciding on a new width or height and then calculating the other dimension in the same ratio as the original. That was time-consuming and would be a bottleneck for other books so I decided this process had to be automated, that is, the program building the book should calculate the dimensions of the smaller version of the picture on the fly so I found some code online that showed how to extract the dimensions stored in JPEG and GIF graphics files and eventually the process actually worked. Many steps, very slow, slower probably than having done it all by hand but then I'd have to go through the same process with the next book with illustrations. I wanted to create an automated system and I did — but it kept me inside at my computer for the better part of two days.

One-hundred-sixty-two: Black Java

"The more I learn about people, the more I like my dog." — Mark Twain

Pulling in close to the corral Yvonne reminded me that the four horses inside were capable of mischief since five years ago when we'd backed into this same spot the van's rear window wiper had been pulled off and the window scratched by some equine prankster. As we got out of the car I saw a rabbit dash under the barn from its position under the domestic rabbit cages where it undoubtedly scavenges successfully for food. Mollie met us on the flagstone walk to the gate and the house, now with a very gray muzzle and tangled red coat. Then Ken was on the porch welcoming us in.

Kate was at the stove starting the asparagus; chicken and potatoes were in the oven. Yvonne handed over her offering bottle of wine and Ken poured three glasses from an already open bottle of "Three buck Chuck." I don't drink. I saw that the chickens were now on the southwest part of the property rather than the north. Ken explained he'd positioned them over and around an aged manure pile. I'd noticed another pile under a tarp close to where we had parked. Four horses produced a surfeit.

The previous year Ken had ordered 25 chicks and they arrived in a box, just a few days old, shipped from the East Coast. I didn't even know that was possible. Twelve remained, ten hens and two roosters. He wanted to put the non-dominant rooster out of his misery because he was too rough with the hens but then he wouldn't have a backup rooster and wasn't sure he could get another one easily. The chickens were Black Javas, one of the oldest American breeds, and in spite of the name were developed from Asian chickens in the murky past, and now virtually extinct. When he was planning his chicken foray he took into account island raptors, mink, and raccoons and wanted birds that were big, strong, smart, and dark colored (so as to be less visible from the air) and be good egg and meat producers. Of the original 25 a mink had gotten one. Ken tracked the mink to its hideout and blasted it. The Black Javas liked the manure pile, full of small red worms and had scratched in it so much that they'd begun to flatten and spread it. Sometime in the future he'd cart the second manure pile to the northwest corner of their property, to the west of the house, and move the chickens there, surround their run with a fine-meshed electric fence that (mostly) kept pests out. He'd then have the original pile rototilled and plant it in potatoes. He explained that modern commercial chickens were bred for fast growth and all-white meat and slaughtered very young or to be extremely productive egg producers. The Javas could do both but excelled at neither. What they were good at: flourishing in the environments close to natural and requiring little care, perfect for small farms and here on Orcas living an ideal chicken life. Their brown eggs were very good — we got a pair to take home — and they made good slow-cook and soup chickens, their meat not nearly as tender as commercial breeds. Ken would soon pick a promising broody hen, separate her from the rest of the flock but close by, and let her incubate eggs from the other hens. The chicks would have to be kept separate from the grown chickens until they were big enough to defend themselves from the curious and sometimes malign adults. He had housed his chicks-in-box in his horse trailer until they were big enough to run, fenced, under the sky.

Talk turned to the local economy and its problems, the perfidy of Wall Street (they had just watched "Inside Job," and how the government wasn't doing enough of what we wanted and too much of what we didn't. That segued into Wall Street's new focus on commodity speculation and with it the dramatic rise in wheat prices, the effect that's had on small bakers (put them out of business) and the chokehold the seed producers, with their patented seeds, have on agriculture, favoring the huge over small producers, and making it almost impossible for a farmer to have any control over their businesses. Yvonne brought in what she'd learned about new wheat strains and small wheat farming in Washington that served small bakers and new, small mills that did the same, some of the motivation coming from the locavore practice that was beginning to have some traction. Kate showed us a video Ken had shot of her interacting with her four big stallions and it was fascinating to

162: Leak Search at Wellhouse #4

watch. Two were lying down, two standing as she walked among them, clearly fascinated with her and attentive to her every move, huge, friendly, quiet, beautiful, intelligent souls — their size giving Yvonne and me a sense of danger, for Kate belied by their real presence and conduct. Kate was so close to and well-accepted by this little herd that she could take them for walks, without halters and leads. The topics moved on to Andrei Codrescu and Dadaism and to the Multiverse — where everything that can be already is — a thought Ken found disturbing since it seemed to obviate the possibility that he could make changes for the better in the world. Then we were back home in the moonless dark on the silent Salish Sea gliding to our Island, our home.

One-hundred-sixty-three: Soup 'n Service

"To forgive is to set a prisoner free and discover the prisoner was you." — Lewis B. Smedes

As I walked to Howard's "Honeymoon cabin" up the stairs and inside his fenced garden I could see that he had been busy; one big bed was raked and ready for planting. With daytime temperatures nudging the 60s, the soil well watered by the winter rains, it wasn't too early, here in late March, to plant hardy cool weather crops like spinach, chard, and lettuce. Brian, David, and Howard were already inside the little cabin and Howard handed me a mug of hot, strong, English breakfast tea as I came in and took my customary seat. Chris hadn't shown up for a few Wednesdays — no one knew why and hadn't pestered him about it when we'd seen him in the interim.

More on the Orcas Island economy — Howard listing businesses that had failed or threatened to. Vern's Bayside restaurant and bar in Eastsound had closed. Our favorite pizza place, Portofino's had closed. It had? Why? The Island Market was laying off staff, the parking lot and store often nearly empty. Virtually nothing was happening in real estate even with asking prices dropping. Jim's Crane holdings were now on the market, all attractive at what would have been very low prices three years before but perhaps now priced too high. Why was he selling now — when prices were low? Was his heretofore successful international business struggling? David had been studying real estate prices around Lake Minnetonka in Minneapolis and had found that $10 million properties were actually selling for $5 million. Detroit had lost 25% of its population. Hard times.

163: Huginn in a Rush (2008 August)

When I had responsibility for services for our Unitarian Universalist fellowship I had attended some of the occasional brown-bag clergy lunches and had enjoyed this small group of good people who were interested in UUism and found a great deal they resonated with but whose congregations would not. From meeting to meeting almost nothing happened, at least from my point of view, until the focus was brought to the Food Bank, an increasingly important island resource that had been started years ago by a well-intentioned but increasingly ineffective older couple, that this clergy group was now helping to let go and pass to a younger, energetic, and more imaginative group. It was at this transition point that Yvonne joined the Food Bank board as secretary. She had organized the Unitarians, our small group, to serve at the Tuesday lunches in the Community Church basement, every fifth Tuesday, and the ten UU women and sympathizers that brought soups and salads and casseroles and even desserts to this Tuesday meal, had been amazed that all the food — every bit — was gone by noon — even though serving was to go on much longer. Yvonne thought 100 people had come to the lunch; someone else told me 120 — in any case at least 2% of the Orcas population. Hard times.

Besides the social action around the Food Bank, the Orcas clergy group, a council of churches, sponsored a Lenten Soup and Service program, on successive Wednesday evenings, the first with the Community Church, then the Seventh Day Adventists Church, this evening the Emmanuel Episcopal Parish, then the UU Fellowship, ending up with the St. Francis Catholic Church. Each evening would start with soup, bread, and conversation, followed by an informal interdenominational service that this year had the theme "Forgiveness." I'd retired from the group when I retired from being UU program planner or lay minister or whatever I was and Suzanne, taking my place with the UUs, had also been attending clergy meetings and had volunteered the UUs to do one of the Wednesday supper services — so Suzanne and Yvonne and I thought we better attend one at another church to know what to expect and to plan, so here we were among a group of 50 or 60 in the Episcopal hall next to the church — with East Sound, our local fjord, right outside the big windows.

Craig Anderson, an Episcopal bishop, had come to Orcas after serving, among other places, at the Sioux reservation in South Dakota and had been made an honorary member. His presentation about the realities of reservation life had been eye-opening to our UU group when he did a service for us several years before. This evening, with the theme of forgiveness, he began his homily with a discussion of the film "Get Low," one that Yvonne and I had recently watched and appreciated, using it as an entry point to talk about self-forgiveness — which Robert Duvall's character, Felix Bush, had tried to do for 40 years as a hermit and hadn't succeeded because it really required the community. Almost all of Craig's talk could have been given by a UU minister, in good conscience. The service was patterned after the Ecumenical Community of Taizé in France, informal, with music and silence and Craig stressed again as I'd heard him do many times that faith meant action — something UUs could wholeheartedly agree with. He suggested each of us think of something we were clinging to, unwilling to unload ourselves of, and look for ways to find forgiveness — in whatever ways were appropriate. Another evening out, on Orcas, away from our comfortable space, our island home, and glad to have been out.

One-hundred-sixty-four: Ties That Bind

"Sometimes you have to let go to see if there was anything worth holding on to." — Anonymous

Up again before 4:00 a.m. with the aim of producing a second draft of *The Metamorphosis* book that Jens, David, Chris, and Natasha could review and if satisfactory we would proofread and get on with securing permissions for or document the public domain nature for the 30 images that appeared in the book. At about 9:00 Yvonne had left for Eastsound, I can't remember why but she hoped to be home by noon. By 10:30 the second draft was complete and I sent it off and then sent my Gmail account copies of the software source code, the database, and all the images, so that in a pinch and if my Mac's Time Machine backup software failed I could continue the formatting process with little interruption. The predicted rain hadn't appeared and the sky was partly clear with some high hazy clouds and the temperature was heading for 60. Time to go for a walk around the island.

What a pretty day! A red squirrel crossed in front of me as a I climbed Circle Road just past the community center and then I turned to look through the trees to see the black square hanging down the side of the water tank: about 11 feet — where it had been more or less since we discovered the location of the big leak at well house #4 (a rarely used well) and isolated it from the rest of the system. Gary would return, perhaps on the weekend to continue his process of finding the exact location of the leak in a complex of underground piping used to expose the water to chlorine before releasing it into the island water system. Friday, April 1st Wilma would be on the island to take month-end meter readings.

At the other end of the island I could hear and see, in snatches through the trees, a crew at work at lot 40, doing a general cleanup there after finishing at lot 50 the site of the burn pile excitement a few days earlier. I left Circle Road at Sunnyside Lane, a spur that passed by Lou's — though it being

Thursday he was likely on Orcas visiting friends, picking up groceries and perhaps doing his wash. Sunnyside was muddy, showing the results of the frequent passage of a front-loader tractor that was now in the big meadow carrying branches to what I assumed would be the site of a burn pile. At one time Marilyn and Rachel's cow had grazed here and provided the island with all the milk it needed, its home a center pole octagonal barn the two women had raised. But that was years ago before they sold their little farm and moved to Orcas, deciding they were too old to cope with the boat trip backs and forth to Orcas and the responsibilities of their acreage and since then the land and the house and guest house and barn and chicken coop and other small out-buildings had lain fallow but now were on the market again, seven acres on three lots for $1.9 million.

I passed a worker in a blue jacket and asked whether Chris, the foreman who I had badgered about his burn pile, was around someplace. Down by the steel-roofed house. That guest house was right above a lovely west-facing beach we had spent some time on with Noah, Natasha, Morgan, and Opal the previous June, basking in the sun and enjoying the beauty of the western San Juans spread out in front of us. The main house had a sod roof — there were others on Orcas at the Helsell farm — bright green with soft new grown grass in the late March sun. Chris was raking with two more of his crew, six in all. The wind, out of the southwest, not so common here, was blowing hard enough to pay attention to. Had he found water sources he needed to have handy for a burn pile? Yes, no problems. I told him I appreciated his having been conscientious about the burn pile on lot 40 once we brought our concerns to his attention. He replied that the Fire Marshall who had been so responsive to me had been a fellow employee of Earthworks for several years and when he found out Chris was the cause of the unattended, un-permitted burn pile on Crane he teased Chris, now somewhat embarrassed. Chris then went on to say that he was calling in to the Fire Marshall every morning reporting that he had a fire and the crew was staying late in the now lingering sun to put it out before leaving. I told him that made things better for everyone because diligent observers on Orcas Island north of Crane had a tendency to call in reports of fires they saw on the island and if the sheriff had information about it on record it wouldn't need to be investigated — perhaps by Tom or by me after being called or being paged on the 911 system. He said because of the wind they wouldn't be having a fire. Good.

164: House Full (2008 April)

One of the two workers raking next to the house walked toward me and I recognized Demetri, a young man who had come to Orcas about four years before with his wife and daughter from Wyoming, Jennifer, daughter to Ken and Kate returning to the island she grew up on. They were now divorced and I had heard that Demetri was struggling to find work. He had been very helpful to me four years before when I needed to install double French doors and wide windows into the space that had been the garage door when finishing the garage-to-studio conversion. We talked very briefly and then recognizing that Chris wanted him to work, not chat, excused himself and went back to work. I liked Demetri and wished we had the resources to hire him for projects. He was a competent carpenter and hard worker and he was reduced to taking a general laborer job which I assumed paid poorly — but it was work at least. On the way home, not far from the community dock, a very fat red squirrel sat in the middle of Circle Road (a road wanna-be) eating what looked like grass seed that had been spilled the week before. I expected it to dart away but it didn't, apparently expecting no trouble from me, only moving when I was two steps away. I wasn't a threat but the eagles and owls were to a squirrel sitting on the road oblivious.

Back home and after lunch I was too sleepy to do anything but flop down on the love seat in the living room, leaving the couch vacant for Yvonne who I expected home at any time and who often enjoyed shutting her eyes for a few minutes on the couch in the afternoon. I dreamed I couldn't get my eyes open and then heard Yvonne and did open them but only for a few seconds and then fell back to sleep. At dinner, Black Java eggs from Ken's chickens (the deep yellow-yoked eggs were delicious), fried potatoes, and homemade one-hour-bread toast, Yvonne told me about the problems she'd had docking at Orcas in the strong southwest wind — the boat simply wouldn't turn the way she expected and she ended up docking across from where we normally parked, a transient area Yvonne had marked by painting the bull rail yellow three years before.

And then she talked about a sobering instant when crossing from boat to dock — with the wind pulling the boat she held with two lines (fore and aft) and pictured herself pulled backward and crashing against the hull of the *Huginn* and then falling into the water, maybe unconscious — but the moment passed and she hadn't fallen. But Dick had the last summer, face first on the Crane dock, and his whole face turned black and blue. She said she still felt agile at 60. What did I think? I thought she was, more than me, as she always had been. We talked about the sense one has of knowing how the boat will move as you move and timing getting in and out of the boat so that it's one smooth motion. And we talked about how mooring lines try to curl around your feet to trip you and the need to be very sensitive to anything around your feet when coming or going, not moving if a line is touching you until you understand what it might do to your balance. No falls are good falls. Tom claims that by 75 all Cranians will have fallen into the water. Yvonne had her kayak swamping at the Orcas dock a few years back. We'll see.

One-hundred-sixty-five: Less is More

"Less is more." — Ludwig Mies van der Rohe

Less than two weeks after the spring equinox, sunrise to sunset had lengthened by about 50 minutes, about 3 1/2 minutes per day and will continue to increase, progressively more slowly until the summer solstice when the sun will be in the sky for 16 hours — and because it rises at a shallow angle, there's light enough to see an hour before sunrise and an hour after. So, as we like think about it, we have very long days at the best time of the year to enjoy them, summer, but with today's continuous rain, there was no sun to enjoy.

Chris wanted us to discuss our eNotated Classics priorities and strategies so we met at David's intending to leave operational questions for our monthly meeting in two weeks. We concluded, without surprising ourselves, that at the top of the list was completing the steps to publish *The eNotated Metamorphosis..* With it we would have something to show eNotator candidates — both to attract them and to provide an example of high-quality eNotations and a rich, complex structure. I would continue working with Jens on the text, images, and formatting but we'd need a quality cover design, professional proofreading, and permissions for the 30 images we were including. I'd looked at Amazon's CreateSpace and noted that they offered cover and proofreading services at reasonable prices. Chris talked to a rep and found out that their cover service provided multiple cover candidates we could choose among — all submitted by independent contractors. Once we chose a submitted design, that graphic artist would get the job and receive (some part of) the $250 fee. Given that we'd have a choice and we wanted a quality cover, we decided to go ahead and I would make arrangements with Amazon — investigating their proofreading service as well, also, I assume done by independent contractors participating in the CreateSpace ecosystem.

We had talked about but were now becoming more clear about the value of having a paper version of *Metamorphosis* with the same structure and formatting as the electronic version we'd been working on — but without the links of course — which would have to be done the old-fashioned way with fingers, bookmarks, slips of paper — whatever was handy. CreateSpace had a solution here as well; books wouldn't have to be printed until they were sold, what Amazon calls Publish-on-Demand, a promising approach to having to pay in advance for print runs and then need a place to store them until — or if — they were shipped. Most people still read paper books after all. So here we were, backtracking, sensibly we thought about the focus of our business — it would be publishing — not just electronic publishing. We thought one advantage of our approach over others was that both electronic and paper editions would tag each paragraph and each eNotation with a unique ID so that group readers — a book club or a class — could use a combination of paper and electronic editions and still always be able to find their way to exactly the same text — not depending on page numbers or the lack of them. This would be possible even if we published for the Nook or any other environment. Extending the publishing to paper would extend the time to publication but we might find that the extra care we'd need to give the cosmetics of the paper edition might have application for the electronic edition.

The rain continued, not the drizzle we're used to, but real rain, along Crow Valley Road, and plumes of white cotton candy drifting at an angle, the top edge leading, from south to north through the forest on the flanks of Mt. Woolard, where Rachel and Marilyn live in an updated version of the sod-roofed home they left on Crane about eight years ago, now being put on the market after being vacant all that time.

Because I had a few minutes before I would meet Jens' at Rose's, I stopped in the Library and talked to Phil, the director, briefly, catching up on the latest issues I no longer needed to worry about, having been off the Board for 15 months. Phil was especially interested in sustainability and was a founding member of the group on Orcas, as was Ken. Phil would take what he had learned and share it with other library directors at a meeting in Yakima, across the mountains, where Yvonne and her friend Julie had seen Bob Dylan in concert the previous summer, sustainability questions here relating to the dependency of ebooks on petroleum, rare earths, and power in the manufacturing process. Phil had a sense that our complete dependence on fragile and energy-hungry high tech was not sustainable and that had implications for libraries.

165: Canada Goose at Crane Dock Breakwater

I was seated at a table along the south windows in Rose's, a very pleasant place for meeting and eating that had been converted from a fire station when the department got a new home near the airport. Just off the dining area, Rose's maintained a bakery and wine and cheese shop that had become a favorite of part of the Orcas retiree population who had cultivated their palates and could afford to do so. Jens arrived in a few minutes and we talked about the Orcas economy, Jens having heard about the same business closings I had. We both ordered the free-range chicken soup — with Rose's French bread — and turned our conversation to eNotated Classics' plans for the future. Jens had recently got a Kindle and wasn't impressed with it — especially when I explained that functionality he and his wife Susan, who was a web expert, expected wasn't possible on a Kindle — or through Kindle software on other devices, even though the hardware and operating systems were. Kindle technology was very conservative and as he was becoming aware and the rest of us had known for some time it was not friendly to reading that was much more than page-turning — and we wanted to offer much more than that. I told him a bit about our ideas for extending our publishing beyond the confines of the likes of Kindles and Nooks but that we needed to finish *Metamorphosis* first and were intent on doing a very good job with it. He and Susan had reacted negatively to all the cross-section links I had put into this second draft. They had, like Chris, quickly gotten lost in the text and didn't know how to get back to where they started or even remember where that was. As I'd done before in other contexts I had confused the possible with the useful or the complex-useless-more with the simple-useful-more. After letting him cite every problem he'd had with navigation, I suggested to Jens, as I had with Chris, that I cut out all cross-text links except those between Kafka's writings and Jens' eNotations. All other sections of the book, essays, expanded versions of images, and so on, would be accessed through the table of contents. Rather than jumping across the text — fast but with the possibility of becoming lost — the reader would go up to the table of contents and then down, to the bibliography, for instance. Jens liked the idea, as had Chris and David. I'd prepare a third draft, implementing the simpler navigation ideas, and we'd all look at it. Jens would proofread and I'd make the changes. Lots to do again.

One-hundred-sixty-six: Timber!

"Only those who will risk going too far can possibly find out how far one can go." – T.S. Eliot

The rainy morning gave way to afternoon sunshine and Yvonne had an idea: we could take advantage of the mild and sunny afternoon to cut down a few of the trees she'd marked with blue tape for removal almost a year ago. They were fairly small, the largest a Douglas fir with a diameter of 8" and about 50 feet tall. One acted as a post for her deer fence. She wanted it cut down to post height. We'd already cut or had cut for us at least 30 trees, all within 100 feet of the house, and all providing unwanted shade to Yvonne's vegetable garden (vegetables, herbs, and cutting flowers to the south) and the entry garden (evergreen ornamental to the north). Last summer had been disappointing in the vegetable department, partly because the summer had been cool and partly because there was too much shade. She had three alternatives in mind for whatever we cut: firewood, timbers for the tree house, and support for climbing beans, larger to smaller sizes.

I was ready for a break, semi-comatose from staring at a computer screen all morning as I recoded my program to implement the book structure changes I'd talked about with Jens and David and Chris the day before. I retrieved my chain saw from my shop and two-stroke gas and chain oil from the tool shed, carrying that kit to what had been the driveway, now overgrown with grass and moss and inspected the saw. The chain was a little loose — the new chain had less than an hour's use on it and they stretch when new — and that lead to noticing deposits of oil-soaked sawdust that I scrapped out of the area around the clutch.

The first tree was just to the south of the three compost bins, hastily constructed out of recycled 2 x 6s that had come from the 15-foot high tower that supported an 8-foot analog satellite dish I'd demolished almost two years earlier to make way for a raised platform and treehouse Eric and Noah had helped build at the 2009 Borgfest family gathering. My plan was to drop the tree to the south between several other trees. But I wasn't careful with my cutting and the tree which already had a bias to the north tilted that way, its branches hanging up in another fir immediately adjacent to the compost bins. I called Yvonne and we tried to push the tree back toward the south; I didn't want it to fall on the compost bins and wreck them; then I'd have more work to do. What a fool!

166: Logs from Beach Drying Out

We tried shaking the errant back and forth but the upper part of the tree, about 30 feet up, remained tangled with its neighbor. I told Yvonne to be ready to run fast at a 90-degree angle to the trunk because it could fall without warning and it might not fall straight down but could be deflected by the branches of the other tree. Then we tried to lift the bottom and slide it south, changing the angle with the supporting tree and maybe dislodging it. We could barely budge the bottom of the trunk and I was worried that we might get in the way. In the past, I'd cut down partially fallen trees by taking out trunk sections and having the remaining trunk fall another four feet down. Eventually the trunks were short enough that the top branches were lower than the branches of the other trees holding them. But it's a very bad way to get a tree down and liable to unexpected gyrations.

I brought a 100' yellow poly rope from my shed we'd commandeered about seven years before when Yvonne ran over it with the *Gumption*, fouling the prop on our pocket trawler near Spenser Spit on Lopez Island. Someone had used poly rope — which floats — for their crab pot line — ridiculous! We limped to the south side of Spencer Spit and I backed the boat as close to the shore as I dared, anchored and then jumped into the water holding a kitchen knife to cut the line and free the prop. The water was very cold, maybe 52, and I had no goggles and couldn't see clearly. Barnacles clung to the prop shaft and the metal skeg that protected the prop and held the bottom end of the rudder and my hands were soon bleeding. Yvonne watched anxiously. I didn't enjoy the experience. After several dives, I freed the rope from the prop shaft and Yvonne pulled the line into the cockpit. As we pulled in the rest of the line we found a float and crab pot attached. We took it all, entitled to it for the trouble it had caused us.

I tied poly line as high as I could reach on the leaning trunk and after yanking in a way that caused the tree to sway the top suddenly came free and the trunk crashed down on the corner of the compost bin, about the best place it could land, doing no damage. In the past I'd always tied a rope to a trunk that was to come down and had someone on the other end pulling as I made the final cut on the back side of the trunk, slightly higher than the notch I'd cut out on the side that faced the direction I wanted it to fall.

The next tree was quite a bit bigger. I didn't want any more trouble so I stationed Yvonne at the end of the rope but well out of the way of the tree I wanted to fall in her direction — but the tree chose a different angle almost hitting the corner of the polycarbonate rain shelter roof I'd constructed three years before. OK — I'd have to be more deliberate about how I made my cuts. They should be horizontal — with the horizon. If they're not, the tree will give way to the low side. I knew that. I'd explained it to Tim when he cut three trees in January. He'd followed my instructions conscientiously and the trees had fallen where we intended. I had cut nine more trees, taking my time to position the saw bar horizontally, and they fell where they were supposed to.

One more to go: the tree Yvonne wanted to be turned into a post for her deer fence. That meant cutting it about 8 feet off the ground. And that meant cutting from a ladder. Not a good idea. I used an extension ladder to tie the yellow poly line about 12 feet up on the trunk and Yvonne took her position about 50 feet south holding the line. I used a step ladder leaning against the tree to get high enough to make the notch cut — on the south side of the tree. That wasn't easy to do because I had to hold the chainsaw above my head. That can't possibly be a very smart thing to do. With the notch complete I took the ladder inside the fence and set it against a tree about four feet north of the tree I was cutting, and once I had the saw running crawled up the ladder and then turned around so I could face the tree I needed to finish cutting. As on the front side, I had to lift the saw above my head. I've been conscientious about wearing goggles and ear muffs but they make it more difficult to interact with the trees I cut. The goggles steam up and the ear protection makes it impossible for me to hear sounds from the tree or from Yvonne should she need to warn me about something. I took the earmuffs off. I didn't like what I was doing but the tree soon fell — just where I'd intended. Yvonne gave me the two-arms-up-making-muscles sign. Sigh.

When I talked to Yvonne later about how unsafe I felt doing that last tree she downplayed the danger. She is willing to take certain kinds of physical risks that I find highly problematic. On the other hand, she's terrified when our boat bounces around and I'm not, knowing that there's little real danger. It was her opinion that any man would have done what I did with that last tree. I replied that didn't mean it was safe — only that some men, like me, are foolish.

One-hundred-sixty-seven: Burn Pile

"The fire is the main comfort of the camp, whether in summer or winter." – Henry David Thoreau

The day before we'd left ten mostly Douglas firs lying scattered around yard, some criss-crossed over one another like a pile of pick-up-sticks. At Yvonne's urging I left my MacBook Pro and the demanding programming I was doing to conform the next draft of *The Metamorphosis* to the ideas I had talked about with David and Chris and then with Jens, in way that was flexible and generalized and could be applied to future books, like *My Antonia* which Barbara had reported she was well into the annotation process for. It was sunny outside, cool but would be warming up and we'd left a mess outside. I was soon outdoors.

Yvonne likes to manage a burn pile. I'm content with my 18" Craftsman (Poulon) chainsaw. Months before Yvonne had bought a burn pile permit at the County site online — so we were legal. She'd created a dead branches pile and a live boughs pile about 20 feet from our campfire/burn pile site in the open area created by the rain shelter and our hers-and-his shops. She'd feed the fire while I brought her more material to burn. But first we needed a hot fire — or green boughs thrown on it would smother it or burn ineffectively and create billows of smoke. One surprise for me years ago was how quickly green fir boughs can burn, the water boiling out of the needles almost immediately and what remained almost exploding into flame. That experience, as well as the persistence of a hot fire, the coals still capable of restarting a fire even when they seemed dead, was sobering and made me even more concerned about the consequences of a fire gone wild on Crane.

But before the fire — we needed a hose handy to bring water from the house 150 feet away. Yvonne suggested I retrieve the new hose from near the 400-gallon water tank we'd bought and brought to Crane almost a year before and to which I needed to direct house roof water so that Yvonne could irrigate her front garden in the summer drought without using community well water. Another project waiting for nicer weather.

167: Yvonne Tends Burn Pile

How to light the fire? Yvonne had her method — which involved newspaper and split firewood — the remaining small cache stacked outside the garden fence under a brown tarp — but that didn't make sense to me. The cache should be saved for special occasions when we wanted a cheery fire in the wood stove — for instance during Noah's family's visit. It made more sense to me to create a small pile of broken-up fir branches and dowse them with used motor oil and a little gasoline to get them started. Yvonne objected, certain a useless fire would be the result. I was confident. Two experts head to head. We'd just have to see who was right. This time I was.

Yvonne cut the boughs into smaller sizes with her long-handled clippers, carefully keeping the fire within its three-foot diameter bounded by dark grey island basalt rocks she'd picked up around the yard. In most places on Crane the soil is thin and filled with broken basalt that forms the island and which speaks of its volcanic past in the same ring of fire that caused the deadly Japanese quake and tsunami. The dead branches and the larger boughs — with needle-carrying branches cut away — would be reserved for a future trip to the chipper, now under a tarp amongst the stacks of green unsplit firewood waiting in the front yard.

I dragged green bough piles from their sites near the felled trees where Yvonne had cut and stacked them the day before and cut others away from the trees, piling all of it near Yvonne and the burn pile she was managing. Then I began to cut the trunks into sections I could carry the short distance to the open, former driveway area. The trick in cutting trunks is to do it in a way that the area you're cutting doesn't sink and bind the saw. I looked for places that were already supported and wouldn't collapse when cut — for instance lying on another log or raised above the ground. I could then manage the smaller sections, placing something underneath so I could make another cut. Each time I had a section I could carry I took it to the driveway and laid these sections, eight to fifteen feet long, in stacks. After moving all the trunk sections to the driveway, I began to cut them into sixteen-inch long pieces appropriate for splitting. The stacks of parallel trunks acted like a sawbuck, holding the top log in place while I cut it. Each time I finished a log I'd throw the sixteen-inch pieces into a stack to be transported to the firewood area in front of the house. By noon, after three hours outside, much of the time using my chainsaw, my right shoulder started to get sore from pulling the rope on the chainsaw to start it again after intermissions of carrying or arranging logs. Yvonne had by that time finished feeding the burn pile. We had had enough exercise for the day and were hungry for lunch.

After lunch, Yvonne took a nap and I went back to my programming, which though a slow process was, I thought, going well. Several times during the afternoon Yvonne checked on her burn pile. With little wind and a light drizzle, it posed no danger. I had more logs to cut up and all of it to transport to the north firewood area but I could do that another time. Looking out the kitchen windows at the stacks of wood I'd worked on for the last two days I was struck at its insignificance compared with the scores of trees in the yard, the hundreds behind them on the little hill that rises to the south, and the hundreds of thousands that cover most of Crane Island's 250 acres.

One-hundred-sixty-eight: Let the Rumpus Begin

"The best way to make children good is to make them happy." – Oscar Wilde

After Sunday's clear sky and seeing the Big Dipper clearly from the hot tub before going to bed, I was surprised to wake up at about 3 a.m. to a steady rain. Now in my third day of intense focus on the software routines that would create the *Metamorphosis* book in a different format than the first four we had published and serve as a foundation for future books, I wanted to at least get to the point of building a MOBI version (what I'd been able to do before tearing the program apart and putting it back together in a different way) that I could look at through Kindle software and hardware before taking time off for family and fun. By 3 p.m. I had something that worked. From here on the issues would for the most part be minor changes to the cosmetics of the book, the result of tedious experiments (How would this look?) but not a challenge to my limited programming skills. Then it was time to prepare for the arrival of Noah, Natasha, Morgan, and Opal — who hadn't been to Crane since last July for Kelley and Tim's wedding — when Noah somehow injured his back and had to spend most of the time lying down.

We suspected that they'd prefer to stay in the studio, with its bedroom, loft, and foldout couch. It didn't have a bathroom but one was available just outside off the deck and another in the house proper off the kitchen so I adjusted the studio thermostat up to the same timing and temperature levels as the house. The first ferry from Anacortes they could conceivably have made was at 10:35 a.m. but that didn't seem likely since they'd have to leave Harstine Island by 6:00 a.m. The next ferry was at 3:30 in the afternoon and about 2:00 Noah called to say they were in the ferry line. They were driving on because we'd all pile into their Highlander Thursday morning to cross to Sidney by the Sea on Vancouver Islanded in British Columbia and then drive down to

Victoria and spend two days before they took the Black Ball Port Angeles ferry to return to the Olympic Peninsula and drive home while Yvonne and I would take the bus back to Sidney and then the ferry back to the San Juans. McKinley and Sugar would spend the five days they were gone in a kennel in Shelton.

168: Versatile SeaSport

About 2:00 Sunday afternoon Yvonne had said she wanted to go to the market at Orcas Landing to buy a few items for dinners the next two evenings — shepherd's pie and chicken and cheese quesadillas — and would I drive. Of course. Though raining the water was calm — ideal for zipping across and after holding the *Huginn*'s speed down until we passed the No Wake buoy between Bell Island and Caldwell Point I took the boat up on plane at about

20 knots and headed straight east across the mouth of West Sound, the bottom of which, about two miles north, was home to the West Sound Community Club building where we had our UU services and the West Sound Marina where I had the *Huginn* scheduled for routine maintenance in mid-April when we'd be gone to Colorado and New Mexico. About a quarter mile east of the ferry landing I saw that we'd be encountering a good-sized wake coming from the other direction and that it would likely give the *Huginn* a good rocking as we crossed it — and it did. I looked over at Yvonne on the bench seat on the other side of the cabin and I could see that she had not found it exhilarating — like a carnival ride — but perhaps slightly nauseating. I took the *Huginn* to the north side of the county dock, the shoreside, where the *Huginn* would be protected from the wakes of other boats and Yvonne jumped out and tied us up. The market wasn't busy. When traveling off-island in the morning we sometimes pick up a breakfast (for me scrambled eggs, cheese, and bacon on a croissant) or sometimes sandwiches for lunch and when I pick up our visitors at the landing they often want to stop at the market for beer or wine before we walk down to the *Huginn* moored at the county dock and speed back to the Crane Island dock. While Yvonne shopped — and she didn't need my help or want it except perhaps to carry the basket, I volunteered to find the *Sunday Seattle Times* but the shelf that usually held them was bare so I exchanged two dollars for eight quarters and walked up to the ferry parking area and found the blue metal *Times* dispenser box. One left.

When the ferry pulled into the dock at Orcas Landing about 5 p.m. Monday I left the house to cross to Orcas so I could meet Noah and family and bring them over to Crane Island. Walking up to the parking lot, I took the van out on Deer Harbor Road, almost a one-lane road here near its terminus, wanting to visit the Post Office and return before our visitors arrived in the lot from the ferry — but there they were in their white Highlander just south of the Deer Harbor hamlet coming to meet me. We stopped, rolled down our windows, and I told Natasha that I'd meet them in the lot in a few minutes.

Opal and Morgan and Noah and Natasha all gave me hugs. It was good to see them back in our neighborhood. I couldn't believe how much they'd packed into the vehicle. Noah and I each took a cartful down to the *Huginn* and Natasha carried several bags as she shepherded the kids down the ramp to the boat. Morgan and Opal, apparently, hadn't slept much in the last two days in anticipation of coming to Crane Island. Back at the house, Yvonne got her hugs and they moved their baggage into the studio and then at Opal's urging I brought the marble-slide construction kit into the house from the studio loft and Noah brought in the big Lego plastic storage box and Yvonne found American Girl doll Samantha and her accoutrements (including a brass bed) to join Opal's Cressa. The kids were happy playing with the toys they associated with our house on Crane and we were soon eating dinner and catching up. What a pleasure to be with this young family. What fun we'd have.

One-hundred-sixty-nine: Skate Park Rain-out

"In time of test, family is best." — Burmese Proverb

Morgan ordered five strips of turkey bacon and Yvonne made enough so that the rest of us would have our fill and then took egg orders. Opal's breakfast had been another piece of homemade gingerbread that Yvonne had served with sliced strawberries the night before. Morgan had some cereal and milk. I'd had my usual oatmeal at 6:00 a.m. Now Yvonne asked who wanted a fried egg and how many. Morgan wanted two. In fourth grade and a 70-pound beanpole Morgan can't seem to consume enough food to stave off hunger.

Noah and Natasha wanted to do a Circle Road walk/run and Morgan wanted to go along but ride a bike so I opened the fence around the storage tent that was supposed to keep out mink and otters (but was effective only with the latter), unzipped the left side of the front door, pulled it open and went inside. More mink scat but not stinky. I would ignore it. We had two mountain bikes — mine a red Scott and Yvonne's a light green. We'd ridden them only a few times in the 10 years or so we'd had them. I pulled the red Scott out of the tent, zipped the door, and refastened the fence just as Morgan came over from the house. We checked the tires and found them a little low so I walked over to my shop, opened the sliding doors and picked my way through what I had used and not put away, picking up a compressed-air carry can I kept charged for a need like this and topped up the tires as Morgan watched. When I finished I handed him a helmet and lowered the bike seat and he took off up the driveway finding it tough going where it meets the end of Eagle Lane. And then they were off around the island, Opal staying home to play with the dolls.

169: Monopoly Fun

On their return they reported a tree across Circle Road at the Clark's cabin, site of the Annual July 3rd picnic. I'd have to do something about it later. Then we left for Eastsound to buy a new battery for my camera at Radio Shack, do some shopping at Island Market, and take Morgan to the skateboard park near the Orcas schools — built several years after a fundraising effort by Warren Miller. Radio Shack did not carry camera batteries — too many to cope with according to the owner. But I didn't miss the sign outside saying the store would close on April 23rd and everything was on sale at a sizable discount. Radio Shack was closing. They'd been for sale for a while but apparently found no buyer. Hard times. The Market wasn't quite deserted but customers were scarce and we picked up some items to eat in the car out of the rain while we watched Morgan at the skate park. Most of his skateboard practice was in the garage at home where Noah had made him a ramp. Their driveway wouldn't work because it was gravel. The Orcas skateboard park is elaborate and big. Judy, working at the Market, with four kids and some grandkids at home, told us that when the park first opened, EMTs made many trips there in their ambulances, the most serious injuries to skateboarders who weren't wearing helmets. Morgan had his. We ate our sandwiches brought from Crane while Morgan skated the periphery and when he was thoroughly soaked we all went home.

While Yvonne cooked dinner in the late afternoon the rest of us walked Circle Road, Morgan on my red Scott mountain bike. Noah reminded me about the tree across the road and I took a bow saw with at his encouragement — a chain saw unnecessary because the diameter of the tree was less than six inches. It turned out that the tree was really a large branch that had peeled off the massive maple nearby, planting its heavy end in the soft soil and falling across the road. Noah made some cuts and we could drag the sections off the road. One purpose for the walk was to get the kids tired — and it worked. After dinner while Yvonne and Opal were dancing, the little girl collapsed in a heap and was soon in bed, Morgan following almost immediately. That gave the four adults time to talk and one subject was the problems some boys seemed to be having growing up — launching themselves into the world. Something new?

One-hundred-seventy: Soup and Service

"Forgiveness does not relieve someone of responsibility for what they have done. Forgiveness does not erase accountability. It is not about turning a blind eye or even turning the other cheek. It is not about letting someone off the hook or saying it is okay to do something monstrous. Forgiveness is simply about understanding that every one of us is both inherently good and inherently flawed. Within every hopeless situation and every seemingly hopeless person lies the possibility of transformation."
— Desmond Tutu, The Book of Forgiving: The Fourfold Path for Healing Ourselves and Our World

Chris had met us at the Crane Island parking lot on Orcas when we returned from Eastsound where we had taken Morgan to the skate park but had been rained out. Chris wanted to create some videos he could post on YouTube and link to from our eNotated Classics website that described where the ideas came from for the product and how it worked. He thought that Natasha could interview me — ask me questions — and he'd edit the raw footage into something usable. Natasha wasn't excited about being the interviewer and wasn't sure what to ask so I talked for a while while Chris did his setup — moving us close to the living room windows where he could take advantage of the natural light — the sky cloudy but the Salish Sea bright with reflected light. The session took about 90 minutes — was unrehearsed and rough. I took Chris back to Orcas and he drove home to begin an editing process. By evening he sent me a link to the first video — about the origins of the ideas for eNotated Classics — and it was better than I had expected — although the popups he used at the opening identified Natasha as "Natalie."

That was Tuesday. Wednesday our focus was on the "Soup and Service" meeting in the evening sponsored by the Unitarian Universalist Fellowship.

Natasha did an early Circle Road morning run around Crane and later our four visitors walked the short distance on the now very wet and muddy path across Och's meadow to Pole Pass and scrambled out on the breakwater to the big rock that marked the south side of the pass. Twice they saw a seal fishing in the vicinity of the pass and an otter made a long appearance in the water south of the breakwater. The Canada geese pair was nearby and they saw the remains of the nest where last summer they'd hatched six chicks who soon lined up with a parent at each end paddling across our small harbor. Within a week we could only see three chicks and then later they were all gone — the parents and chicks perhaps finding a safer environment. The sun was out and now higher in the sky felt very warm, so the young family decided that Morgan needed another chance to try out the skate park on Orcas.

After lunch Yvonne worked on preparations for the UU dinner, making a garbanzo bean and spinach soup and handling last-minute calls from the other women who had volunteered to bring soup. Suzanne had called to ask me if I'd do a reading at the service — on forgiveness — the theme of the five Lenten soup and service sessions our little group was participating in. As I was thinking about the sources I had available to look for an appropriate reading, Yvonne suggested Desmond Tutu, the Anglican bishop in South Africa who had been instrumental in the success of the Truth and Reconciliation process that was effective in preventing much of the violence and retribution that was expected when apartheid gave way to something more democratic. I'd heard him interviewed years ago about why they approached the problem in the way they did — the practical, moral, and religious reasons — and I was enormously impressed with how radical and how right he was. I spent some time on the web — on Wikipedia — reading his biography, other sites quoting him, and on the Forgiveness Project site, seeing for the first time — or perhaps noticing for the first time — references to the concept of "ubuntu," a native African approach to forgiveness and reconciliation that had the goal of communal healing rather than revenge or retributive justice.

170: Soup and Service - Opal, Yvonne, Noah, John, Mogan (Photo by Margot Shaw)

We arrived at the West Sound Community Club building about 4:45 and found a dozen cars in the parking lot, most belonging to high school students (or their parents) who we could see out on West Sound, paired up in a dozen small sailboats engaged in their Wednesday evening sailing practice, apparently oblivious to the cold, though certainly useful wind blowing out of the southeast. Behind us, I could see that they'd left their packs on tables on the grass outside of the yacht club shelter, and the area had been invaded by gulls and crows who were very busy going through everything looking for food and in some cases finding it, one gull making short work of a sandwich pulled from a pack. Did this happen every time the kids went sailing?

Inside Suzanne had done some of the set up, Mary, the pianist for the evening helping. The six of us got busy setting up more chairs and then tables pushed to the side that we'd line up after the service in two rows with chairs on both sides. Women began to bring in soup pots and Yvonne put them and Natasha to work slicing bread. By 5:30 it looked like the evening would be a bust — but as it turned out most everyone was late and we ended up with close to 50 attending — very respectable for our little group. Suzanne had prepared an order of worship and printed up copies for every chair, a service that resembled our typical service except omitting our time of sharing joys and concerns. As it turned out she was also focusing on Desmond Tutu, his work and philosophy, impressed as I was with this remarkable man because of his focus on action more than words. On our boat trip back to Crane the water was calm, the sun just setting through Pole Pass, shining through broken clouds over Vancouver Island. Dark sky, bright hope.

One-hundred-seventy-one: Victoria

"The real voyage of discovery consists not in seeking new landscapes, but in having new eyes." – Marcel Proust

We had moved most of our luggage to the Highlander's Xcargo roof storage pod the day before so we didn't have much to carry as we boarded the *Huginn* at 6:20 to make the 6:50 interisland ferry to Friday Harbor where we'd pick up the Washington State ferry to Sidney by the Sea on Vancouver Island and then drive down to Victoria, about 20 miles south. We'd drive our van to the Orcas ferry landing so that when we walked off the interisland on the way home we'd have transportation back to the Crane Island parking lot on Orcas. Tea and coffee in the market at the landing and we were good to go. The *Evergreen State* docked on time and we were soon on our way to Friday Harbor, the car deck about 25% full.

Cruising through Wasp Passage, Yvonne pointed out our house just visible through the trees south of Pole Pass. Disembarking at Friday Harbor to wait for the ferry to Canada, Yvonne and Natasha bought the ticket for the Canadian passage, only $25.00 for the car and all of us. In the meanwhile Noah and I had taken the kids to King's market to find something for breakfast for them — which turned out to be a six-pack of tapioca pudding. We were soon on our way north and then west on the *Elwah*, pointing out Crane and then Yellow Island, a Nature Conservancy property west of Crane, that was covered with yellow wildflowers in the spring and served as a kind of vegetable garden for the Salish peoples during the millennia they lived summers in the area.

Then there was Speiden Island, grassy on the south side facing Speiden channel through which we cruised, but forested on the north side, still owned by Jim Jannard who had put his Crane Island properties up for sale and in the process of preparation had a crew clean and burn brush — which resulted in the minor kerfuffle about burn piles, permits, and safety on Crane Island.

We'd come through Speiden Channel many times, almost always on our own boat, bound for Roche Harbor at the northwest corner of San Juan Island or just as often on our way to Sidney by the Sea, and its quality marina, a place we'd come ten or more times over the years. Past Speiden, Stuart Island was visible, a few miles away, and shortly the lighthouse and tender's house, now restored and maintained by a local foundation — our destination for many walks over the years with friends and visitors when we'd cruise to Reid Harbor, a long narrow bay on the south side of the island or the prettier but more exposed Prevost Harbor on the north side, both supplied with mooring buoys, floats, or dock space that provided access to the state park — with its beaches and camping areas. Salt Spring Island, in Canada, was visible to the north, its two massive escarpments rising steeply in the west, falling to near sea level in the east, with Ganges, the island's main town, artist colony and popular tourist area toward the east end, up a long bay studded with islands. Another place we'd spent many pleasant days.

As we passed the Boundary Line buoy we pointed out that we were now in Canada. The Canada-US border, established by Kaiser Wilhelm, defusing a potential war between the US and Canada in 1872, proceeds northeast here from the Straight of Juan de Fuca up Haro Straight and then just north of Stuart Island turns east, where we'd seen huge freighters alter course to the east on their way to Vancouver, BC, perhaps a quarter mile off the Turn Point lighthouse site on Stuart Island.

Less than an hour's travel from Friday Harbor, the *Elwah* docked at Sidney and we made our way through Canadian Customs, Yvonne and I supplied passports, Noah and Natasha special Washington State driver's licenses and birth certificates for the kids. At Safeway we bought some groceries and took them down to the waterfront, having a picnic lunch of sandwiches we brought from Crane. The sun was warm but the wind cold, sitting on benches looking east toward Stuart Island, Speiden, and Orcas, with Turtleback Mountain and Mt. Constitution visible behind it. Clouds obscured Mt Baker, when visible an impressive white-capped peak dominating the Cascades west of Bellingham. Gulls and crows, drawn to our picnic on the Sidney waterfront waited patiently for whatever might come their way — Noah advising Morgan not to feed them while we were eating — or we might find them becoming unwelcome pests. Morgan did finally begin to offer them corn chips, hoping they'd take the offerings from his hand but we couldn't stay long enough to develop the rapport it would probably require.

We'd intended to visit the Mineral store next but found it closed — but then inquiring at a dive shop nearby were directed across the street. The diversion was satisfying for the kids because Yvonne had brought along what Canada coins and bills she could find at home, so they each had an allowance of more than $10 CAN to spend during our time in Canada. They shopped deliberately, each finding something they wanted priced under $2 — leaving a balance for further shopping in Victoria.

A half-hour drive brought us to Victoria and the Queen Victoria Hotel on Government at Douglas, across the street from the Royal BC Museum and very close to the historic Empress Hotel (a Fairmont property) and the inner harbor. When we left Orcas the sky was cloudy. By the time we got to Sidney the sky was partly cloudy and now it was clear. Approaching Victoria on route 17 we'd all been impressed with the view of the Olympics across the Straight of Juan de Fuca, snow-covered, seemingly rising 6000 feet out of the Straight, in reality not quite that dramatically since Port Angles, 20 miles south of Victoria lay at the foot on the mountains that rose gradually over miles to their impressive height.

Yvonne had booked a two-bedroom suite at the hotel with a living room and small kitchen — where we could prepare breakfasts and lunches. Having deposited our luggage and supplies we headed for the Inner Harbor and the wax museum we'd visited perhaps 15 years earlier with James and Yvonne's nieces Sarah and Samantha. We took the young family through the Empress lobby and showed them the original lobby now devoted to serving a formal afternoon tea we'd done perhaps eight years before when in Victoria with Loren and Janelle during the winter — at that time staying in the Empress. We crossed Harbor and walked down the stairs to the marina, mostly devoted to sailboats, two large catamarans, one Camano Troll like the one we used to have, and some classic wooden sailboats including one that offered three-hour afternoon cruising. Climbing the southwest stairs back to street level at the wax museum building we watched a young man practice parkour (I assumed) jumping up and walking on railings, climbing the wall from the lower area, and generally looking for strength and balance challenges to which passersby could become an audience.

171: Empress Hotel Above the Inner Harbor, Victoria, B.C.

 The Royal London Wax Museum was closed and surrounded by scaffolds covered with plastic sheeting. What a disappointment. I inquired next door at the Black Ball Ferry terminal, where Noah and family would depart for Port Angeles on Saturday morning, and the woman clerk reported that the museum had closed in September. We descended again to the inner harbor level and walked around to the other side, Natasha and Morgan stopping in a souvenir store, Noah buying Opal an ice cream cone at a stand, and Yvonne and I walking along and looking toward the side of the harbor from which we'd just come, the BC Parliament and Museum across the way. We all walked farther down the quay and once at the end heard a loud horn blast announcing the arrival of the Black Ball Ferry from Port Angeles. We watched it dock, starboard side against the dock, a sliding door opening in the hull near the bow, the matching door on the port side facing us closed. The harbor water was calm and there was little wind but having a sense of what it takes to dock a large boat I wondered aloud how they managed it reliability. Bow and stern lines pulled the boat close to the dock and perhaps bow and stern thrusters played a part.

Yvonne and I talked to a clerk in the information office nearby while the kids — with attentive parents — watched a busker do sleight-of-hand tricks — something they reported enjoying greatly. Then up Government, a main shopping street with two certain destinations in mind: a hotel Yvonne wanted to inspect for use when we returned in the summer with friends from Boulder and the Ming Chinese food restaurant Natasha had in mind for ordering take-out the next evening. We stopped first at a deli for clam chowder, hot chocolate, and other victuals to sustain us and the process revived Morgan a bit after he had begun to descend into a low blood sugar funk. Out on the street again, Noah and I got distracted at the Stormex outdoor clothes store, a brand he didn't know, and a clerk was soon hovering around us trying to engage us in conversation. Out on the street, we saw no sign of the others so consulting a map walked up Government to Yates and then walked east toward the restaurant and hotel and spotted them coming back our direction. The kids were tired of walking around so far to no purpose, so Yvonne and I suggested they go directly back to the hotel while we did more reconnoitering. We beat the family back to the hotel, Morgan having followed us without our knowledge and Natasha soon had the kids in the pool downstairs. They were happy. In the natatorium Natasha struck up a conversation with a Vancouver woman whose husband was in a nearby hospital recovering from surgery while she and a grandson stayed at the hotel, subsidized by the Canadian medical plan. She admitted that their services for non-critical care could seem slow to be provided but she had nothing but praise for the system overall, both she and her husband having benefitted greatly from it.

Yvonne had packed her homemade spaghetti sauce and pasta, and had bought bread and salad fixings in Sidney and we sat around the coffee table in the living room enjoying it. After dinner, I played 21 and then gin with Morgan and shortly the kids were in bed. A long interesting discussion ensued about how people change and don't change over their lifetimes, Natasha noticing that her journals seemed to come back again and again to the same questions and I attested to that from my own experience. We talked about writing — fiction and non-fiction — and about what is or should be told and what shown, about evoking a feeling or sense or perspective versus describing it to the reader, of the concrete and specific versus the general. A long day, the kids were troopers, and we were all ready for bed.

One-hundred-seventy-two: Butchart Gardens

"Nature is not a place to visit. It is home." – Gary Snyder

We'd heard good reports about Miniature World a few blocks away and so after a breakfast of bagels Yvonne and I had picked up at the Bagels on Broad shop the day before — and coffee — and Irish tea for me — and after Noah and Natasha had gone out for more coffee — bringing back a report on what people had been doing the evening before under the glass roof of the building across the street — not moving — a bridge tournament — we walked to Miniature World, a Victoria attraction since 1939 — and spent 90 minutes marveling at the complexity and detail of the historic and fantasy worlds created there. It was beyond me that anyone would have the patience or interest to create these dioramas but I was impressed that they had — a way to look at the world from an Olympian perspective through which one could notice an enormous number of details about what past worlds looked like, even felt like.

Back at the hotel, clear blue skies carrying a warming sun we packed up to drive a half hour north to Butchart Gardens, parked, and walked to the cafeteria where Yvonne had planned for us to enjoy lunch — but it was closed — though later in the day on the way out we could see it was being set up for opening the next day — the beginning of a busier season at the Gardens. The coffee shop sufficed, the kids each having a huge hot dog, the women chicken gumbo soup, Noah an egg salad sandwich and me a chicken and bacon club sandwich. Sated, we started our tour through the Gardens beginning with the sunken garden, the largest and most elaborate part of Butchart. Jennie Butchart conceived of turning her husband's quarry into a garden not long after the turn of the 19th century, transforming what had become a rocky wasteland into a Pacific Northwest premier garden, personally involved in the work to the extent that she was lowered in a bosun's chair down the quarry walls to plant ivy — which now — a century later has covered the gray limestone with green.

Morgan, who I half-expected to be bored in the Gardens was very interested, remarking at the beauty and fascinated with the transformation concept. He said something about taking pictures and I handed him my little Nikon and he and I took turns taking pictures over the next two hours, Morgan alive to visual potential and framing scenes. I restrained myself, for the most part in offering any advice and told him I'd post all his pictures online — so he could look through them, download what he wanted and generally get a sense of what worked and what didn't. Though it had been cool when we started our tour, the sun, caught in the quarry that also excluded the wind, warmed to the high 50s. We climbed to the top of the rock island in the quarry and at the south end spent ten minutes watching the fountain, with its changing pattern, at the far end of a lower level of the quarry.

Here the beds were planted in blooming daffodils and primroses — the tulips for the most part still in bud. The hundreds of rhododendrons that provided a backdrop would bloom in the next week or two, making the third and fourth weeks in April perhaps the most flower-filled here (this year) of the entire year. Once the spring flowers have bloomed, the grounds crew will swap in summer flowers and given the hundreds of thousands of transplants they must do several times a year, it seems impossible that it could be done so well and so unobtrusively. Leaving the quarry area we passed the always-full dog water bowl and remembered that on our first trip to Butchart in 2001 we had left Samantha on the Gumption but then understanding that she would be welcomed at the Gardens took her with the three other times we had come to the Garden's backdoor by boat.

172.A: Butchart Gardens

An indoor carousel had been added near the bandshell and Yvonne and Opal were the only riders for the fastest revolving speed I'd ever seen on a carousel. We all liked the Japanese Garden area, Yvonne talking about how those gardens address all the senses and focus more on shrubbery and trees than flowers. A bamboo water feature continually filled from above, tips, dumps — banging against a rock and then repositions itself to receive more water — the hollow thunk audible all through the garden. We walked out the back gate to look at the float plane and dingy dock — with four mooring buoys nearby where we had tied up twice when we'd come to Butchart this way. Back at the coffee shop the adults each enjoyed a pot of Earl Gray and shared two scones — while the kids finished their gelato.

172.B: John, Opal, Natasha, Noah, Morgan, Yvonne at Butchart

Back at the hotel, Natasha coordinated with Ming's Chinese restaurant for take-out delivery while the rest of us took the kids downstairs for pool time, Morgan an enthusiastic swimmer who was expected to benefit from lessons in the summer and Opal cautious but willing to descend repeatedly to the bottom of the pool, five feet deep where she spent most of her time. We were back upstairs just at 6:00, Noah detecting the aroma of Chinese food as we rode the elevator to the second floor. After dinner, Yvonne and I played crazy eights and then pig/spoon with the kids until it was time for them to go to bed. Relaxed time for us adults and then we too had to retire after a full and satisfying day.

One-hundred-seventy-three: Walk Aboard

"People don't take trips, trips take people." – John Steinbeck

Noah and family would take the Black Ball ferry from the Victoria Inner Harbor to Port Angeles on the Olympic Peninsula and head home, stopping on the way to visit Natasha's father, Gene and friend, LaRonge. We would catch the noon ferry from Sidney back to Friday Harbor and then the Interisland ferry back to Orcas, where we'd left our van Thursday morning. The *Coho* would leave Victoria at 10:30 and arrive at Port Angeles 90 minutes later. Though they had a reservation, they wanted to be in line well in advance of departure so they expected to leave the hotel before 9:00. Their trip home was uneventful and the visit with Gene and LaRonge satisfying.

An express bus to Sidney was due at 8:40 right outside the hotel on Government St so by 8:30 we had said our goodbyes, got our hugs, and were waiting at the bus stop. Within a minute or two a double-decker bus stopped and opened the door. It was running route 71 and we were waiting for 70 but both went the same place; the double-decker was a local and might take fifteen minutes longer in drive time but was leaving earlier. We hopped aboard and I deposited $5 in coins — two toonies and four quarters — I'd traded a US $5 bill for at the front desk of the hotel a few minutes before. We hadn't ridden a double-decker since one London trip more than 20 years before. As it turned out the express bus caught this local just as we turned into Sidney from the highway.

We climbed the narrow stairs to the upper deck, me carrying the roller bag we shared for this trip, forgetting my pack where I set it down so I could retrieve coins from my pocket to pay the fare. Later I had a moment of panic when I realized I had the suitcase but no pack — which contained my MacBook Pro and Kindle — but it was right where I'd left it and I took it with me upstairs.

On the way out of Victoria, on this Saturday morning the 71 pulled over at about every third bus stop and picked up or discharged passengers while we sat at the upper-level windshield ducking our heads, unnecessarily, when passing under low-hanging branches or traffic lights. Seattle has double deckers too but they're all on one level — basically a bus dragging a bus-trailer. The horizontal approach might carry more passengers but it has a larger footprint, thus perhaps reducing the total potential traffic flow during any period. On the other hand, going up and down those narrow stairs on the double-decker isn't simple — or even possible for some passengers. The height did command the view though and we could see more and farther returning to Sidney than when we'd driven to Victoria two days before.

173: Black Ball Ferry to Port Angeles, WA

Driving south we'd passed the Elk/Beaver Lake Regional Park, noticing some single and crewed sculls in use and others coming out from the boat house — as well as some small fishing boats on Elk Lake. On Saturday, when the bus stopped across from the recreation center at the lake, we could see two dozen young people, mostly girls, in team uniforms, it looked like, running along a trail toward the lake. The lake was covered with at least 100 fishing boats averaging two fisherpersons per boat, seeking the rainbow trout the lake is stocked with. It felt a bit like our Miniature World visit Friday morning, watching the bustle in the area as the population was intent on getting the most benefit possible from this dry but cloud-attracting morning.

Half-way to Sidney we left the highway and traveled a local, mostly parallel road, getting a look at the countryside and the houses of the locals, some commuting to Victoria, seat of the British Columbia government. Victoria is small, with a population around 80,000 and the greater Victoria area four times larger. It's an out-of-the-way area, this Canadian banana belt or Mediterranean or Southern California — lying in the rain shadow of the Olympics and warmed by the Japanese current, mild enough for palm trees though with a latitude north of St. Johns, a more challenging environment. On a hillside several hundred feet and a half-mile west of highway 17 we could see San Juan Island and Orcas Island and a hint of Mt Baker, the snow-capped volcano perhaps 50 miles west in the Cascades.

While Yvonne did a little shopping in Sidney, I sat at Starbucks, enjoying a cup of tea and a muffin while doing some writing, disappointed though that free WiFi wasn't available. Yvonne joined me after 45 minutes and we walked three or four blocks to the entry point to the Washington Ferry landing, buying our tickets — $25 for walk on — about the same as Natasha spent getting us to Sidney from Friday Harbor. We walked into the customs office and waited while the only clerk worked with a couple and their young adult son to find a way to let them through the checkpoint. The clerk finally took a break with his mysterious efforts, examined our passports and waved us through. The gift shop held nothing of interest for us and the waiting room, though clean, was beige enough to steal one's soul so we moved outside and stood along the chain link fence watching Saturday fishermen launch their boats at the ramp just south of the ferry landing.

Aboard the *Elwah*, not half-full on its cruise to Friday Harbor, we ate our Starbucks sandwiches in the galley — with a french fry side. I wrote some more and Yvonne continued with her knitting project and soon we were walking off at Friday Harbor and had to explain ourselves to a customs officer who wanted to know where we'd been, what we'd done, where we lived, where we were going and whether we needed to declare something. The Interisland ferry, the *Evergreen State* was due to depart in about 45 minutes so we sat at a nearby ice cream/coffee shop and shared a hot chocolate. We were back home before 4:00 and I turned on the water, turned up the heat, fed chlorine to the hot tub, and felt happy to be back home — so we could reenter our day-to-day island rut. We relaxed in the evening by watching the movies, *127 Hours* — and then talked about how foolish I'd been how many times climbing 14ers in Colorado — me maintaining I had been very responsible because I always hiked with someone — Yvonne pointing out that I often went way ahead or climbed some other mountain nearby and then met my climbing partner on the summit he had scrambled toward all day. So I had climbed alone — it's true — and several times I had found myself in a pickle — but always found a way out. When you're strong and love moving from rock to rock, it's hard not to test your limits.

One-hundred-seventy-four: Talking about Walking to the North Pole

"Stories are the communal currency of humanity." – Tahir Shah

The UU Fellowship poetry service was meeting this morning but we'd miss it. I would be going for a walk around Mountain Lake, organized by Gordon, and Yvonne would be catching up on seemingly hundreds of small tasks. Ken had withdrawn from leading the poetry service because the prior year only six people had shown up. It was his opinion that the group should disband.

My goal was to send out a near final version of *Metamorphosis* during the day — for review of the formatting and organization especially, so I found myself up working not long after 4:00 a.m. Before 9:00 Yvonne reminded me that I was due at the Mountain Lake parking lot in Moran State Park by 10:00 — from portal to park might take 50 minutes and I needed to stop at Island Market to pick up sale items on the list Yvonne had put in my wallet and the *Sunday Seattle Times*. A windy morning, not the worst but the ride to the Orcas side dock was bumpy and it was a struggle to pull the *Huginn* backwards against the southeast wind to a spot in the transient area — where Yvonne had painted the bull rail yellow three summers ago — the paint now chipping off and some showing up on the *Huginn*'s hull. I hadn't had time to take a shower and as it turned out wouldn't all day — but I did brush my teeth.

No cars on Deer Harbor Road and I stared at the construction site on the west side of the road at Massacre Bay, the site of a 19th-century mass murder of local Native Americans by the Haida who had come several hundred miles south from the Queen Charlotte Islands, apparently with the knowledge of local authorities but left for the Indians to settle amongst themselves. The lot had been dug out and pipe laid, apparently for a ground-based heat pump system, a very efficient heating/cooling system appropriate to this area and much superior to an air-based system that would require resistance heating once the ambient temperature dropped below 40 — not uncommon in the winter in the San Juans. I caught up with a slow-moving flatbed truck driving north on Crow Valley road but as I expected it was soon exceeding the 35 mph speed limit and I followed along in its wake a polite distance behind. Nothing going on at Island Hardware and Supply, the lumber yard. They were closed on Sundays but business was slow during the cold and rainy months — probably slower this year than usual.

Turning off Orcas Road, I noticed that the Washington Federal clock showed 9:35. I would take a least 15 minutes to drive to Mountain Lake in Moran Park on the east side of East Sound. Better to be a little early than late — though I usually made the other choice. Bill had arrived and then Gordon, David, and finally Jens — having come from Orcas Highlands nearby where he and Susan had bought a second home and were trying it out over the winter while he was on sabbatical from Wellesley. We knew Gordon through Sylvia who Yvonne had worked with through the Master Gardeners and the Garden Club, Sylvia again in charge of the Garden Tour fundraiser this year.

There was some question about what route to take — a 90-minute circle of Mountain Lake or a walk to Twin Lakes, an uphill route, or even to the summit, a long and demanding hike. Jens had plans later and I didn't want to spend the whole day — so Gordon led us to the trailhead for a counterclockwise hike around this beautiful lake, a reservoir built by Robert Moran as part of a system that fed his water turbine electrical system at the Rosario mansion several miles away and hundreds of feet lower. As we waited for Jens, David and I had talked briefly about the weather, cool, cloudy, and on the water, windy though the wind wasn't evident here. David agreed that soft light and the wispy clouds, ghosts, drifting through the big firs and cedars across the lake was more attractive than bright sunlight that hurt the eyes, alternately making some of the landscape invisible and other washed out looking.

174: Canada Goose Incubates Eggs Near Pole Pass

For the most part the trail would only accommodate two walking abreast, sometimes only single file. Given that Yvonne and I had watched *127 Hours* the night before I wanted to talk to David Schermerhorn about his reaction to that film, David, from my point of view having been an intrepid explorer, having hiked many times to the North Pole, the last time a few years ago when he was injured crossing broken ice that by this summer had too many water gaps to allow continuous hiking. Had he seen *127 Hours*. No — but he knew the story. Did he ever have a sense that his Arctic treks were dangerous? No — usually it was David and a guide — but they had radios. His sense was that the *127 Hours* story wasn't the most interesting kind of survival story — it was just a question of whether one valued staying alive over having a right hand and whether one could stand the pain of doing a self-amputation. The *Alive* story, the soccer team that had crashed in the Andes, some resorting to cannibalism and others refusing and starving to death, was in his mind the interesting kind of story — survival versus disgust and taboos. He pointed out that some of the survivors rationalized eating their dead companions by comparing it to the Catholic Mass where the blood and the body of Christ are consumed. He went on to talk about the Communist influence on burial practices in Siberia and then their disappearance under Gorbachev so that they could revert to leaving the dead for the wolves. I brought Bill into the conversation — we were now about halfway around the Lake and scooted ahead to Jens. Jens and I talked business for a while — the state of *The Metamorphosis* and that I'd soon supply him with *The Trial* to begin work on and a colleague who he said was an expert on Chaucer's *Canterbury Tales* — and then I turned the conversation to what it was like growing up in post-war Germany, for him Hamburg beginning in 1949. Back in Eastsound at Island Market, I saw Larry, in a short-sleeved shirt outside the store and we talked about their new house in Tucson (101 degrees but they got lots of painting and floor projects done) and then the status of the new Food Bank building due to come over by ferry about now from Anacortes — except the ferry people wouldn't give him a definitive answer about scheduling — so he was going to take another route to find out. I suggested Kevin Ranker our local representative to the Washington State legislature, once a county commissioner and someone Yvonne and I had confidence in. That was just what Larry intended to do — his daughter, he said was a good friend of Kevin's. What about layoff at the Market — Larry had been manager before retiring. Not that he knew though hours were always cut back in the winter. But in his 30 or more years on the island he hadn't seen so many businesses closing in such a short time.

 Gordon had come into the store too for shopping but disappeared among the shelves and I put on my glasses and consulted the list Yvonne had put in my wallet. Two oranges — on sale. They were navel oranges and I could tell many were too soft — so I picked what I thought were two that were firm enough to last a while. Mayonnaise — on sale — but not the right kind. Yvonne thought light mayonnaise was disgusting. Then canned vegetables — two corn, two beans, two peas — at 10 for $5. Really? Maybe I should get more. No, that's not what the list said. It said six. Then grapefruit juice — if it was on sale — and it was — two for $5 — so I got two. Chips — the list said — our favorite a local brand that made corn chips that included sesame seeds — more nutritious and better tasting — what's not to like? And then peanut butter on sale. Where was that? I looked up and down almost every isle and then asked for help from a young woman stocking a freezer. Over by the bread on the last aisle. Of course! Putting the *Seattle Times* in the cart, I parked it at an open lane — they were all open — and pulled out the two cloth carry bags Yvonne had sent with me. Well past noon and starving I opened a bag of chips as I drove out of the parking lot and headed back to Deer Harbor.

Tom was in the lot loading his canopy-covered truck bed with recycle and he reported that he and Gary had done more work on the leak at well house #4, tracing the leak to the line to the main. I'd noticed the pink dayglow paint streaks on the road and grass in the vicinity — assuming OPALCO and CenturyLink had left them because Gary intended to dig in the area and Tom confirmed that adding that he had already put in almost 16 hours and Gary, with Ruby part of the time, certainly more. Fixing the leak was turning into a big project. Then Tom said he had been worrying since last fall that he had left the wrong impression with me about a conflict in Suncrest, a subdivision on Orcas where he owned a lot, and where I knew one couple had drawn the ire of others because they had violated the covenants when they'd built their home. In fact I had just seen Gerd, who was now working at the Market. Tom wanted me to know he hadn't ganged up on them having bought the lot after the dispute had taken place. I wasn't sure why he was telling me all this. Then Steve appeared and wanted to talk about the No Wake Zone fundraising letter he'd just sent out and I reported we'd already received a check from Cal — and he opined that Cal wrote the check as soon as he heard the fund drive was open. Then Tom began talking about how he was disappointed because we hadn't put a No Wake Zone buoy in the water out from his house at the southeastern part of Crane to protect his dock. I excused myself, saying I needed to go home and have lunch, with a grocery bag in each hand, suggesting that they work it out.

After lunch, we called James and sang "Ja må hon leva," our family and a traditional Swedish birthday song, and talked to him and then to Keith about their birthday doings — which would be at a nearby LA restaurant recently written up in the *New York Times*. They'd found a cat sitter for Leo and Fyo, their Russian Blue kittens, and wouldn't need to leave them with us when they came by in the summer on their way to Europe. And they had gone ahead and had the timing belt and other repairs done to James' Honda — for $800. And the day before as he waited at a traffic light a plumber in an adjacent lane had motioned to roll down the window and proposed that he fix the right side of the front bumper that Keith accidentally pulled off its mounting when backing out of their parking space at their apartment and which duct tape had failed to keep from flopping about. The plumber followed him home, drilled a new hole in the plastic and then secured it with a bolt. James said he appreciated getting the *Proust Was a Neuroscientist* book and that he'd been in a discussion about it a few days ago — before he got it.

By 3:30 *Metamorphosis* was in good enough shape to send out. I'd applied all the fixes Jens had told me about as well as some others I pursued (double spaces where there should be only one) and though the annotations cited within the Topic essays didn't show a blank line between paragraphs the fix would take too long and I was too eager to send this third draft out for reactions — having made many formatting changes — I hoped all for the better.

Tessa called from Boulder and she and Yvonne caught up — it had been months — and Tessa thought maybe she and Alan could join Barb and Dean and Yvonne and me at the Mabel Dodge Luhan House in Taos Wednesday before arriving in Chimayo for our Good Friday walk. Then a truly delicious chicken curry dinner with basmati rice, and carrots and broccoli on the side. Mmm! And fresh baked chocolate chip cookies Yvonne brought into my office — still warm from the oven — while I toiled over *Metamorphosis* in the afternoon — and then while we watched *Made in Dagenham*, a feel-good dramatization of the struggle for equal pay for women at a Ford plant in England in 1968. Sitting in the hot tub after I pointed out how different this story and setting was from other contemporary English stories we'd seen. The "estates," one new and attractive, the people hopeful and energized, had become dilapidated, even slums and the English cynical and discouraged. Yvonne pointed out that perhaps it had always been that way — never quite as optimistic as the film had portrayed. Perhaps. Done with Codrescu's *Posthuman Dada Guidebook*, but not quite sure what to say to him about it, I returned to Thompson's *Merchants of Culture*, immersing myself again in this story of the publishing business — something about which I wanted to have a much better understanding.

One-hundred-seventy-five: Roots Revealed

"A budget is telling your money where to go instead of wondering where it went." – Dave Ramsey

About 9:00 the sun topped the clouds to the east over the mainland, 20 miles away, and the day turned lovely, the wind out of the northwest broken by the forest in that direction so that we enjoyed almost calm air. After catching up on a long list the day before Yvonne spent some of the day tending to the deer fence protecting her raised bed cutting garden just south of the studio deck. The main deer fencing material was a stranded nylon four inch mesh and did a fine job keeping the deer out — except for their snouts. When something just inside the fence interested them they would stick their noses through the fence and nibble what they could reach. In order to discourage them — where something was planted close to the fence as it was with the cutting garden, Yvonne added another layer of fencing material, this time half-inch plastic mesh, much more difficult to work with and much less attractive but very effective. The trunks of the trees I had cut down and in some cases cut up into 16" sections the week before lay where I left them, on what had been the driveway to what had been the garage, content enough to wait for me to finish cutting and then to carry them to the firewood area at the front of the house. Because we had run very low we hadn't been using firewood this month, except for two-morning fires when Noah and family visited and since I had set the thermostats to begin raising the house temperature earlier — 6:00 a.m. — and letting it drop earlier — 7:00 p.m. — and also raising the daytime temperature from 68 to 70 we'd been comfortable enough but we were using more power than before. I'd find time to analyze the difference later on.

Because we were leaving for Seattle and then Colorado and New Mexico the coming Saturday, I needed to prepare whatever I'd be reporting to the Crane Island Association Board at their meeting in 12 days — that I'd miss while traveling. Gary had finally sent the meter reading list and I updated the month-by-month, year-to-date report I provided to the members from time to time so they could see their usage and know what the water had cost them so far this fiscal year. The report had a second purpose: to provide some social pressure for members to be careful about their usage, even if they could afford the higher rates per gallon that came with usage above 100 gallons per day. Overuse of a well could ruin it — salt water would intrude — and a new well would be expensive for the community and perhaps not even possible — physically or because the state wouldn't approve it. The Board had approved a Cross-Connect Control Plan a few months back and the first step in implementing it was to survey the members to identify where there was a risk of backflow from their property into the community system. An appropriate backflow prevention device would have to be installed at those locations, for instance at a hot tub, or the property as a whole would need a prevention device. I sent the survey form and cover letter along with the YTD water report to Martha for distribution to the membership.

As treasurer, I was obligated to keep the Board up to date on how we were doing relative to budget. The bookkeeper had sent me a cash report and general ledger as of April 1st and copies of checks written after so since our fiscal year ran August to July we now had more or less nine months of activity and overall we were doing well and would end the year with enough cash to make a $30,000 deposit into our reserves, what we'd budgeted and had done regularly for a number of years. The reserves would be drawn on for dock and water system improvements or replacements that went beyond normal maintenance — and could be very expensive — docks costing $200 to $400 a square foot. I wrote up a report on our financial status as well as a water report and sent them to Martha for distribution to the Board — having forwarded the bookkeeper's financials earlier in the day.

175: North End Front Yard

The principal news in the water report was the discovery and remediation of the leak between well house #4 and the main line across Circle Road. In the evening, after a dinner of leftover curry, Yvonne and I had walked around the island, stopping at well house #4 to examine the ditch that Gary and Tom had dug so that Gary could run a new line from the main to the well house line where it emerges from the chlorine contact assembly. I noticed an exposed electrical cable crossing the ditch about two feet down at the end of the ditch close to the road, imagining that was the 7200 volt cable OPALCO had marked on the ground with paint and had warned Tom about. The ditch, apparently dug by hand, and not quite straight, ran about 25 feet from the road to where the new line would need to be connected to the well house system. What was especially striking was the enormous number of roots that crossed the ditch, mostly less than a foot from the top, some as large as three inches in diameter, all at a 90-degree angle to the ditch, most broken or cut through perhaps by an ax. Tom had told me they would be digging and I told him to call me but neither he nor Gary had and the truth was that I really didn't want to do ditch digging anyway — even if I hadn't had a great deal to do before traveling. Where it isn't cut back and there is some reasonably drained soil, vegetation grows thick on Crane with roots snaking back and forth out of sight, though for the most part not going deep, one of the reasons wind can blow over big firs but not break their trunks. On the walk around Mountain Lake the day before we had come upon ten or more big firs that had recently fallen across the trail and then cut through by the park staff to restore access.

Yvonne and I had exchanged emails with Noah and Natasha about our recent time together — and then an email appeared in my inbox from ten-year-old Morgan, thanking Yvonne (Grandma Bon) and me for doing the trip with them — our first thank-you email from a grandchild. What a pleasure! I wrote back promising I would put the pictures he'd taken with my camera into an album on the family Website — though I might not have time for a week or so.

One-hundred-seventy-six: What's That?

"Your body hears everything your mind says." – Naomi Judd

Because I hadn't seen a doctor for more than two years, I made an appointment for a physical exam with Tony Geifert, the one full time family practice physician at the Orcas Medical Center. He'd solved my painful right shoulder problem with a shot of cortisone and I was very grateful. Six years before I had been coming downstairs to the kitchen in our Cayou Valley Road house in Deer Harbor holding my open Averatec notebook computer out in front on me. I missed the bottom step, pitched forward and deliberately landed on my right shoulder to save the computer — which I still use. For the first half hour or so I thought I broken something — the pain so was so intense — but it became bearable and so for a month I tried to ignore it — but finally couldn't.

Nurse Raven measured my height and weight: I was shrinking and now about a half-inch shorter than i had been at 20. I had gained a pound or two but was still lighter than I had been in college — where I lived on bread, potatoes, eggs, and dessert. My blood pressure, 120/70 and my pulse, 60, as usual, didn't suggest any new areas of concern.

Then Tony came in and we talked for a while about getting old — I'd be 68 in a few weeks — and he examined me, not finding anything he was concerned about. In the past my lab tests hadn't shown anything that required attention and he saw no reason to do another series of lab tests since the odds were strongly in favor of their coming out the same. But if I wanted lab tests he'd have them done. But I didn't. Because I hadn't had a colonoscopy he recommended I have one and explained why. I said I'd think about it.

176: Red Sky in the Morning - Ferry Docked at Orcas Landing

But there were two items that did need immediate attention: I should have a diphtheria, tetanus and pertussis booster shot; and I should have the wax cleaned out of my ears. Carol came in shortly with the vaccine and then Raven returned to squirt warm water into first my left and then right ears to soften the wax and flush it out. The process took at least half an hour and yielded unattractive globs of wax the size of a small pea. When I'd been examined for hearing aids two years before at Costco by an audiologist he recommended I have the wax removed from my ears; my ear canals were nearly plugged up. I worked on it at home making no noticeable progress and ignored it. But once the wax was actually removed I could hear much better without my hearing aids — and with them was startled at the loudness of everyday sounds. I tried going without my hearing aids and decided I could get along without them in a pinch — though they'd been absolutely necessary before the de-waxing.

No bad news, a vaccination that could be important, and better hearing — a good morning at the medical center. When I entered the building about 9:00 a.m. the lobby was empty and I sensed little activity while I was in the building. The Medical Center, built with donations and subsidized by generous islanders, was intended to provide facilities and administrative help for all Orcas physicians but for the last five or six years hadn't. One doctor, unhappy with the Board, had moved out and set up his own offices. Another, hired by the Center, had worked there for a year and then gone out on his on. And off and on other physicians practiced part-time, sometimes using the Center. Orcas actually had too many physicians given its population and that meant that Orcas medical care was actually being subsidized — by doctors who couldn't earn what their peers would in Anacortes or Burlington — or by a foundation dependent on donations. It seemed to me, and to others, that though the surfeit of doctors appeared to benefit the Island population it probably couldn't be sustained. If the existing doctors retired or went elsewhere to make more money, Orcas could find itself underserved instead of over-served.

Yvonne had spent the afternoon in Eastsound at the Food Bank Board meeting. The Washington State Ferry service hadn't yet been able to commit to a schedule for bringing the new building to Orcas for installation at the site in the Community Church parking lot. Apparently ongoing overhead repairs at the Anacortes ferry landing might make it impossible to bring the two building sections on to the ferry. If the service allowed the loading but it turned out to be impossible, the ferry could be delayed and management unhappy that the staff had encouraged the debacle. Larry reported that he was becoming more demanding — of at least an informed answer — and was hopeful they'd know something definitive soon.

One-hundred-seventy-seven: The Carrion Next Door

"The greatest threat to our planet is the belief that someone else will save it." – Robert Swan

We left the house at 7:30, Yvonne on her way to Seattle and me on my way to Howard's for our weekly Graybeards session. A weak sun barely penetrated a high thin formless cloud layer above scattered clouds below, especially in the east over the Skagit Valley mainland. Later the rain would come down hard, though without the force Yvonne drove through in Seattle and farther north. A cormorant emerged from the waters of Pole Pass as we approached, startled to see a boat coming its way, and lifted itself out of the water, feet walking on the water as it took off to the south, its long neck extending straight out from its streamlined body, wings beating furiously. Returning home later, the same or a different cormorant went through the same exercise at the same place although this time I was coming from the east instead of the west. In the evening, returning to Orcas to pick up Yvonne, a young seal floated contentedly on the surface facing the Orcas' shore paying almost no attention to my passing.

Chris was in Pasco representing OPALCO for a utilities meeting and wouldn't return until Thursday sometime. David had picked up Brian, who was again without a car, having driven his Volvo into a ditch two weeks before. Howard had his camera and used it to illustrate a story about the cycles of nature in the Islands. On Friday his neighbor to the north had called to say that a dead deer lay next to her house and she didn't know what to do with it but didn't want it around. Howard said she should call the Fish and Wildlife office for advice — since the deer may have been killed out of hunting season. Their reply: if it doesn't have an arrow sticking in it or a bullet hole we won't be involved. Howard and his neighbor inspected what turned out to be a yearling, its eyes still open and not clouded over. It had died within the last few hours and the body offered no clues as to the cause.

177: White Path on the Water

They dragged the deer uphill away from the house, leaving it as carrion for whatever animals might want to make a feast of it and Howard took a picture, returning each day to see how long it would take nature to clean up the dead. First to arrive were the crows; they could only peck out the eyes and work on soft tissue like the anus. They would have to wait for the bald eagles to tear through the hide and open up the body cavity. After 24 hours the deer was open and as many as three eagles working on the remains, the crows waiting for their chance when the eagles left. Howard was surprised that the turkey buzzards hadn't made an appearance. The eagles are often tipped off by circling buzzards that carrion lies below — but not this time since the buzzards hadn't picked up the scent, perhaps because the deer was so newly dead or perhaps because the buzzard population was still small and would increase as the weather warmed. By Monday the deer had been reduced to skin and bones, everything edible having been removed by the scavenging team and the remains no longer a public health issue. Though Yvonne and I hadn't seen bald eagles scavenging, though we knew that was a principal food source for them, we had seen rapacious vultures in the Ngorongoro Crater violently fighting over an unidentifiable corpse. They were big and they were mean.

This example of the cycle of nature triggered other related topics, one being whether clear-cutting in Pacific Northwest forests was sustainable or whether carrying the wood off — and thus minerals — would deplete the already poor soil leading eventually to hilly and mountainous terrain bereft of trees and subject to erosion from the northwest rains. It seemed obvious to three of us that clear-cutting was not sustainable but Brian, who had been a professor of forestry at Oregon State, said we were mistaken. His research over the years showed that clear-cutting made little difference to the mineral content though it could affect the availability of fixed nitrogen — but that could easily be treated with fertilizer, not uncommon in forestry practice. Clear-cutting, Brian said, was a matter of aesthetics, not sustainability. David, Howard, and I remained skeptical.

Yvonne called from the ferry line in Anacortes about 6:00 just as I was looking for leftovers to heat up (chicken curry, basmati rice, broccoli). I'd pick her up at the Crane dock on Orcas about 7:45, taking our dock cart to the dock on Crane and leaving it there to use when we came back — to carry the cases of wine and rice milk and other heavy supplies Yvonne had picked up on the mainland. She'd gone to downtown Seattle for a haircut, returning to Jeni's stylist after she had helped Yvonne recover from a bad haircut she'd gotten in Eastsound six weeks or so earlier. This time the cut wasn't a recovery; it was the real thing, a bob that looked very good on Yvonne, the best haircut style for her that I'd seen in our 33 years together. She was happy and I was happy because she was happy. And she'd look good when we traveled to Colorado and then New Mexico beginning Sunday.

One-hundred-seventy-eight: Lonely houses

"The best thing for being sad," replied Merlyn, "is to learn something. That is the only thing that never fails." – T.H. White, *The Once and Future King*

Daffodils inside Yvonne's deer fence trembled in the gentle morning breeze off the water and lingering from the overnight rain, drips fell sporadically from the eaves outside the living room windows, diamonds in the new day's new sun now risen above the bank of clouds over Blakely Island, independent fragments drifting north through its forested flanks. The *Chelan*, in the middle of Harney Channel and a mile east of Blind Bay where it had loaded vehicles from Shaw Island, was headed for the Lopez Island ferry landing and then on to Anacortes, the second mainland ferry of the day. To get a better look I took our binoculars from the window sill in the living room and brought the ferry into focus. In doing so I scanned the upper reaches of Blakely Island, the summit reaching about 1100' out of the Salish Sea — and saw two broad fields of snow — areas that had apparently been clear-cut not so long ago. Here at sea level the temperature was 38. I found out later that Bellingham had received a dusting. By afternoon the temperature had risen to 48 — still much cooler than average for this time of year by almost 10 degrees. In the hot tub after "Morning Glory" that evening Yvonne told me that she read El Nino weather conditions were moderating and temperatures were predicted to rise. Good!

In the late afternoon, Yvonne took the *Huginn* to Orcas to attend the Rock on the Rock choir practice, now working on the Beatles *Because* from the album *Abbey Road*, not concerned that the southeast wind had risen considerably since morning. After heating up leftover quiche for dinner, I walked up the driveway and then around the island, first checking the tank level (12'), then whether more progress had been made in fixing the leak at well house #4 (the ditch through a tangle of roots to lay a new line was untouched from earlier in the week) and finally, at the other end of the island, walked down the now muddy Sunnyside Lane to see whether John Thompson's crew, the burn pile problem people, had finished their cleanup at the two properties for sale at the end of the road (they had — to good effect). I walked down the driveway for lot 42, not having looked at this vacant house for four years, and found it sadder than before. It was actually two connected houses, the smaller one guest quarters, I assumed. The deck was disintegrating and the inside of the house looked cold, abandoned, bereft of life. As I walked back to Circle Road, passing Lou's driveway, I thought about how his deck and reports that it was falling down, his overgrown yard, and his inability, in his old age to properly care for it. Perhaps our family could make it a morning project during our family gathering, Borgfest, in August.

178: Outfits for Opal

Deer were everywhere on the island, alone or with a companion or two, noticing my approach, and then prancing toward the thick forest in the center of the island. A few nights before, Yvonne and I had seen at least 20; this evening I counted 14. Though the grass is green year round on Crane, it grows very little during the cooler months, was now rising, and in May would grow a foot or more. I assumed this new growth would be a feast for these white-tailed browsers — but according to Howard — cows and deer going to grass from hay or at least drier foods can suffer severe diarrhea and even starve in the midst of what I assumed was a kind of plenty. It isn't. Howard had said that deer like to eat a variety of foods, some woody like new salal growth. I had been watching the deer in their early morning rounds past Yvonne's garden over the last few weeks and I noticed they nibbled, a little here and a little there, not like cattle that move slowly across the ground mowing everything in their path. Josh had left Ilse's remodel project for the weekend, Ethan having retired from the project a week or two earlier and I wondered what it would be like to work alone all day and then stay alone all night as Josh was now doing — except on long weekends. I wouldn't want to do it but some Island construction or remodel projects had been handled that way, though it was usually a small team, two or three that might spend six months living out of a tent while putting up a house. The crew that built Doug's house told me they enjoyed camping out on the island. Maybe so.

I'd sent Jens new software and Kafka's *The Trial* in a database for him to begin work on. He'd need to assemble a library of source material and could do that by taking advantage of the interlibrary loan service at the Orcas Island Public Library but first he'd make a pass through the book, entering what amounted to bookmarks for followup. At 7:00 I received an email that the program had displayed a message that an out-of-bounds condition had occurred — that is something was trying to access an array beyond its limits. Hmmm. His note said he'd put in about 30 notes in Chapter 1 before he encountered the problem. Since *The Trial* has very long paragraphs I suspected the problem was related to the number of notes per paragraph and was able to duplicate the problem. Sure enough — when I had raised the limit from 20 to 50 per paragraph — which I had done for *The Metamorphosis* — I had raised the input limit but not the corresponding size of the array that held information about them for temporary use by the program. I fixed the problem and sent him a new version of the program.

Yvonne was home just before dark — she wouldn't have wanted to operate the *Huginn* in the dark. Everyone at choir practice had wanted to keep on talking. What could be more fun?

One-hundred-seventy-nine: Remembering Grandma Opal

"A boat is safe in the harbor. But this is not the purpose of a boat."
— Paulo Coelho

It would have been Yvonne's mom's birthday — she would have been 96 this year. Yvonne missed her. Her brother Ron, who had seen his grandson, Raphael, and his ex-wife, and called to tell Yvonne about the session, missed their mother as well, gone 11 years. We all missed her — even her granddaughter, Opal Ashenhurst, age 6, who never met her.

Chris and I showed up at David's, at 9:00 for our third Friday, eNotated Classics monthly "Executive Committee" meeting and after fixing myself a cup of tea sat at the dinning room table, huge windows to my right, the tops of firs and madronas outside, with a view of Crane Island and Pole Pass about a mile away across the water of Deer Harbor to the southeast. From time to time during our meeting I'd glimpse a turkey buzzard (the same one?) floating among the trees on the lookout for carrion below and saw a small gray squirrel on a branch eating something tasty.

The most important questions for the morning related to the upcoming publication of *The eNotated Metamorphosis* — especially how we would handle proofreading and how we could have a cover made. I'd talked to Amazon's CreateSpace two days before and they could provide both services. An Orcas woman, who had been trained in proofreading was also a possibility. I'd assembled all Jens' *Metamorphosis* related writing into one Mac Pages document and found it contained about 28,000 words. At $0.0175 per word, CreateSpace would charge about $500. Linda charged by the hour and her charges, given what she could typically accomplish per hour, would come out about the same. We decided to approach Linda first. I'd create a PDF file with all the text in it, we'd have it printed, let Linda proofread and pass on her marked-up document to Jens who would approve, reject, or change Linda's recommendations, pass the document to me and I would make the changes to the database. Later after unsatisfying email correspondence with Linda, Chris volunteered Lynn, printed out the manuscript and put it on the table where Lynn couldn't avoid seeing it. The price was right, at least.

CreateSpace wanted $500 or $1000 to create a cover and perhaps two months to complete it. That wouldn't work so Chris volunteered to take the dummy cover I'd done and see whether he could make something out of it that would satisfy all of us, including Jens.

179: Raised Bed Project

After lunch Yvonne took Margaret's boat to Orcas and would pick me up at West Sound Marina at 3:15. About 2:30 I took the *Huginn* through Pole Pass and once past the No Wake Zone buoy between Caldwell Point and Bell Island brought the boat up on plane. I had turned on the GPS and could track the boat's speed, something I hadn't done since having the rebuilt engine installed in early December. Before the boat would cruise at 21 knots (about 23 mph) at 3600 rpm. Today it moved along at 23 knots — a gratifying improvement. Approaching the head of West Sound, I could see 25 to 30 small sailboats, all the same class, out on the water, practicing for weekend races, the wind blowing from the southeast, up West Sound, enough to satisfy the young sailors. The weekend races, the NWISA District HIgh School Double Handed Championship hosted by NWISA, Sail Orcas, and the Orcas High School Sailing team. The young people and their coaches would stay at the Four Winds camp on the west side of West Sound adjacent to the old Kaiser property and use the Orcas Island Yacht Club grounds, shelter, and dock. Burke, the principal organizer, had done a wonderful job in recent years with the Orcas Sail Team, now competitive with the best teams in the country even with very limited resources compared with some other areas.

Mooring at the visitor/fuel dock at the West Sound Marina, I could see a couple with a son (?) looking at a 30-foot sailboat (to buy?) and that the Marina was now in spring mode, the platform where boats were worked on, pulled from and returned to the water by a movable lift. An eight-inch diameter mast, at least 50 feet long lay on blocks waiting for installation. I found Betsy in the marina store/office and she explained the mast belonged to a catboat, a single sail design for wide work boats that could be singlehanded. Over the last few days the *Huginn* idle had been sticking so Betsy put it on the list — along with a pullout, hull cleaning and painting if necessary, zinc checking, oil change, fluid topping up, and general inspection and the repair of the gel coat on the starboard corner of the swim platform where a few months before I scraped the gel coat off by turning too sharply when leaving the Orcas dock, exposing the porous fiberglass underneath, something green and growing beginning to flourish there. Ian came out from the back office and I told him I was very happy with the *Huginn*'s performance now and intended to bring her in twice a year for servicing, that being his advice as a way to minimize total maintenance and service costs over time — something I was now willing to believe. For years I had been conscientious about auto oil change cycles; I would do that with our boat as well.

Having gotten to the West Sound Marina and taken care of all my business by 2:50 I had 20 minutes to wait for Yvonne to pick me up after leaving her Friday knitting group at the Deer Harbor Community Club at 3:00. I sat on a trailer in the boat yard, among a dozen boats and a half-dozen empty trailers. Each boat represented someone's dream — and a running meter — clicking over each month for storage fees and less often but for more substantial charges — maintenance and repairs. Some boats sat years — or indefinitely — without being used. Crane had several, their decks and roofs turning green, the only water they saw was from the sky. I'd read somewhere that boats are the single most disappointing major consumer purchase. Certainly most boats were underused and very expensive on an hourly basis.

One-hundred-eighty: Seattle

"Every exit is an entry somewhere else." – Tom Stoppard

We left the house at 7:30 a.m., stopping at the Deer Harbor Post Office to put our 2010 Federal Tax filing in the mail, and driving along West Sound just east of Crow Valley Road could see many high school sailors out in the water in their Vanguard 15's and FJ's, more congregating at the yacht club shelter, vans and cars bringing in more kids, some having breakfast. In the low 40's, it wasn't so cold but the air was calm. Perhaps it would pick up as the sun, through the clouds, warmed the air. The day before when running the *Huginn* to West Sound Marina and with the Furuno GPS/depth sounder turned on I noticed that the mid-April Salish Sea temperature was 47.6 degrees. Any high school sailer that capsized would be doing so into very chilly water.

At the Orcas Hotel coffee shop Yvonne had her breakfast, a lemon custard danish and an 8 oz regular Starbuck's latte — she was returning to caffeine but in smaller doses — and I sipped my 12% Tazo Awake tea — and there was Julia, picking up drinks and breakfast for her and Jay in the car. We were surprised to see her on a Saturday morning eastbound because she and Jay lived in Seattle and came to Orcas on weekends. They had bought an 8 by 10 greenhouse kit, a show special, at the February Flower and Garden Show in Seattle and were on their way to pick it up at Charlie's Greenhouse in Mt Vernon. We described how we'd put together our greenhouse in February about eight years ago at our house on Cayou Valley Road, one that Yvonne had bought from Costco, and which had been delivered to the house. The kit included directions but also a videotape demonstration of each step in the process. I ran an extension cord from the boathouse, a large shed where I had my office in the loft, and plugged in our TV and a videotape player and we watched the tape, pausing it between each construction stage. The weather was mild and not too wet, though when it misted we'd drape a tarp over the electronics. We'd finished in two days, happy with the result.

180: Corrina, Jeni, Kelly, Tim, Yvonne

On the *Chelan*, Julia and Jay found us on the upper level, Yvonne knitting and me just starting to type into my MacBook Pro. We spent the rest of the voyage talking, Jay reporting on how busy he'd been with his work and me responding that I was busier than I'd ever been, admitting that it was by choice. We hadn't talked since eNotated Classics published its first book. He was familiar with Slocum's classic, having read it twice and immediately understood what we were doing when I showed the eNotated version on my Kindle, a device he'd seen but hadn't tried. I then showed him the book on the iPad, demonstrating the advantages of a touch screen, for our kind of book, and then on the iPod, where he was surprised at how readable it was on such a small screen. We went on to talk about photo and video archives, and the pleasure they can bring, potentially for succeeding generations. And then we'd arrived at Anacortes. Yvonne told me later that Julia suspected that

Sylvia and Gordon might choose to move from Orcas to Seattle because Sylvia was there so often helping their children, including taking care of grandchildren, leaving Gordon home to take care of the dogs and deal with the troubled homeowners association — with members unwilling to participate or to spend money but vociferous in their complaints with Gordon who struggled with the community water system and roads. Julia told Yvonne that her homeowners' association was a mess as well, no one willing to work on the one hand and the president, who was operating like the Lone Ranger, making decisions without any input.

Yvonne made a dash through Target in Burlington while I sat in the food court at a table, Burger King and Starbuck's competing for attention. On to Costco for a return and me to visit the hearing department to see about having the volume turned down on my hearing aids, the removal of wax from my ears a few days before making them unbearably loud, especially in groups, but no one was available to talk to. Eating the sandwiches Yvonne had brought from home as we drove I-5 to Seattle, we were soon at the new home of Elliot Bay Books, Seattle's premier bookstore, and its new home on Capitol Hill a block east of Broadway between Pike and Pine, pleased to see it more crowded than it had been in its first home in the Pioneer Square neighborhood, the space more efficiently used, with its coffee shop on the main floor. What a great bookstore! As I reviewed its shelves, not as extensive as a Barnes & Noble, I was struck by the quality of the offerings as well as how many titles had employee recommendations and descriptions. I was looking for a paper copy of Andrei Codrescui's *The Posthuman Dadaist Guide* that I'd already read on my Kindle but wanted to write him back intelligently about his book and found the electronic version inadequate to review because I couldn't see enough of it at one time — or quickly move around in the book — for me an inherent problem with the way electronic readers are programmed and something perhaps eNotated Classics could address in the future. A clerk quickly found a copy for me in the Essays section and I was surprised initially at its narrow shape, much narrower than tall and then realized that it was supposed to be a guidebook and fit in one's pocket. Yvonne showed me *The Wittgenstein Family* on the discount table for $6 and I couldn't resist, having written my undergraduate thesis on this influential, perhaps mystic and certainly very difficult to understand early Twentieth Century British/Austrian philosopher — whose life was as much a testament to his philosophy as his writings.

About eight years before I'd thoroughly enjoyed *Wittgenstein's Poker*, ostensibly about an incident when Karl Popper spoke at Cambridge and Wittgenstein could barely contain his contempt or at least strong disagreement. Yvonne didn't buy a book but I had bought Paula McLain's *The Paris Wife* (historical fiction about Ernest Hemingway and his first wife, Hadley Richardson) and downloaded it to the iPod for her to read on our trip to the mountain states.

We were at Jeni's a bit after 2:00, Corrina and her cat, Gypsy, now in residence with Jeni, and her cat, Lola. After hugs, Corrina answered our burning question: had she made up her mind among her three acceptances for MFA programs in Rhode Island, Philadelphia, and Seattle? Yes. She had chosen Philadelphia. We were surprised, like everyone else she had shared the news with. Because, she explained, it most closely fit her intentions about what kind of role she sought in the community of art — namely teaching at the university level. She'd start in June, and have residence over the next three summers and thought she could work out the financing.

On to MOHAI, the Museum of History & Industry, Seattle, near UW, featuring a "Now & Then" photo exhibit mostly on the work of Paul Dorpat, who has become a local master of repeat photography, understanding objects by displaying photos taken at different times. After being kicked out at 5:00, the four of us met Kelly and Tim and then Ron at Machiavelli on Pine and enjoyed the food and conversation in a very noisy environment. I learned more about Corrina's program, Ron's growing acupuncture practice and his visit with his ex-wife and then Kelly's plans for delivery of her baby and finally Tim's thoughts on semantic searching finally becoming practical with the help of tools like the database service Freebase — a fascinating development that wasn't possible when I worked on the SilverPlume reference library and search system as late as 15 years ago. I want to know more. Finally arriving at the Radisson Hotel across International Blvd from SeaTac, Yvonne and I could finally relax, soon lapsing into unconsciousness.

One-hundred-eighty-one: Brown and White

"We don't remember days, we remember moments." – Cesare Pavese

As is often the case, air turbulence over the Colorado Front Range added a little excitement to the descent to DIA, the brown plains stretching east as far as we could see toward Kansas, always a shock after leaving the verdant Pacific Northwest. And on the ground it was 70; that was nice, but the dry west wind wasn't. Coming down the long hill on Route 36 into Boulder, the town and university with its red-tiled roofs standing out in the middle of it, we had a modest sense of homecoming to the place we lived for 25 years.

The trip to Denver from Seattle included no hassles. As we walked from the Radisson across International Blvd, our suitcases in tow, we saw little traffic on the broad road and almost none as we approached the terminal. The desk clerk at the hotel had been friendly, the young man who checked us in at the Frontier counter was friendly — offering to check our bags for free, the TSA security people were in a good mood, and a flight attendant handed out warm chocolate cookies during the flight. Though it took years the SeaTac concourses are mostly remodeled and much more pleasant to spend time in than they were. We made our way to the atrium close to Concourse B and immediately got in line at Starbucks. A young man took our orders while we waited in line and besides tea and a cinnamon scone, got a ham and cheese sandwich to carry on board for lunch. While Yvonne shopped for small gifts to take to our Boulder friends and a carry-away lunch, I sat at a table taking advantage of SeaTac's free WiFi service.

181: Sunrise before We Leave Crane for America

Yvonne had found that Advantage Rent-A-Car had the best rates for our rental period. It would cost $150 for a week's rental — a bargain. We had the choice of a Nissan Versa or a Toyota Yaris and since the former was a little larger we chose it. The clerk offered us the prepaid gas option, a savings of $.25/gallon and Yvonne and I argued briefly about whether to take it or not, the clerk throwing in his two cents from time to time. The tank holds 13 gallons. If we opted for the pre-paid plan and we brought the car back with the tank empty, we would save $3.25 versus with the other plan and returning the car with the tank full. With the first plan any gas left in the tank would be a gift to Advantage; we would get no credit for it — so with one gallon left in the tank we'd break even — anything more and we'd lose money on the deal. Since it's much simpler to bring a car back with the tank full than plan for it to have less than a gallon of gas left, it was clear to me the prepaid plan didn't make sense for us. I insisted over Yvonne's skepticism.

In Boulder, our first stop was for wine and the second for bagels — which we hadn't been able to find a good source for within 50 miles of Crane Island. Washington bagels were not boiled before being baked and were not, for us, a source of gustatory pleasure. Alan and Tessa came to the door as we came up their walk and we spent the next six hours talking continuously. One of the first orders of business was to look at the New Zealand slide and video show Alan had put together of their recent trip immediately after the Christchurch earthquake. They spent four weeks, most of it on the south island, as tourists, because the earthquake had so damaged the university, rather than involved with the academic matters Alan had expected. The photos showed a paradise of mountains, seas, lakes, fertile fields, jungle, wildlife, and friendly people — more friendly and welcoming than any they'd encountered over their extensive travel. The people seemed happy, they had productive lives, their society appeared more cooperative than competitive, they had a deep sense of community, medical care was free and readily available, and there wasn't much of the stress, even desperation we often see in America. On the other hand, New Zealand Society discourages standout performance and lacks the edge and influence of American society. Alan and I agreed we wouldn't want to live in that apparent utopia, because disagreement, ferment, trouble, and change — all part of American life — is stimulating, not just emotionally but of ideas, business, the arts — but perhaps that's rationalization.

Over the evening we went down the list — coming up to date on every child, grandchild, sibling, friend, and project — bringing each other up to date. Alan was very curious about the situation with Richard and wasn't aware that Richard had gone into competition with us. They'd met Richard and his on-again, off-again romance, Maggie, when they'd come to Chimayo four years before, at my invitation, to walk with us. In some respects neither Alan nor Tessa was surprised since Richard's history was a series of betrayals of people that cared about him. We know Alan and Tessa so well and find it so easy to have extended quality conversations that its always a pleasure to spend time with them. Then we were all worn out. Tomorrow we could begin again.

One-hundred-eighty-two: Jobs I Have to Do Today

"Friends are the family we choose for ourselves." – Edna Buchanan

I made a pot of Tessa's gluten-free, wheat-free, dairy-free, R5 Elisa Certified Pedigreed Pure Seed Dedicated 100% Whole Grain keeps-best-refrigerated-or-frozen Bob's Red Mill Old Fashioned Rolled Oats — enough for both Yvonne and me because, surprisingly, she wanted my boiled oatmeal rather than her micro-waved version, which turned out to be too much, except that Alan was happy to clean the pot, covering his portion with fruit and yogurt, something that didn't even occur to me, in part because I'm lactose-intolerant and don't eat yogurt and also because I like the satisfying taste of the oatmeal on its own.

Alan was on sabbatical but very busy, this morning reviewing dissertation-related offerings from several of his advisees, and Tessa, though retired was very busy, this morning getting in an early swim at the nearby Boulder recreation center. She had just gotten a new Honda Fit and Yvonne and I, at the beginning stages of thinking about a new high-mileage car, were interested in a test drive and so took her Fit to Safeway to pick up food for the dinner Alan and Tessa would make that evening and to Big Daddy's Bagels to buy sesame bagels they were missing the day before and for me to pick up a breakfast bagel for lunch. This Fit, a hatchback, had better storage options than the Versa we'd rented at the airport but my first impression was to find the Versa seating more comfortable and the interior more attractive.

182: Yvonne and Tessa on Our Neighborhood Walk

About 10:00 the four of us took off for a three-mile neighborhood walk, much of it on paved bike/pedestrian walkway, Alan and I falling into conversation about Freebase (a database), semantic searching, and its applicability to educational research, and SilverPlume, the insurance text database I'd been instrumental in developing in Boulder now almost 20 years ago. We went on to talk about the research project he and his colleagues had conducted and just finished with the Denver Public Schools to identify factors that made some schools more successful with immigrant children, a significant part of the system's enrollment, and besides the expected factors, the good schools did a great deal of explicit, shared, vocabulary building. I have no idea what Yvonne and Tessa talked about. When Yvonne and I sold our Boulder Wonderland Hill home in 2000, planning to live most of the time on Orcas Island, we bought a condo not far from where Alan and Tessa lived and my morning runs, now in south rather than north Boulder sometimes threaded through the same paths we were taking today though more likely to be along South Boulder Creek on a trail that runs for miles to the southwest, often seeing coyotes, hawks, prairie dogs (a controversial resident), meadowlarks and other fauna of this riparian ecosystem.

In Victoria, Noah, Natasha, Yvonne, and I had talked about the general in thought (philosophy) and the concrete (literature, poetry) and since then Noah came across a quote he wanted to share that neatly expressed the difference, by Kevin Clark, in *The Mind's Eye*, a book on poetry: "One specific image can often render a multitude of ideas, not just one general concept. Most of us prefer concrete picturing to abstract reflection. That's why literature relies on concrete language to imply meaning about human experience. Philosophy typically uses abstract language to state meaning explicitly" and then Noah offered an example: "Opal is in the living room with me composing her own poem."

Jobs I have to do today
  I have to do the dishes
  I have to cook all the fishes
  I have to cook all the pancakes
  I have to cook all the hamcakes
  I have to cook all the things
  before the bell rings
  I have to cook the buffalo stew
  oh, all the things
  that I have to do
  I have to put the wood
  on the fire
  I have to sing with the choir
  then I will eat a big meal
  oh, how I will feel
  (Opal Ashenhurst, age six)

Yvonne and Tessa went to meet Ann and Barb at the Boulder Dushanbe Teahouse, a gift from the people of Dushanbe to the people of Boulder that opened in 1990, a Central Asian venue at the foot of the Rocky Mountains. Alan spent the afternoon at a university meeting in Denver and I worked on the provenance of the images Jens wanted to include in *The eNotated Metamorphosis*, amazed at the number and imaginative nature of Kafka-related images on the Internet.

Alan, Tessa, and Yvonne worked on dinner preparations late in the afternoon; chicken, rice, and a kale salad with a meringue for dessert and at 6:00 Dave and Ann appeared at the door, not long returned from Rio de Janeiro where Dave had hosted a conference and then a trip to Iguazu Falls on the Argentine border. Dean and Barb showed up soon after with their daughter Karen and her 2-year-old, Darren, on their way to DIA for the young mom and son's return trip to Eugene, though they would soon be moving to Boise, following her husband's new job.

One-hundred-eighty-three: Morning Sun Come My Way

"A human being lives out not only his personal life as an individual, but also, consciously or subconsciously, the lives of his epoch and his contemporaries." — Magic Mountain by Thomas Mann

Perhaps it was because we were getting old but rather than greet the sun on its rising at about 6:15, the women had decided that the time of sunrise on the spring equinox, the day we'd traditionally have this gathering, made more sense, especially because it was 45 minutes later. As we had for 30 years (the Phillips and the Ashenhursts and later the Davises and the Beasleys), we sang up the sun (although it had already risen well above the horizon) with a chant some of us had learned from Forrest Whitman — who had been minister of the Boulder UU Church for about 25 years. Its provenance is unclear. It goes this way:

Morning sun, morning sun, come my way, come my way (repeat four times)

Morning sun, morning sun, take my pain, take my pain (repeat four times)

Take my pain, take my pain, down below, down below (repeat four times)

Down below, down below, to cool waters down below (repeat four times)

Morning sun, morning sun, bring us joy, bring us joy (repeat for times)

We followed with *Morning is Broken*, (Eleanor Farjeon), *Canticle of the Sun* (St Francis) and a multipart *Alleluia* based on Pachelbel's *Canon in D*.

Clouds in the east obscured the sun but the sky above was blue. It would be a beautiful day in the 60s. From the Phillips' house on the flank of the Dakota Ridge hogback, we could see downtown Boulder to the south, Flagstaff Mountain, a Ute holy site, and behind and above it Green Mountain, rising about 2500 feet above the town (the same relative altitude as Mt. Constitution on Orcas above the Salish Sea), the Flatiron monoliths I'd climbed a few times propped against the mountain, a dramatic and beautiful view we'd been used to for the 25 years we'd lived a bit north of the Phillips.

This morning we came to the Phillips' in a roundabout way from the Davises', Yvonne wanting to look at my ex-wife, Jill's new house on the edge of the neighborhood she and I had lived in briefly before separating a year later and then divorcing.

The eight of us took our seats in the Phillips' family room, as we had done perhaps 100 times before and Tessa introduced the topic of transitions. Dave talked about retirement from his association executive duties after a tenure of more than 30 years, now perhaps a year away, during which time he would bring on and train new staff to replace the three who were retiring. Barb had just retired from her nurse duties and was both relieved and at a loss. Dean, a family practice physician was working half-time but discouraged with the oppressive administrative duties that were crowding out medicine. Alan, after the surprise retirement of a colleague, said he was considering retirement from his teaching role. Tessa and Alan talked about the selling of Alan's family house, the memories, and the room-by-room ritual the two of them with Alan's brother, Glen, had conducted before letting the house go. Yvonne talked about what she was trying to do for and with her grandniece, Cressi, a high school junior in eastern Washington, practically speaking, abandoned by her parents, both disabled by drugs, but who wanted to go to college and didn't know how. Yvonne would take her to colleges in Western Washington, help her with college applications and preparing for the SAT test. I reported on my first email from a grandchild, Morgan, age 10, and how I intended over time to nurture direct communication with him. And then Tessa prompted me to talk about how Richard had gone into competition with us, a kind of betrayal, that only Alan and Tessa had heard about — though all had met him several years before when I'd invited him with his friend Maggie to join us all in Chimayo for our walk.

And then the usual breakfast we'd shared for years on every solstice and equinox: Ann made a chilaquiles casserole, Barb a bacon and cheese quiche, Tessa brought sliced fruit, and Yvonne Cowboy coffee cake, though she was disappointed in it because the brown sugar didn't melt into the cake the way it normally did but crystalized on top. Ann and Barb wanted to hear about the multiverse, responding to the email summary of my Orcas UU talk I'd sent all of them in February. Barb, having read Brian Greene's *Elegant Universe* some years back was familiar with the terrain and it turned out that later in the day they listening to Terri Gross' interview with the physicist. I talked in very general terms about several different ways physicists thought about the multiverse and was prompted by Ann to talk about the way different areas of the multiverse would duplicate one another or be slightly different in a few details. Alan was dubious and told us it was all nonsense — just irrelevant fantasies spun out by narcissistic people who wanted to feel more important by having other versions of themselves someplace. Then we talked about the scientific method generally, how this was the best current thinking of physicists, an implication of Einstein's work that had been corroborated in many ways, the most being experimental data that showed the universe was "flat," a precondition of it's being infinite and only one of zillions of shapes it could have but somehow didn't. This wasn't goofy fantasy. It was the best available science and it made more sense to me than a single finite universe, a source of serenity, not angst. I talked about the possibility of empty universes, nearby brane universes (in other dimensions), universes with physical constants different from ours, the anthropomorphic principle — or fallacy. Alan, who would have none of it went on to talk about how an infinite number of monkeys typing over an infinite period of time would never, never compose the works of Shakespeare; infinitesimally small probabilities would never occur, even in an infinite amount of time.

Each time we returned to Boulder I would have my teeth cleaned and checked and sometimes repaired by people in whom I had a great deal of confidence, so at 11:00 I reclined in the chair and Charlotte began to poke, scrape, buff, and finally floss — following up on the quick flossing I'd done the night before so that it would look like I flossed regularly — which I didn't. She asked about James and then talked about her son and daughter and then about how dry it had been in Boulder and the problems with fires, the results of one Yvonne, Tessa, Alan, and I had viewed the previous October, and the cool, wet winter and lingering spring we'd had on Orcas. That led to pine beetle problems on the other side of the Divide where dead trees extend for miles so that the Front Range is no longer green topped by white.

183: We Visit Lopez Island with Boulder Friends Visiting Us on Crane (2009 August) - John, Ann, Dean, Barb, Yvonne, Tessa, Dave, Alan

Yvonne had lunch with Cathy and Mary at the Tea House and after a brief update on all the players in our lives, talk turned to the problem Katie was having deciding on a wedding dress for her summer wedding in Montana. I was happy to have been absent. Yvonne found me in the Boulder Public Library writing, after printing out a discount coupon to buy a pair of Keen sandals, ahead of our Chimayo walk and we spent a few minutes in the shop owned by the father of my nephew Kevin's girlfriend. Back with Alan and Tessa, Yvonne made dinner and we spent time talking about eNotated Classics, Andrei Codrescu, and Alan's research project. In the morning Yvonne and I would drive south to Taos. Alan and Tessa would follow as soon as they could get ready. A continuing topic at their house was why the newly installed dusk-to-dawn outdoor light didn't work as expected. The installer had been back but couldn't find the instructions. Late in the evening Tessa and I experimented with the settings — needing a flashlight and magnifying glass to read the little LCD screen — but had no luck. Shortly after Yvonne and I had gotten in bed and started reading, Tessa knocked on the door to tell us she'd found the instructions online. The dawn to dusk switch wouldn't work with fluorescent lights and that's what they'd installed. Tessa's other source of irritation was the squirrels in the backyard who defeated every security measure she'd deployed to prevent them from getting purchase on the hanging bird feeder and then denuding it of seeds that she intended for her feathered friends. Tomorrow we would decamp for New Mexico and our Chimayo pilgrimage

What's Next?

Crane Island Journal is a four-volume memoir covering October 19, 2010 through October 18, 2011.

This is *Vetur (Winter)*, the second volume of *Crane Island Journal*.

Find information about *Haust (Autumn)*, *Vor (Spring)*, and *Sumar (Summer)* on the Journal's website, www.craneislandjournal.com.

www.ingramcontent.com/pod-product-compliance
Lightning Source LLC
Chambersburg PA
CBHW070418010526
44118CB00014B/1811